Quality of Work Life and Mental Health

Jewels for Workplace Spirituality

Quality of Work Life and Mental Health

Jewels for Workplace Spirituality

Dr Rishu Roy

ALLIED PUBLISHERS PVT. LTD.

New Delhi • Mumbai • Kolkata • Chennai • Bangalore • Hyderabad

ALLIED PUBLISHERS PRIVATE LIMITED

D-5, Sector-2, **Noida**–201 301
Ph. Nos.: 0120-4320295/2542557/4352866 • E-mail: delhi.books@alliedpublishers.com

17 Chittaranjan Avenue, **Kolkata**–700072
Ph.: 033-22129618 • E-mail: cal.books@alliedpublishers.com

15 J.N. Heredia Marg, Ballard Estate, **Mumbai**–400001
Ph.: 022-42126969 • E-mail: mumbai.books@alliedpublishers.com

No. 25/10, Commander-in-Chief Road, Ethiraj Lane (Next to Post Office)
Egmore, **Chennai**–600008
Ph.: 044-28223938 • E-mail: chennai.books@alliedpublishers.com

P.B. No. 9932, No. 15, 3rd Floor (Next to Vijaya Bank), 5th Cross, Gandhinagar,
Karnataka, **Bangalore**–560009, Ph.: 080-41530285 / 22386239
• E-mail: bngl.journals@alliedpublishers.com / apsabng@airtelmail.in

Sri Jayalakshmi Nilayam, No. 3-4-510, 3rd Floor (Above More Super Market)
Barkatpura, **Hyderabad**–500027
Ph.: 040-27551811, 040-27551812 • E-mail: hyd.books@alliedpublishers.com

Website: www.alliedpublishers.com

ISBN: 978-93-90951-35-2

Published by Sunil Sachdev and printed by Ravi Sachdev at Allied Publishers Pvt. Ltd.,
D-5, Sector-2, Noida–201 301

Foreword

Human Resource is one of the most crucial asset that determines the success of any organization as they can make use of the other resources to create avenues which has a profound impact on organizational performance. In this VUCA (Volatile, Uncertain, Complex and Ambiguous) world, it is essential for the organizations to have an inclusive and diverse workforce as it allows wider perspectives to be integrated and leads to better decision making. But as organizations continue to diversify, there is more probability for workplace issues to intensify. Most of the workplace issues arising in organizations are human and social rather than physical or technical which affects mental health of the employees. Pandemic has also forced employees in many ways to come out of their comfort zone and the concept of QoL (Quality of Life) and QWL (Quality of Work Life) have changed—possibly forever.

If an organization provides good quality of work life, it will not only attract new talent but also retain the existing ones that can help the businesses to achieve their objectives in terms of market share and goodwill. To cope up with intense competition, jobs have become more demanding and in quest to meet deadlines and grab market share, the mental health of employees is deteriorating. Employees' mental health problems and their impact on an enterprise's productivity and disability/medical costs are critical human resource issues. These issues throw new challenges in managing people and market places. So there is a need to adopt new approaches to unleash the hidden the human potential. It therefore calls for a paradigm shift which can be substantiated by making a new room for 'Spiritual Aspect' in organizations.

Spirituality brings another dimension to organizations, a dimension that focuses on human development and encourages choices that transcend organizational self-interest for long term growth and sustainability. Spirituality is thus considered as an important ingredient of the overall well-being of an individual. Given the significance of spirituality in one's life, organizations are increasingly making efforts to ensure that employees use spirituality to engage themselves physically, emotionally, and cognitively in their work. Engaged employees volunteer to engross themselves cognitively, emotionally, and physically in their work and affects organizational effectiveness.

The book is quite useful in understanding quality of work life, mental health and spirituality at work place. Mid-life soul searching, quest for stability in this VUCA world, spiritual needs of an individual at workplace—are some of the reasons for embracing this subject. This book also focuses on corporate wellness programs and happiness at workplace which helps to mitigate occupational stress and enhance individual and organizational performance.

Case studies are incorporated at the end to instill the interest of the readers and better understanding of the concept. The book has evolved with the teaching and research experience of the author and her interactions with various practitioners and policy makers. This book will be provide a framework for building *'Spiritual Organizations'* and is primarily designed for HR students, research scholars, policy makers, practitioners and industry experts.

Acknowledgements

Writing a book is harder than I thought and more rewarding than I could have ever imagined. None of this would have been possible without **Dr Sushma Bahre**, my very own Superhero, my dearest mom. My first friend, she has stood by me during every struggle. That is true friendship.

I'm eternally grateful to my father **Dr Surendra Bahre** who taught me discipline, love, manners, respect and so much more that has helped me succeed in life.

Special thanks to my mother-in-law **Mrs Gouri Roy** who has helped me develop a positive attitude towards life. My beloved husband **Amit** has helped me grow both as an individual and as a professional. He has supported me in every phase of my life.

Being professionally inclined, I have at times neglected my response-bilities at the personal front. I could not be there when my son **Aditya** needed me most. I take this opportunity to thank him for his under-standing.

Having an idea and turning it into a book is as hard as it sounds. The experience is both internally challenging and rewarding. I especially want to thank the individuals who helped make this happen. Profuse thanks to my brother **Dr Skand Bahre** and sister-in-law **Dr Aparna Bahre**. It is because of their efforts and encouragement that I have a legacy to pass on to my family. They have always stood by my side and helped me in whenever I needed them most.

To all the individuals I have had the opportunity to lead, be led by or watch their leadership from afar, I want to say thank you for being the inspiration and foundation of my professional life.

A special thank you to my mentors **Dr Santosh Dhar and Dr Upinder Dhar** for giving me a platform to perform and to chart my growth with their sharp intellect, keen sense of observation, deep knowledge and profound wisdom. I have also come to appreciate, admire and respect their leadership.

Finally, to all those who have been a part of my getting there: **Dr Vanita Joshi** (for being my soul sister and confidant), **Dr Rakesh Chouhan** (for being my go-to friend in sticky situations), **Dr Vikas Pathak** (for eternally motivating me), **Mr Vikram Agnihotri** (for he is inspiration personified), **Mr Prateek Sanghvi** (for confiding in me) and **Dr Abhijeet Chauhn** (for helping me realize my dream).

Dedication

to

My Mother – Dr. Sushma Bahre

For being a strong and gentle soul
who taught me to trust in God Almighty,
believe in hard work and that much
could be achieved with little.

For being my first teacher.

For being the guardian of my educational career.

For imbibing the seed of inspiration
in me to do quality work.

Contents

UNIT–I

Introduction to Quality of Work Life (QWL)

Introduction

Quality of Work Life (QWL) is cooperative in nature rather than being authoritarian and evolutionary, it is open rather than being static and rigid, it is informal rather than rule-bound, it is impersonal rather than mechanistic, and it is mutual respect and trust rather than hatred against each other. Since its origin in early 1970's, quality of work life has become an aspect in work organisations.[1]

Quality of Work Life has become inevitable for the present day organizations to successfully grow and gain a competitive edge. It enables organizations to function smoothly by ensuring that the employees are motivated to perform better. A good QWL ensures that the employees are happy and healthy, enabling them to take sound decisions, which improves turnover and leads to successful goal accomplishment.

An improved QWL also helps attract competent and proficient talent and to retain the existing experienced talent. It is important to assess QWL in an organization at regular intervals as it provides information regarding working conditions and physical work environment, salary and other benefits, career growth opportunities, inter-personal relationships, work and rest schedules etc. It also helps to enhance QWL for further improvement in employee morale, motivation and performance.

Origin

Although, work life programs have existed since the early 1930s, people did not recognise them. It was during the 1960s–1970s when QWL became an important HR intervention in the United States and Scandinavia. It was discussed for the first time in 1972 at an international labour relations conference. In 1986, the term 'work life balance' was first identified but its use in everyday language was still sporadic for a certain number of years.

Before World War II, the W.K. Kellogg Company created some flexible work hour shifts for their employees that replaced the traditional working hours. It resulted in increased employee efficiency. The first waves of these programs were mainly to support women with children. QWL programs of today are less gender specific and identify other obligations.

By the mid of 1990s, QWL had become a fundamental issue for individuals and it became a necessary part of the strategies of all organizations all over the world. In India, QWL offers a value frame and the social technology of organizational change leading to task effectiveness of micro entities through utilization and unfolding of human potential.

QWL can also be understood as those working conditions which are conducive to create a favourable and purposeful organization, and cater to the personal needs of employees by moulding their values, improving their health and wellbeing, ensuring job satisfaction and security, developing their competencies, and maintaining work-life balance.[2]

The management must, therefore, pay attention to employees' well-being as a strong workforce will be beneficial for the organization. Employees who are satisfied and happy with their work are often more committed to their work and perform better. QWL is of immense importance for both the employees and employers.

It has become increasingly important in the present era due to bottleneck competition, increased stress at work, rapid technological advancements, deskilling of jobs, artificial intelligence (AI) and emerging challenges like VUCA (volatility, uncertainty, complexity and ambiguity).

These and numerous other factors have necessitated the improvement in QWL of employees so that they have a good and healthy experience at work. Every organization must, therefore, strive to provide a work environment which is propitious to the human resources of that organization. Various measures can be adopted to ensure a better QWL in an organization.

Fair and adequate remuneration, fringe benefits, bonus and other incentives, proper working conditions, balance between work and personal life, no discrimination among employees on the grounds of caste, colour, creed, race, religion or sex, ample opportunities for professional growth, employee autonomy, better interpersonal relationships, effective performance appraisal system etc. can help improve QWL of employees. QWL is a term which encompasses most of the relevant aspects affecting employees and their work.[3]

In 1996, Emery and Thorsurd identified six psychological requirements of working people. However, they cautioned that these could be met differentially at different work places.

These six factors are:

1. The need for variety in the content of a job (not necessarily novelty).
2. The need for being able to learn on the job and to go on learning.
3. The need for some minimal area of decision-making that the individual can call his own.
4. The need for some minimal degree of social support and recognition in work place.
5. The need for an individual to be able to relate to what he does and what he produces to his social life.
6. The need to feel that the job leads to some sort of desirable future.

Concepts

A multi-faceted aspect, it is inter-related with several set of ideas. Its general premise is having a work environment where an employee's activities become more important. This means implementing procedures or policies that make the work less routine and more rewarding for the employee.

These procedures or policies include autonomy, recognition, belonging, progress, development and external rewards. QWL is an indicator of how free the society is from exploitation, injustice, inequality, oppressions and restrictions on continuity of the growth of man.

What is more important in India at this stage is developing consciousness among all sections of industry including workers, unions and management. The success of any organization depends a lot on the quality equation amongst these three players.

It embodies the following inter-related set of ideas:

1. Ideas dealing with a body of knowledge, concepts and experiences related with nature, meaning and structure of work.
2. Ideas dealing with nature and process of introducing and managing organizational change.
3. Ideas dealing with outcomes or results in the change process.

Therefore, QWL is a process by which all members of an organization, through appropriate channels of communication, have some say about the design of their jobs in particular and the work environment in general. Quality of Work Life not only improves the job content but it also moves towards participant management.

QWL concept views work as a process of interaction and joint problem solving by working people-managers, supervisors and workers.

This makes the QWL process:

1. Cooperative rather than authoritative.
2. Evolutionary and changing rather than static.
3. Open rather than rigid.
4. Informal rather than rule-based.
5. Interpersonal rather than mechanical.
6. Problem-solving.
7. Win-win rather than win-lose.
8. Based on mutual respect.

Elements

QWL focuses on creating a human work environment where employees work together with satisfaction to achieve the objectives collectively.

The four basic elements of quality of work life are:

1. The program is meant for enhancing human dignity and growth opportunities.
2. Employees are to work together to achieve the collective goal(s).
3. Employees decide on work-related issues through total participation.
4. The program integrates people with organization by assimilating individual and organizational goals.

Figure 1: Elements of QWL

Importance

Improved QWL was not considered an important factor in India until recently as there were important impending factors like resource deficiency, environmental threats and some services of financial problems. The quality of work life program has become important in workplace for the following reasons:

1. Increase demands at work
2. Loss of long-term employee guarantees
3. The need for enhanced workplace skills
4. Greater competition for talent
5. Increased women in work force

Good quality of work life leads to an atmosphere of good impersonal relations and highly motivated employees who strive for their development. Though monetary benefits still occupy first place in the cost of elements like physical working conditions, job restructuring and job redesigning, career development, promotional opportunities etc are gaining importance rapidly.

As such, workers expect the management to improve all these facilities which thereby improve Quality of work life. If provided with good QWL, employees concentrate more on both individual as well as group development which in turn leads to overall development. Walton (1975) proposed eight conceptual categories, which are as follows:

- Adequate and Fair Compensation
- Safe and Healthy Working Conditions
- Immediate Opportunity to Use and Develop Human Capacities
- Opportunity for Continued Growth and Security
- Social Integration in Work Organization
- Constitutionalization in Work Organization
- Work and Total Life Span
- Social Relevance of Work Life.

Successful organizations are turning through the introduction of Quality of work life strategy to the people who work in them to maintain competitive advantage. The benefits to both management and workers comprise:

1. Improved organization performance through the development of people.
2. Increased cooperation and team work within and across all levels of the organization including movement towards management or trade union partnership.

3. Increased environment in doing a good job.
4. Improved quality performance.
5. Increased commitment to organizational values and goals.
6. Anchoring of the development of a quality organization.

Effects

The quality of work life affects job involvement, sense of competence, job satisfaction and job performance. A favourable quality of work life results in positive consequences of these factors. These four effects of QWL are listed below:

- ***First Effect (Job Involvement):*** Job involvement indicates the extent of people's identification with, or ego involvement, in the job. Job involved people spend more time on job and turn out better performance. Challenging jobs influence employees to get involved with their jobs. Similarly, people with high need for achievement and high work ethics feel involved in jobs.

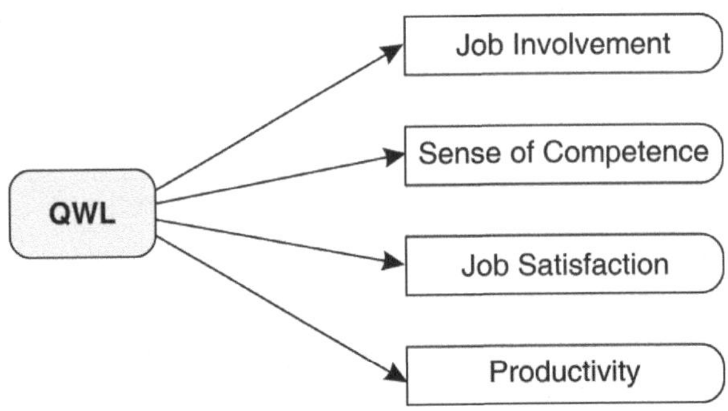

Figure 2: Effects of QWL

- ***Second (Sense of Competence):*** A sense of competence denotes the feelings of confidence that an individual has in his own competence. By engaging in a work that calls for a variety of skills, abilities and talents, individuals gain mastery over their work environment leading to better feeling towards the quality of work life. This leads to a development of sense of competence.
- ***Third Effect (Job Satisfaction):*** Job satisfaction is a set of favourable or unfavourable feelings with which employees view their jobs and the environment in which these are performed. Favourable feelings lead to job satisfaction while unfavourable feelings lead to job dissatisfaction. Better quality of work life makes both jobs and the

environment, in which these are performed, favourable resulting in a higher job satisfaction.

- ***Fourth Effect (Productivity):*** Job involvement, job satisfaction and a sense of competence affects the productivity of employees. When the level of these factors is high, productivity of employees tends to be higher. In the alternative case, it tends to be low.

Assumptions

The concept of QWL is based on the assumption that a job is more than just a job.[4] It is the centre of a person's life. In recent years, there has been increasing concern for QWL due to several factors such as.

1. Increase in education level and consequently job aspirations of employees
2. Association of workers; significance of human resource management
3. Widespread industrial unrest
4. Growing of knowledge in human behaviour etc.

Objectives

The main objectives of the quality of work life are to:

- Improve employee satisfaction
- Improve physical and psychological health of employees which creates positive feelings
- Enhance productivity of employees
- Reinforce workplace learning
- Improved management of the on-going change and transition, and
- Build the image of the company as best in recruitment, retention and in general motivation of employees.

Basic Issues

The quality of work life is concerned with the following questions:

1. How to develop careers that allow employees to realize their full capabilities and interest?
2. How to design jobs to provide meaningful, interesting and challenging work experience?
3. How to utilize group dynamics and participative management to improve the quality of life at the workplace?
4. What supervisory strategies help to improve the quality of work life?
5. How can the desired organizational changes be carried out?

Parameters

One of the principal problems with this term is that Quality of Work Life is not a single or a specific notion. Rather, it consists of a whole parcel of terms and notions, all of which really belong under the QWL umbrella that comprises the following:

- Industrial Effectiveness
- Human Resource Development
- Organizational Effectiveness
- Work Restructures
- Job Enrichment
- Socio-technical Systems
- Working Humanization
- Group Work Concept
- Labour Management Cooperation
- Working Together, Worker's Involvement and Worker's Participation
- Co-operative Work Structures.

Each of these, in varying degrees of inadequacy, identifies a part of the large whole that the quality of work life seeks to identify. QWL is actually the sum of all these various attempts to label a general new direction for work organizations in the late 20th century.

Barriers

Barriers to QWL are resistance of employees to changes due to their pre-conceived notions regarding schemes, plans, tools and techniques developed by the management and lack of financial resources which prohibits implementing any HRD intervention strategies for improving the quality of work life. Managements do not tend to learn to adopt the 'Paternalistic Approach'.

Every organisation is an interdependent social and technical system. Today's organizations need to be more flexible so that they are equipped to develop their work force and enjoy their commitment. The scope of term quality of work life is so vast that it covers almost all areas of the human resource management.

QWL is gaining momentum every day. With good quality of work life, employees concentrate more on their individual and group development. The management can get their attention with their high motivation and morale which paves way for rapid and smooth human resource development.

Employees who are provided with good QWL can concentrate more on their development and it ensures a congenial atmosphere between different layers of employees and management.

The sustained vitality and profitability of any company is clearly linked to the satisfaction of workforce. QWL addresses the concerns of improving employee satisfaction, strengthen workforce learning and better manage the ongoing change and transition.

Strategy

The results of implementing QWL in organizations have produced positive returns from across the globe. Quality of work life strategies can be initiated in organizational working via programs, policies and services. Some of its profound outcomes are listed as follows:

- Improves communication with employees
- Strengthens family friendly programs
- Provides employees with Internet access
- Increases investment in workplace learning
- Improves effectiveness of supervisors and team leaders
- Evaluates effectiveness of diversity management practices
- Improves ability to manage change and transition
- Supports faculty and staff efforts to manage competing demands of work and personal life
- Supports health promotions and wellness
- Expresses appreciation for faculty and staff contributions to the university
- Highlights outstanding individual contributions
- Recognizes long-term commitment.

One of the important strategies to improve QWL is to create work rules that can help in maintaining an orderly atmosphere that is pleasant for employees to work effectively.

Strategies to Improve QWL

By implementing some changes, organizations can create a sense of involvement, commitment and togetherness among the employees which paves way for better quality of work life.[5] It also leads to:

1. Job enrichment and job redesign
2. Autonomous work redesign

3. Opportunity for growth
4. Administrative or organizational justice
5. Job security
6. Suggestion system
7. Flexibility in work schedules
8. Employee participation.

Quality of work life improvements are defined as any activity that takes place at every level of an organization which seeks greater organizational effectiveness through the enhancement of human dignity and growth.

A process through which the state holders in the organization, management, unions and employees—learn how to work together better to determine for themselves what actions, changes and improvements are desirable and workable in order to achieve the win and simultaneous goals of an improved quality of life at work for all members of the organization and greater effectiveness for both the company and unions.

QWL and Productivity

The general perception is that improvement in QWL costs much to the organization. But it is not so as improvement over the existing salary working conditions and benefits will not cost of QWL. Thus, increase in QWL results in increase in productivity. But continual increase in QWL eventually leads to reduction in productivity due to increase in cost of output.

This is because the employees' output does not increase proportionately after a certain level, even though QWL increases. Improved QWL leads to improved performance. Performance means not only physical output but also the behaviour of the worker in helping colleagues in solving job-related problems accepting orders with enthusiasm, promoting a positive team spirit and accepting temporary unfavourable work conditions without complaint.

QWL and Personnel/HRM

The quality of work life is broader than motivation though these two terms seem to be similar. All personnel-related activities affect quality of work life. Some examples of this are as follows:

P/HR Activity	*Effect on Quality of Work Life*
Job Analysis	Analysing the job in such as way that human needs like freedom, challenging work, autonomy can be satisfied.
Selection	Selecting the right man and placing him in the right position. This satisfies his needs for reward, interesting work etc.
Job Enrichment	Satisfies higher order needs like pride and ego.
Job Evaluation	Equitable Wage.

Role of HR

The role of human resource department in QWL efforts varies widely. In some organizations, top management appoints an executive to ensure that QWL and productivity efforts occur throughout the organization. In most cases, these executives have a small staff and must rely on the human resource department for help with employee training, communications, attitude survey feedback and similar assistance.

In other organizations, the department is responsible for initiating and directing the firm's QWL and productivity efforts. Perhaps, the most crucial role of HR department is winning the support of key managers. Management support (particularly top management's support) appears to be an almost universal prerequisite for successful quality of work life.

By substantiating employee satisfaction and bottom-line benefits, which range from lower absenteeism and turnover to higher productivity and fewer accidents, the department can help convince doubting managers. The policies and practices of human resource department also influence motivation and satisfaction indirectly.

Rigorous enforced safety and health programs, for example, can give employees and supervisors a greater sense of safety from accidents and industrial health hazards. The motivation and satisfaction of employees acts as feedback on the organization's QWL and on the department's day-to-day activities.

Success Variables

The following variables have led to the success of quality of work life programs:

1. ***Flexi Time:*** A system of flexible working hours that serves as a work-scheduling scheme allowing individual employees, within

establishing limits, to control and redistribute their working hours around organizational demands.

2. ***Job Enrichment:*** Redesigning programmed for employee jobs to allow greater autonomy and responsibility in the performance of work tasks is required time to time.
3. ***Management by Objectives:*** Participation of an employee with his superior in setting employee goals that is consistent with the objectives of organization as a whole.
4. ***Staggered Hours:*** A work hour arrangement of overlapping schedules of predetermined hours established for the total work force. In staggered work-hour scheme a group of employees begin and end work at different intervals.
5. ***Socio-technical System:*** The physical and technological redesign of the work place for employee with human considerations of the work force.
6. ***Job Rotation:*** It is the programme in which employees are periodically given changed work assignments to acquire skill and knowledge and to reduce monotony burden in the organizations.
7. ***Job Enlargement:*** A program in which employees continue their present jobs, but duties are added with the intent of making the job more rewarding.
8. ***Autonomous Work Group:*** A form of participation in which a group of workers is given some control over decision making on production methods, distribution of tasks, recruitment of team members, selection of team leaders, work schedules and so on.
9. ***Employee Participation:*** A programme aimed at a greater sharing of responsibility for decision-making.

Main Constituents

The quality of work life attempts to fulfil the following needs of workers:

1. ***Safer Working Conditions:*** Walton considers QWL deeply concerned with provision of a work environment absolutely free from various hazards arising out of natural and unnatural things. He further encompasses the need for reasonable hours of work, favourable physical conditions of work, age restrictions, etc to be followed by the organizations.

   In India, the Factories Act, 1948 and several other labour laws provide various rules and regulation of protecting workers from health hazards at the working site.

2. ***Equitable and Fair Pay:*** Quality of work life requires that employees must be paid their due share in the firm's progress. The compensation system should create a favourable environment whereby the organization utilizes human resources to the maximum extent thereby helping the employee to maintain himself and his family with a standard in the society.
3. ***Job Satisfaction:*** The workers, as they are living beings, desire to work on the job that will utilize their abilities and talents and provide them satisfaction. The management must enrich jobs and redesign them in such a way that workers feel satisfied.
4. ***Job Security:*** Employees strongly desire stability of their jobs. The workplace should offer security of employment. Layoffs and retrenchment are opposed by all categories of employees these days.
5. ***Autonomy and Control:*** With the work becoming highly monotonous today, workers become more mechanical towards the machines and lack control on them. Researchers observe that when sufficient autonomy as well as control is given to workers, who in turn will use their innate skill and abilities for developing the organization, it will lead to an improvement in organizational QWL.

Influencing Factors

Several factors influence and decide the quality of work life. Some of these are listed as follows:

1. ***Attitude:*** The person who is entrusted with a particular job needs to have sufficient knowledge, required skill and expertise, enough experience, enthusiasm, energy level, willingness to learn new things, dynamism, sense of belongingness in the organization, involvement in job, inter-personnel relations, adaptability to change as per situation, openness for innovative ideas, competitiveness, zeal, ability to work under pressure, leadership qualities and team spirit.
2. ***Environment:*** The job may involve dealing with customers who have varied tolerance level, preferences, behavioural pattern, level of understanding or it may involve working with dangerous machines like drilling pipes, cranes, lathe machines, welding and soldering machines or even with animals where maximum safety precautions have to be observed which needs lot of concentration, alertness, presence of mind, quick with involuntary actions, synchronization of eyes, hands and body, sometimes high level of patience, tactfulness, empathy & compassion and control over emotions.

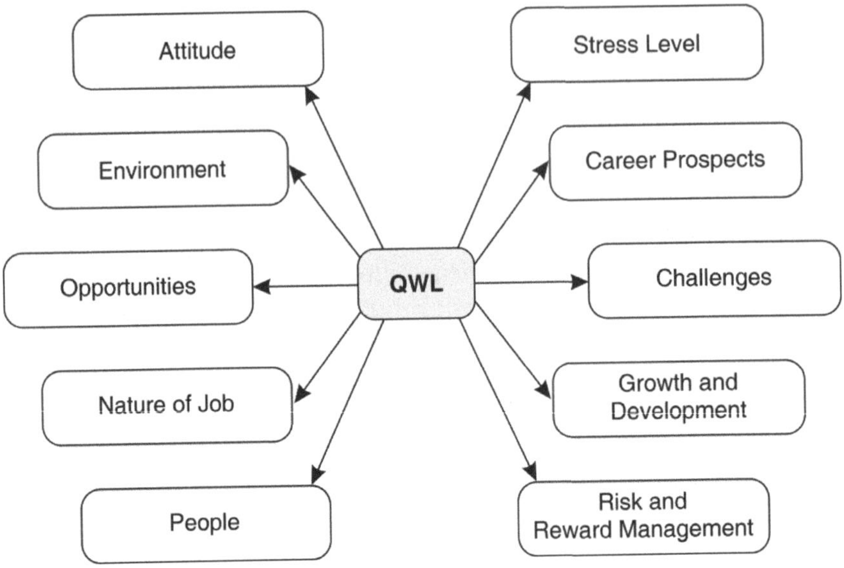

Figure 3: Factors Influencing QWL

3. ***Opportunities:*** Some jobs offer opportunities for learning, research, discovery, self-development and enhancement of skills, room for innovation, public recognition, exploration, celebrity status and loads of fame. Others are monotonous, repetitive, dull, routine, no room for improvement and in every sense boring. Naturally, the former types are interesting and very much rewarding as well.
4. ***Nature of Job:*** An example in this regard can be that of a driller in the oil drilling unit, a diver, a fire-fighter, traffic policeman, train engine driver, construction labourers, welder, miner, lathe mechanic etc. They have to perform dangerous jobs and remain constantly alert in order to avoid a loss of limb and/or life which is irreparable.

   Meanwhile, a pilot, doctor, judge and journalist have to be more prudent and tactful in handling the situation. Though, a CEO, professor and teacher have more responsibility and accountability but they have a safe working environment.

   A cashier or a security guard cannot afford to be careless in their jobs as it involves loss of money, property and wealth. And a politician or a public figure cannot afford to be careless for their reputation and goodwill is at stake.

   Some jobs need soft skills, leadership qualities, intelligence, decision making abilities and finesse to train and extract work from others while some jobs require forethought & vision, and yet some other jobs need motor skills, perfection and extreme carefulness.

5. ***People:*** Almost everyone has to deal with three set of people in the work place, namely, boss, co-workers in the same level and subordinates. Apart from this, some professions need interaction with people like patients, media persons, public, customers, thieves, robbers, physically disabled people, mentally challenged, children, foreign delegates, gangsters, politicians, public figures and celebrities.

   Such situations demand a high-level of prudence, cool temper, tactfulness, humour, kindness, diplomacy and sensitiveness.

6. ***Stress Level:*** It need not be directly proportional to compensation. Stress is of different types—mental, physical, psychological or emotional. A company's Managing Director will have mental stress, a labourer will have physical stress and a psychiatrist will have emotional stress. Mental and emotional stress cause more damage than physical stress.

7. ***Career Prospects:*** Every job should offer career development. This is an important factor that decides the quality of work life. Status improvement, more recognition from the management, appreciation etc are motivating factors for the employee to keep on taking keen interest in their job. Workplace atmosphere should be conducive to achieving organizational goal as well as individual development.

   It is a win-win situation for both the parties—an employee should be rewarded appropriately for his good work, extra efforts and sincerity while a lethargic and careless employee should be penalized suitably. This will motivate the former to work with more zeal and deter the latter from remaining lethargic.

8. ***Challenges:*** Jobs should offer some challenges at least to make it interesting. This enables an employee to constantly upgrade his skill, knowledge and capabilities. This is because the monotony of a job makes a person dull, non-enthusiastic, dissatisfied, frustrated and complacent. Challenge is the fire that keeps innovation and thrill alive. A well-accomplished challenging job yields greater satisfaction than a monetary perk and it boosts self-confidence as well.

9. ***Growth and Development:*** An organization that does not give opportunities for growth and personal development, faces difficulty to retain talented personnel. It also has a hard time finding fresh talent.

10. ***Risk Involved and Reward:*** The reward or compensation is directly proportional to the quantum of work, man-hours, nature and extent

of responsibility, accountability, delegated powers, authority of position in the organizational chart, risk involved, level of expected commitment, deadlines & targets, industry, country, demand & supply of skilled manpower and even the political stability and economic policies of a nation.

Although, every job involves a risk but it varies in nature. All said and done, reward is the key and a major factor to lure prospective workers to the organization.

QWL Programs

During the early seventies, many projects were launched in order to move labour and management toward cooperation in the improvement of QWL in the workplace. This was also strongly supported by the governments, which led to such activities as the creation of a Federal Productivity Commission in the United States and the sponsorship of a number of joint-labour QWL experiments in Europe.

As a consequence of these projects, the term QWL became synonymous with certain approaches. A second definition of QWL emerged defining QWL as an approach, and focusing still on individual, rather than organizational outcomes. During this time, QWL improvement was often considered to proceed in two separate, but not mutually exclusive, directions.

One direction concerned the alleviation or removal of negative aspects of work and working conditions to diminish fatigue, boredom and psychological stress. The other direction concerned the modification of aspects of work and working conditions to enhance capabilities of job holders and to relate jobs to some desirable future, in order to promote behaviour deemed desirable or valuable for the individual and society.

QWL was seen as the extent to which workers were able to satisfy important personal needs through their experiences within the organization, not only in terms of material matters, but also in terms of self-respect, contentment, an opportunity to use their talents, make a contribution and for personal growth.

Although QWL began as a variable focusing on the level of worker satisfaction, it developed during this period, into an approach and series of programs designed to increase worker productivity.

Corporate education programs, including training and development, are seen as an integral part of human resource management in firms recognized for their outstanding QWL. Experts argue that the issue is not whether productivity and high QWL are related, but rather to define the circumstances in which they can be increased.[6]

This is why four distinct strategies have been proposed, which represent sets of beliefs and findings about the causes of productivity and QWL.

They are:

- Autonomous Work Groups
- Job Restructuring
- Participative Management
- Organization-wide Change.

Indian Scenario

Indian people are in fact, hard working, industrious, painstaking, knowing fully their duties & responsibilities and ambitious. They have high morale and are group-orientation compared to other countries. Yet, these qualities mainly remain at home for a large section of employees as they do not carry them to the work place.[7]

They cannot be blamed wholly for this shortcoming. Managers do not use these qualities in their organizations. A proper understanding of the work force will help the organizations achieve the desired goals. Further, employee productivity in India is considerably low compared to other Euro-Asian countries.

The basic reasons for this state of affairs are:

1. India as a country is undergoing tremendous economic transition. The need for educated and skilled manpower is on the rise. This calls for appropriate equation and vocational training. Though our higher education system is quite impressive, there is dearth of quality primary and secondary-level education. Besides, dropout rates are also very high in this segment. Similarly, a lot needs to be done in the field of vocational and professional courses.
2. A majority of industrial work force in India has their roots in villages. Quite a large member of them have left their traditional occupation and migrated to the cities in search of employment either on a permanent or temporary basis. Most of them still retain their attachment to the land and periodically migrate to their villages. This gravely affects industrial manpower needs. However, a new class of industrial labourers—without roots in agriculture—has started emerging in our towns and cities.

3. Further, industrial labour is mostly uneducated. As a result, they encounter frequent troubles at the workplace. Corrupt unions leaders have further aggravated the situation.
4. The evil of caste, class, region, religion and language keeps the work force thoroughly divided, and thus, open to exploitation by the unscrupulous.
5. Moreover, Indian workers do not remain in the same job for a considerable length of time. Though there is high turn-over, absenteeism and indiscipline among others are also quite widespread. Somehow, they seem to give preference to leisure over employment.
6. Indian culture has not been able to utilize the collectivism of employees in work places as managers are not able to, or at times not willing to, incorporate this cultural trait. This is because Indian employees remain highly dedicated to their in-groups consisting of their extended family, friends, clan and culture and treat the work place as one group.
7. In the industrial sector, western style middle working class division is superimposed on a highly divested caste system. As a result, there exists a fundamental conflict interest the two classes of the industry face. This, in turn, contributes to a confrontational and hostile worker-management relationship.
8. The Indian industrial scenario has had its share of complacent attitudes towards changing times leading to utter failure. One such glaring example is that of yesteryears market leader Hero Cycles literally becoming zero solely due to their failure to read the changing market dynamics. Many organizations have had to pay dearly for misreading the writing on the wall.

Conditions for Successful QWL Programs

The following conditions are highly essential for the success of QWL programs:

- Shared recognition of a need for change.
- Strong leadership.
- Collaborative planning for change.
- Allocation of adequate resources to manage the change.
- Invitation to a third party who can introduce novel ideas, serve as a communication link, help eliminate stereotypes and distrust.

Common Characteristics

The results reported from a number of qualities of work life improvement programs have some common characteristics. These are:

1. Persistent commitment from management to the open non-defensive modus operandi of sincerely inviting collaborative inputs from the workforce regarding problem identification and suggestions for improving any aspect of the organization or the policies, practices and structure of work with incentives provided for such participation.
2. Invited involvement of members of tasks groups in recommending resolution of identified problem.
3. Training of supervisors to prepare them to function effectively in a less authoritative style.
4. Implementation of practicable suggestion and explanations for rejected ideas.
5. Feedback and recognition for good results achieved. Selection of personnel who can be motivated under appropriate conditions to strive for excellence in task performance.
6. Evaluation and analysis of results, including failures, leading to renewed effort towards continual improvement in modus operandi.

Evaluation of QWL Programs

QWL programs can be evaluated on the basis of following points:

1. ***Fair Compensation and Job Security:*** The economic interests of people drive them to work at a job and employee satisfaction depends at least partially on:
   (a) Compensation offered
   (b) Pay should be fixed on the basis of work done
   (c) Responsibilities undertaken
   (d) Individual skills
   (e) Performance and accomplishments

   Job security is another factor that is of concern to employees. Permanent employment provides security to the employees and improves their QWL.
2. ***Health is Wealth:*** Organizations should realize that their true wealth lies in their employees and so providing a healthy work environment for employees should be their primary objective.
3. ***Provide Personal and Career Growth Opportunities:*** An organization should provide employees with opportunities for personal/

professional development and growth to prepare them to accept responsibilities at higher levels.

4. ***Participative Management Style and Recognition:*** Flat organizational structures help organizations facilitate employee participation. A participative management style improves the quality of work life. Workers feel that they have control over their work processes and they also offer innovative ideas to improve them. Recognition also helps to motivate employees to perform better. Recognition can be in the form of rewarding employees for jobs well done.
5. ***Work and Life Balance:*** Organizations should provide relaxation time for the employees and offer tips to balance their personal and professional lives. They should not strain employees personal and social life by forcing on them demanding working hours, overtime work, business travel, untimely transfers etc.
6. ***Fun at Workplace:*** This is growing trend adopted by today's organizations to make their offices a fun place to work.

QWL in India

So far as its relevance in the Indian context is concerned, studies have shown that the realities of acute poverty, high unemployment, unreasonably high disparity between the poor and rich cast some doubts on the authentically of the concept.

Researchers adopt a similar position and question the validity and relevance of only socio-psychological factors in the Indian context. They suggest that management can initiate a number of changes in work procedures and rationalise wage structures to bring about improvement in worker amenities and working conditions—all of which lead to improvement in the quality of work life.

While referring to the Indian context, one needs to keep in mind that the quality of work life is an indicator of how free the society is from exploitation, injustice, inequality, oppression and restrictions on the continuity of growth of man, leading to his development to the fullest.

Studies have shown that in context of redesign efforts in India, workers are willing and able to move beyond their limited ascribed roles and take on additional responsibility.

This means that the basic concept of quality of work life will have to emanate from the idea of liberation from the entrapment of technology because it is the sovereign role of technology that has so far determined the form of organization resulting in not only a segmented work system but much more than that, a jaundiced view of the objective reality of work and life.

Social scientists present four key areas of concern for India:

1. Improving QWL implies improvement in wages, poor working conditions, worker amenities, safety and occupational health.
2. There is need for systematic analysis prior to change.
3. Dynamics of implementation and willingness for participation.
4. Diffusion and strategic considerations.

Despite the fact that unemployment has made work unattractive in the country, three critical elements can be adopted by organizations to become more responsive:

- Technological changes in work
- Educated entrance
- Market uncertainties.

In the Indian context, one needs to recognize an employee's economic, social and self-actualization needs accordingly so that they could develop their potential qualities and experience better quality of work life. A report published in 1981 on the findings of QWL programs in public sectors of India suggested some important implications.

As per the report, some new form of work organization can be applied to developing countries as low education is no problem for work restructuring and monetary incentives can be used for changing work organization for developing countries like India.

One should be wary of applying the western approach of quality of work life in the Indian context without searching the inner and social relevance of the concept. India is still in the grip of extreme poverty, lack of education and exploitation. The vicious cycle continues. Hence, any attempt to study and apply QWL concepts per se will not fetch much significance and relevance.

A look into environmental and other surrounding factors becomes necessary to bring concrete meaning to the analysis of quality of work life in Indian context. Therefore, an effort has been made here not to limit the factors of quality of work life but to also extend its relation to group behaviour so that it can be brought into an integrated whole as far as possible.

Besides ensuring fair pay, fair treatment of employees and safe working conditions, many companies respond to specific employee needs. In India, some companies that emphasize on quality of work life are Hewlett-

Packard, SmithKline Beecham, American Express, Colgate Palmolive, Gillette, Dr Reddy's Laboratories, Reliance and Maruti Udyog Limited.

HP allows flexible working arrangement for its employees and follows certain innovative practices such as allowing employees to avail leave for special occasions (marriage, exams, adoption, paternal leave and bereavement).

Emergence of QWL Movement in India

Following factors led to the QWL movement in India:

1. Changing profile of Indian workers from illiterate, rural, low caste individuals to educated, urban and essentially belonging to upper strata of caste structure has made them receptive towards their hopes and aspirations.
2. Workers differ from other factors of production such as machinery, land and capital as they have feelings and emotions. The establishment of a separate Ministry of Human Resource Development by the Government of India is a testimony to such realization.
3. The unionized aspect of labour force lends evidence that workers are aware of their rights.

Although the debate regarding the relevance of QWL is still raging on, the first known study of redesigning took place in Ahmedabad in 1958. The lessons of the Ahmedabad experiment lingered in a dormant state till a workshop was organised (in which social scientists from India and Australia participated).

The response to the workshop was favourable as some showed interest in undertaking pilot projects on work redesign to overcome employee apathy towards work. A series of workshops were planned across India from 1974, which led to specific thrust from some of the major industrial and government organizations to start action research projects.

On the whole, the seed sown somewhere in 1973 started digging roots in early 1975 through the efforts of resource persons from the academic world and industrial enterprises yielding positive results. Mostly, action researches in India took place in banks, life insurance, post offices and other public sector enterprises.

QWL in India is practised in a variety of operational systems such as workers' participation, job enrichment, quality circles etc. Following are some suggestions that can help in enhancing QWL:

Employers Can

1. Provide physical amenities at work place, health & safety and welfare provisions.
2. Involve workers in decision-making process.
3. Initiate suitable forms of work design.
4. Formalize QWL experience for future use.
5. Develop an appreciation of changing environment.

Employees Can

1. Educate and make employees aware about QWL.
2. Identify areas of collaboration with management.
3. Encourage them to participate in QWL activities.

Organizations Can

1. Organize workshops and seminars to bring about greater QWL awareness.
2. Initiate specific research projects in the field.
3. Provide professional assistance to organizations to help generate internal competence.
4. Develop better QWL profiles.

Government Can

1. Legislate standards and norms in newer areas.
2. Execute in policy to provide greater autonomy experiment with QWL.
3. Execute actions to ensure implementation of legislated facilities.
4. Encourage and adopt appropriate technology.

Social Aspect of QWL in Indian Context

As far as human life space is concerned, QWL and QoL cannot be considered as different entities since both of these depend on each other. Satisfaction in one aspect of human life is reflected in other and vice-versa. An important question arising in this perspective is whether one lives to work or works to live?

According to Indian philosophy, the ultimate goal of human life is self-actualization and attaining 'Moksha', that is, absorbing the soul into the Almighty. In achieving this, one should not leave everything aside and get into meditation alone, but work is considered as a way of life instrumental in achieving the ultimate goal of life. Work and life, according to Indian perspective, is itself a spiritual discipline.

As per the ancient teachings, work is 'worship' and workplace is a 'temple'. The preachings of various saints and the basic philosophy—central theme of the holy 'Bhagwat Gita'—is 'karma yoga'. Karma means 'duty' or 'work' and yoga means 'addition'. What this means serving the humanity through work, adding the soul with the Almighty. During the ancient era, four 'Varns' (social class of people) were prevailing in India.

According to one philosophy, these were broadly divided on the basis of 'work'. Hence it is evident that from the olden times that work remained an important part of societal demonstration in India. Currently, agrarian work culture prevails in India, which influences the industrial work in the country.

In an agrarian society, the work place and home are in close proximity. Work design provides room to take care of the family and to maintain social relations as well. On the other side in an industrialized society, workers have to move away from home and even sometimes their village/city to reach the workplace hence unrest follows dissatisfaction among them[8].

Human relations and QWL plays an important role in any organization irrespective of type of employees. While analysing non-managerial perspective of QWL, social scientists have revealed that in addition to issues of financial nature, certain non-financial factors seem to be of high concern from the perspective of non-managerial motivation. These include 'relational and social aspect of work life' and 'equity, justice and grievance handling mechanism'.

From the organizational point of view, QWL is considered as a philosophy which, although varies with organizations, brings them together under a common denominator: human dignity. Further, all human activities are oriented towards an end (a goal) and certain goals are subordinated to others but the ultimate goal is the pursuit of happiness.

Therefore, QWL and its social relevance in the Indian context is of paramount importance. Since work life consumes 8-12 hours daily on an average of a person and it has also been empirically proved that whatever a person does at work is reflected in the other spheres of his life. Hence, quality of life at work is very important to study.

Moreover, in the present era, dissatisfaction among employees and employers is increasing at a fast pace and the concept of social values & ethics is escaping from the human life.

Quantum Shift in QWL Profile[9]

Quality of work life plays a very important role in every organization. Employees are the force that is behind every successful organization. No organisation can become successful with technology alone as a strong work force is required to manage it.

Beginning on shaky ground in the late 1960's in India, it has been growing in stature and importance in every work place. Initially, quality of work life focussed on the effects of employment on general well being and the health of the workers.

But the focus has changed in present scenario. Organizations today are creating good environment for their workers providing financial and non-financial incentives so that they can be retained for the longest period possible and also for achieving organizational goals.

Factors that influence and decide the quality of work life are:

1. Working conditions
2. Use of capacities at work
3. Opportunities and growth
4. Social integration
5. Constitutionalism (respect of laws and policies)
6. Work life balance
7. Social relevance and importance of work
8. Fair and appropriate salary (compensation).

All organizations and managements must pay heed to the fact that a happy and healthy employee will give better turnover, make good decisions and positively contribute to the organizational goal.

Unique QWL Methods Today

Organizations all over the world are adopting unique methods to enhance the quality of work life in their work culture. Facility for prayer/meditation at the workplace has emerged as an important QWL factor. Some other prominent examples are as follows[10]:

- The ***American Stock Exchange*** has a Torah Study Group.
- ***Boeing*** has Christian, Jewish and Muslim prayer groups.

- *Apple Computers* office has a meditation room and employees are given 30 minutes to meditate or pray.
- *Prentice-Hall Publishing* has a quiet room for employees where they can take mental retreats.
- *Marriott International's* 10,000 workers dedicate a day of service to their local communities each year.
- *IBM* funds childcare centers at 60 of its locations.
- *Intel* offers 22 weeks of maternity leave.
- *SAS* has low absenteeism and only 3% turnover due to no-lay-off policy, 35-hour workweeks, flexi time and on site amenities like gym, medical clinic and message therapists.
- *Volvo* changed its assembly line system which led to greater job satisfaction, low absenteeism and turnover.
- *Tata Group* offers free medical aid, free telephone facility, leave with pay, accident compensation, profit sharing bonus and retiring gratuity.
- *Indian Armed Forces (Army, Navy and Air Force)* provide a two-year fully paid educational leave to all Permanent Commission personnel.
- *Kendriya Vidyalaya Sangathan (KVS)* offers life-long free education to the children of its permanent employees (academic as well as non-academic).
- *Wipro* has instituted paid holidays, maternity leave, free counselling sessions and break-rooms to help redress stress and burn-out.
- *Google India* extends flexible work schedules, massage parlours, outdoor & indoor games and sleep pods.
- *RMSI* provides parenting & relationship counselling, child psychology & self-defence workshops, zumba lessons etc.
- *SAP Labs India* offers 20-week-long maternity and paid adoption leave for women.
- *Hindustan Unilever* has a meditation room, yoga classes, a library and low-cost quality education at Aditya Birla Schools for employees' children.
- *Bharti Airtel* has flexible work hours, day care and grocery centres, fitness & spa facilities, 6 months leave for personnel and educational benefits.
- *Standard Chartered Bank India* provides day care centres for women employees and Happy Fridays.
- *MakeMyTrip* has introduced social engagements with NGOs, theme day, rock and performances and sports activities.
- *Kotak Mahindra* offers Bollywood and Hollywood movie screenings, annual family days, indoor & outdoor games and yoga sessions.

UNIT–II

Approaches to Quality of Work Life

Socio-Technical

In order to understand quality of work life, it is essential to understand the socio-technical approach to an organization as a methodology of change.

Managers, academicians and all those concerned with the workplace are finding that many of yesterday's sure life solutions to personal problems are no longer effective because of today's changing societal values, affecting work satisfaction of humans in the industrial organization.[1]

People are looking for new ways to structure jobs and to organize work in order to improve economic experiences for the worker, basically the development of QWL movement.

The quality of work life represents a blending of these very real concerns for human values in today's society with awareness that all individuals devote the greater part of their mature lives to work, expending time, energy and physical and mental resources to this endeavour.

It recognizes that work is the chief determinant of an individual's freedom, growth and self-respect, as well as his standard of living. Further, the role of a breadwinner is fundamental to the survival of the family and society.

Society has also begun to realize that human resource represents the only remaining plentiful natural resource, and that both the individual and society can clearly benefit from their full utilization. Finally, the most important fact is that production, industrial growth and technical advances are clearly not ends in themselves but simply a means to an end, that is, the improvement of quality of life for all.

The main concept used to explain QWL is that of the 'socio-technical system'. It is based on the logic that any productive system embraces a given kind of equipment, layout and a work organization, but the latter has a certain social and psychological properties independent of technology.

It is further suggested that a socio-technical system must also satisfy the financial conditions of industry, which it is a part of. A productive system comprising the three key dimensions of technical, social and economic, which are all interdependent, are the best.

The socio-technical approach in organizational development is an approach to complex organizational work design that recognizes the interaction between people and technology in workplaces. The term also refers to the interaction between society's complex infrastructures and human behaviour. In this sense, society itself, and most of its sub-structures, are complex socio-technical systems.

The term 'socio-technical systems' was coined by Eric Trist, Ken Bamforth and Fred Emery, in the World War II era, based on their work with workers in English coal mines at the Tavistock Institute in London.[2] It pertains to a theory regarding the social aspects of people, society and technical aspects of organizational structure and processes. Here, technical does not necessarily imply material technology.

The focus is on procedures and related knowledge, that is, it refers to the ancient Greek term 'techne'. "Technical" is a term used to refer to structure and a broader sense of technicalities. Socio-technical refers to the inter-relatedness of social and technical aspects of an organization or the society as a whole.

The socio-technical approach is about joint optimization with a shared emphasis on achievement of both excellence in technical performance and quality in people's work lives. It proposes a number of different ways of achieving joint optimisation.

They are usually based on designing different kinds of organization, ones in which the relationships between socio and technical elements lead to the emergence of productivity and well-being.

This approach refers to the inter-relatedness of social and technical aspects of an organization. It is founded on two main principles:

- One is that the interaction of social and technical factors creates conditions for successful (or unsuccessful) organizational performance. This interaction consists partly of linear "cause and effect" relationships (the relationships that are normally "designed") and partly from "non-linear", complex, even unpredictable relationships (the good or bad relationships that are often unexpected). Whether designed or not, both types of interaction occur when socio and technical elements are put to work.

- The corollary of this, and the second of the two main principles, is that optimization of each aspect alone (socio or technical) tends to increase not only the quantity of unpredictable, "un-designed" relationships, but those relationships that are injurious to the system's performance.

The key elements of socio-technical approach include combining human elements and technical systems together to enable new possibilities for work and pave the way for technological change. Due to its mutual causality, this approach has become widely linked with autonomy, completeness and job satisfaction as both systems can work together to achieving a goal.

The Tavistock researchers' said the employees using the new and improved system should participate in determining the required quality of working life improvements. Participative socio-technical design can be achieved by in-depth interviews, questionnaires and collection of data and the analysis of relevant documents.

The researchers believed that flexibility and speed are the twin pillars of socio-technical approach's future. To transform a business organization, the mindset must first be changed, as companies in the future will have to find a balance between four extremes:

- Hierarchies versus Networks
- Profit versus Meaningfulness
- Control versus Empowerment
- Planning versus Experiments.

The socio-technical approach will continue to be of interest to researchers and therefore will adapt overtime to meet the ever-changing climate. New socio-technical approaches in QWL have endeavoured to overcome the shortcomings of the old approaches, through relying on theories from the social sciences (social science is a scientific study of human society and social relationships, that is, how people interact with each other.)

Although structures are changing within the industry, companies and managers, employees, their rights and needs must always be given a high priority. Job/work design in organizational development is the application of socio-technical approach and techniques to the humanization of work, for example, through job enrichment.

The aims of job design to improved job satisfaction, to improved through-put, to improved quality and to reduced employee problems, for example, grievances, absenteeism.

Evolution of Socio-technical Approach

The evolution of socio-technical approach has seen its development from being approached as a social system exclusively. The realisation of the joint optimisation of social and technical systems was later realised. It was divided into sections where primary work that looks into principles and description, and how to incorporate technical designs on a macro-social level.

Benefits of seeing socio-technical systems through a work system lens—Analysing and designing socio-technical systems from a work system perspective and eliminates the artificial distinction of the social system from the technical system. This also eliminates the idea of joint optimization. By using a work system lens in can bring many benefits, such as:

1. Viewing the work system as a whole, making it easier to discuss and analyse.
2. More organized approach by even outlining basic understanding of a work system.
3. A readily usable analysis method making it more adaptable for performing analysis of a work system.
4. Does not require guidance by experts and researchers.
5. Reinforces the idea that a work system exists to produce a product(s)/ service(s).
6. Easier to theorize potential staff reductions, job roles changing and reorganizations.
7. Encourages motivation and good will while reducing the stress from monitoring.
8. Conscientious that documentation and practice may differ.

QWL's Socio-technical Approach

The socio-technical approach of quality of work life was developed in England during the late 1940s by Eric Trist and his colleagues at the Tavistock Institute of Human Relations.

These researchers conducted seminal studies on the coal mining industry, where the introduction of new technology had shifted the social patterns of work so profoundly that productivity and job satisfaction were negatively affected.

In response, managers and workers fundamentally reorganized their work patterns, returning to small teams and collaborative process that had prevailed before the mechanization of the industry.

In these and subsequent studies across a variety of work settings, Trist and his colleagues found that technical changes in an industry (for example, increased automation) consistently produce profound changes in the social aspects of work as well.

They became convinced that work must be conceptualized as a joint social and technical process and that the so-called self-regulating work group is the essential building block of effective organizations.

Following the initial Tavistock studies, further experiments in the design of work as per the socio-technical approach proceeded slowly in the United Kingdom, India and Europe during the 1950s.

Support for the approach was bolstered in early 1960s when the government of Norway supported a labour and management effort to introduce Trist's principle of "industrial democracy" into the industry there.

In the years since those early efforts, socio-technical approaches have been widely applied in a variety of work settings. The approach is commonplace today and has come to be viewed as a major category of organizational theory.

Although, there are no universally accepted defining principles and assumptions of the socio-technical approach, the following ideas are commonly identified with this approach:

- *Organizations are Open Systems:* They exist as animate entities in an environment of customers, competitors, suppliers, regulators, technology, stakeholders and the broader economy. They must scan that environment, exchange with it (receive inputs and produce outputs), anticipate and react to environmental changes in adaptive ways.
- The Tavistock group was strongly influenced by general systems theory as it was articulated in the physical sciences by Ludwig von Bertalanffy during the 1940s and 1950s. Fred Emery, a noted member of the Tavistock team, brought von Bertalanffy's work to the attention of Trist and the rest of Tavistock group, where it became a pillar of the socio-technical approach.
- *Change is Norm in Work Environment:* The business environment is aptly described as turbulent and uncertain, connoting that change can be sudden, extreme and largely unpredictable. Turbulence disrupts previously stable patterns of interaction and requires a rethinking and redesign of work.

- *Joint Optimization is Essential:* Because work is, by its very nature, an intertwined technical and social process, both aspects need to be integrated into the design of work to achieve the critical objective of improved productivity and quality of work life.
- *Equifinality:* A notion diametrically opposed to Frederick Winslow Taylor's concept that there is only one road to success, prevails. In all living systems, there are many possible ways to achieve the same outcome. Thus, there are many possible work designs that can achieve the joint goals of productivity and quality of work life.
- *Work Must be Designed for Flexibility:* Because the environment is constantly changing, no hardwired design, no matter how well adapted to current conditions, will continue to fit the evolving demands of the environment. The organization must be designed and continually redesigned for flexibility. The design process is never completed. No design is ever final.
- *Design with Minimum Critical Specification:* Work designers should specify only what absolutely must be specified in terms of technical and social job design parameters and allow the organization the flexibility to specify the rest for itself.
- *Stakeholder Input is Critical:* Employee participation at multiple levels is essential in creating a socio-technically designed organization and operating it daily. High levels of employee empowerment are central to the socio-technical philosophy.
- *Teams do the Work:* Teams are the universal, most visible end product of a socio-technical design. The primary production unit is the self-directed work team (also known as the self-managing, self-regulating, semi-autonomous or high-performance team). Team members are usually expected or even required to acquire broader skills and more business knowledge so that they can take on a higher level of decision-making ability and authority.

In practice, such multi-skilled teams commonly complete a whole, meaningful unit of work rather than a subcomponent only. They absorb some functions traditionally provided by support departments, such as managing quality, setting production goals, tracking performance and productivity and making process improvements. Self-managing teams are embodiment of the socio-technical systems approach.

- *Teams Becoming more Capable of Self-direction:* When such a stage arrives, teams become less reliant on daily supervisory control. They can, thus, be allowed to manage the bulk of their daily work internally. Management is then able to step out of team boundaries—to focus more strategically on keeping the team linked with other teams and other parts of the organization helping to build and manage such structures as pay-for-skill and gain-sharing programs, which support the team concept.

- *Arising Problems:* When problems occur, they should be handled at the source by those who directly encounter them. Thus, quality variances are detected and addressed promptly by line employees who are trained in quality as well as production.

QWL Principles

The basic features of organizational socio-technical approach are enunciated as follows:

1. The design of an organization must be compatible with its objectives. In order to adapt to change and be capable of using creative capacities on an individual, a system should provide people an opportunity to participate in job designs they are required to perform.
2. There should be minimal crucial specification of tasks, minimal critical allocation of tasks to jobs or of jobs to roles, specification of objective and minimal critical specification of methods of obtaining them.
3. There should be variance control. This means that wherever possible, people should be allowed to inspect their own work, thereby learning from their mistakes and redesigning a number of communication links across departmental boundaries. Fewer the variances, lesser the levels of supervision and control required.
4. Organizations having a repertoire of different performances to achieve their objectives, multiple functioning should be encouraged. Multiple functioning is achieved by training the same people in repertoire of different performances, each requiring a separate set of rules and role relationships.
5. More control of activities within a department becomes the responsibilities of members. The more a supervisor's role is concentrated on boundary activities assuring adequate resources to the team to carry out its functions, co-coordinating activities with other departments and viewing ahead the changes likely to impart upon them.

   Boundary maintenance is the role of supervisor in a well-defined system. In some cases, responsibility for managing their own boundaries is given to respective teams while the responsibility of coordination is placed on those whose activities require to be coordinated.

6. Information systems should be designed to provide information to the point where action on the basis of it will be needed. This will enable work teams to learn to control variances and to anticipate events likely to have a bearing on their performance.
7. Systems of social support should be designed to reinforce behaviours that the organisation structure is designed to elicit.
8. The objective of organizational design should be to provide a high quality of working life to its members. There are six characteristics of a "good job" that can be striven for in the design of organizations and jobs, that is, variety opportunity to learn on the job, some minimal area of decision-making that individuals can call their own, minimal degree of social support and recognition in the work place, ability to relate what individuals produce in his social life and a feeling that the job leads to some sort of desirable future.
9. There is a change-over period from old to new requiring a transitional organization. Implementation planning should begin with the beginning of design. This needs planning, organising, designing and training. A careful rehearsal of roles should be performed during change-over and especially the continuing training role of supervisor.
10. Design is a reiterative process. The closure of options opens new avenues. As soon as design is implemented, its consequences indicate the need for redesign.

There is a moderate amount of field research on the effectiveness of the socio-technical approach. However, because applications vary widely, it is not always easy to determine what was done and which parts of the design or redesign may have been effective. And there certainly are reports in the literature of failed or minimally effective socio-technical design efforts.

Still, the bulk of evidence from studies that meet the standard criteria of research excellence points to substantial increases in productivity—increased throughput, reduced rejects or scrap, decreased cycle time and decreased machine downtime.

Effects on employee satisfaction and quality of work life, measured directly through opinion surveys or indirectly through data on absenteeism, grievances and job bid-outs, are also generally positive.

The huge body of anecdotal evidence is also strongly positive, showing productivity improvements in the 25 per cent to 45 per cent range and greatly improved employee satisfaction. Such gains, touted in the practitioner literature and lore, are sufficient to keep the approach prominent in contemporary practice.

Critics of the socio-technical systems approach observe that applications commonly accept the technical work process as a given and focus largely on social redesign. Furthermore, despite such guiding principles as equifinality, the social redesign always results in the same solution—the self-managing team.

A further criticism is that the classical socio-technical design process, which relies on steering committees and design teams to do analysis and design, is very slow (24 to 36 months being a common time frame) and costly. However, there are alternatives, such as the "future search" methodology, that compress the timeline for work redesign.

The socio-technical systems philosophy and approach to the design of work continues to spread. The approach forms a central part of the philosophical base of the popular contemporary high-performance organization model.

Job Restructuring

Job restructuring[3] typically means modifying the employee's job in order to reallocate or redistribute non-essential job functions, or altering when and/or how a function of the job is performed. But it can also involve changing the way essential functions have traditionally been performed.

For example, a court decision in 2007 held that the employer may have been able to accommodate the plaintiff, suffering from cerebral palsy, by allowing him to use certain equipment such as a wheelchair, scooter and hand scanner while working as a cashier.

Job restructuring as a form of reasonable accommodation may involve reallocating or redistributing the marginal functions of a job. Job restructuring frequently is accomplished by exchanging marginal functions of a job that cannot be performed by a person with a disability for marginal job functions performed by one or more other employees.

An employee must be able to perform the essential functions of the job. But where it is possible to remove certain non-essential tasks from an employee's work requirements, this should be done.

For example, an agency has two data processing clerks. Typing on the computer is an essential function while using the phone is a marginal one. If a qualified data processing clerk had speech impairment, it would be reasonable to assign the function of using the phone to the employee without speech impairment in exchange for doing that employee's filing.

The agency is not required to reallocate essential job functions. It may be a reasonable accommodation to change when or how the essential functions are done. These include:

- Reassign work at the existing site among co-workers. For example, if a secretary had a vision impairment that prevented her from typing in small spaces on forms, whenever such forms needed to be prepared, they might be assigned to another secretary without vision impairment. In exchange, the secretary with a disability could assume one of the colleague's duties, such as filing.
- Eliminate non-essential tasks. For example, if a part of the job is not necessary, it could be eliminated entirely. A mail clerk, rather than travelling to post office early in the morning, might be allowed to wait for regular mail delivery.
- Reassign visits to accessible sites. For example, a repairperson who uses a wheelchair could service accessible sites, while the other sites could be assigned to someone who does not have mobility impairment.
- Allow work in other than the traditional office setting. For example, a surveyor can make calls on a designated line from home instead of having to come regularly to an inaccessible office to make those calls.

The changes in business world are some of the most testing times for a company to withstand. It is for this reason why adaptability is one of the crucial attributes in the corporate space today. To survive, one must be able to swiftly change course whenever things go bad.

Of these many changes that a company may have to endure, one of the hardest is job restructuring. It is because often restructuring changes a significant chunk of the business. This can be products, employees, ownership or even the original mission and business model.

It is common knowledge that a strong team of employees can help build a business from the ground up. But one can't expect a business to prosper if the workers are not thriving with it. To help keep employees satisfied and motivated, the company management must resort to job restructuring.

Restructuring the workplace and redesigning job is one of the two major thrusts of quality of work life movement. Job enlargement and job enrichment make employees feel more involved in and challenged by the actual content of work. Jobs are designed to use a wider variety of skills by involving them in entire tasks.

This view of organizational efficiency gained a secured niche in the minds of organizational and industrial leaders, and has remained virtually unscathed for years.

Job restructuring is when an employer changes the nature and responsibilities of an employee's position. With job restructuring, one might add similar tasks to an employee's workload or one might give higher-level responsibilities to an employee, even though they are in the same position.

It comprises restructuring the elements including tasks, duties and responsibilities of a specific job in order to make it more encouraging and inspiring to employees or workers.

The process includes revising, analyzing, altering, reforming and reshuffling the job-related content and dimensions to increase the variety of assignments and functions to motivate employees and make them feel as an important asset of the organization.

The main objective of conducting job redesigning is to place the right person at the right job and get the maximum output while increasing their level of satisfaction. Job restructuring can be broken down into two categories: horizontal and vertical restructuring.

Horizontal Restructuring

Horizontal restructuring consists of adding new tasks to an employee's workload that fall into the same level as their current responsibilities.

For example, a company employee working in the accounts department starts taking on more financial-related tasks along with his normal job responsibilities. These new tasks are on the same level as the employee's other duties, but they fall into a different department or category.

Vertical Restructuring

Vertical restructuring is when an employee's position is changed to take on higher-level responsibilities along with their regular tasks.

For example, giving your customer service employee the responsibilities of customer service manager, like balancing the cash register.

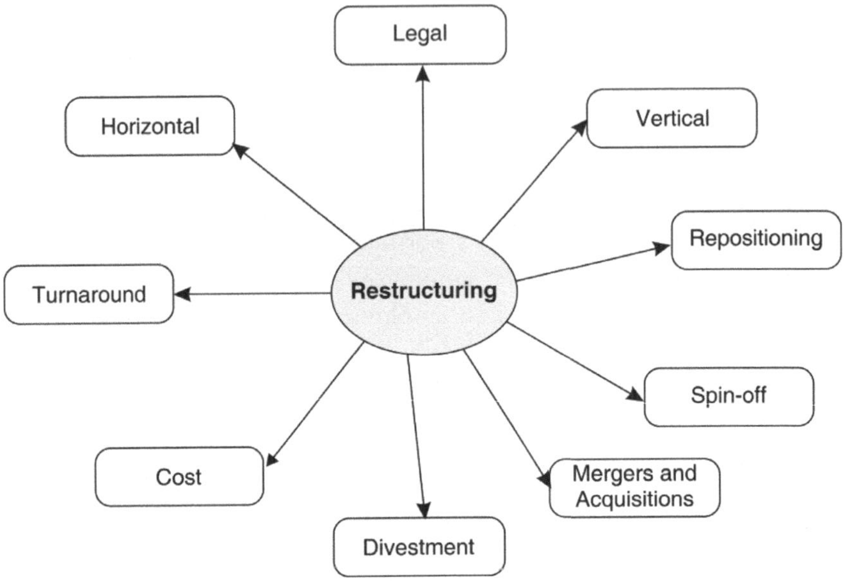

Job Restructuring

Legal Restructuring

In this type of restructuring, company executives use when they decided to make a company its own legal entity. Another purpose of legal restructuring in business is to evaluate the ethical practises and procedures within a company and create a legal structure to ensure each department adheres to legal practices.

Turnaround Restructuring

It refers to any restructuring activities that seek to replace product lines, business models, organizational structure, culture and other areas that do not contribute to a company's success.

An example of this would be when company leaders decide to discontinue a major product due to low sales and consumer interest. From this, they can develop a new product or set of products that match the revised needs of consumers within their industry.

Cost Restructuring

Companies use cost restructuring to maintain operations before or during economic downturns. This means restructuring department budgets, enacting furloughs or lay-offs and other cost-saving measures.

Repositioning Restructuring

It is a type of restructuring that organizations use specifically when they want to change their business model and redirect their focus of their enterprise. An example of this would be if a major clothing retailer expanded their business model to include home furnishings and decor.

Spin-off Restructuring

Spin-off restructuring refers to the process by which a company makes one or more branch locations or company sectors into their own business entities. This enhances the company's value and allows it to take on the role of a parent organization.

Divestment

In this type of restructuring, companies close branch locations, departments or other business units due to revised needs of profitability expectations. For example, a company removes their community engagement department and moves employees to work as members of the marketing department.

Mergers and Acquisitions

It refers to a type of restructuring in business where a company consolidates branch locations or appoints one person as the head of multiple departments.

Reasons for Job Restructuring

Companies may use job restructuring for a number of reasons such as to reorganize a company, meet reasonable accommodation requirement and improve employee satisfaction.

1. *Company Reorganization:* At some point, one may find the need to reorganize the company. To accomplish this business reorganization, one may have to lay-off employees, condense departments and eliminate certain processes. Because of these changes, one likely needs to shift employees' positions and responsibilities. Job restructuring is a good option if one is planning to reorganize the company and switch up employees' work responsibilities.
2. *Reasonable Accommodation:* Many companies change the structure of jobs to help meet reasonable accommodation requirements in the

workplace. It is an adjustment an employer makes to give a disabled individual equal access to employment opportunities.

Job Redesign Process

Vertical restructuring is when an employee's position is changed to take on higher-level responsibilities along with their regular tasks.

- *Revising Job Content:* This process involves recollecting and revising job-related information to determine the inconsistency between person and the job.
- *Analyzing Job-related Information:* Once the job analyst is through with recollecting and revising job content, analyzing discrepancies is the next step. It is done to determine hindrances in performing job-related tasks and duties, and investigate why an employee is not able to deliver the expected output.
- *Altering Job Elements:* The next step is to amend job elements. It may include cut-back on extra responsibilities or addition of more functions and a higher degree of accountability. The basic aim of restructuring a job content is to design it in such a manner that encourages employees to work harder and perform better.
- *Reformation of Job Description and Specification:* After restructuring job elements, a job analyst needs to reform its description and specification in order to make sure that the worker placed at a particular place is able to deliver what is expected of him.
- *Reshuffling Job-related Tasks and Duties:* This is followed by reallocation of new or altered tasks and functions to employees. It may be done by rotating, enriching, enlarging and engineering the job. The idea is to motivate the performers while increasing their satisfaction levels.

Therefore, thc purpose of job restructuring is to identify task significance and skill variety available in the organization, and realloca-ting job-related tasks and responsibilities according to the specific skills possessed by an employee.

Some reasonable accommodation modifications include:

- Revamping a position to accommodate a worker's needs.
- Allowing individuals to work from home.
- Modifying an employee's work schedule.
- Making changes to the workplace (such as a wheelchair ramp).
- Providing job coaches.

Restructuring a position can give disabled employees equal opportunity in the workplace and allow them to thrive professionally. Job restructuring also helps the business stay up-to-date with central government guidelines.

Satisfaction and Benefit Aspects

Job restructuring does not always result from other changes in the workplace. Sometimes, employers restructure positions to satisfy or benefit an employee.

Job restructuring may benefit workers who:

- Have strengths in various areas or departments.
- Need motivation.
- Don't like routines or repetition.

For example, an employee, Atharv, has many skills and strengths. However, he prefers handling a variety of tasks and wants to expand his area of expertise. To meet Atharv's career goals, the management might restructure his position a bit. He now works 30 hours a week in customer service and 10 hours in sales if he enjoys up-selling products to customers.

Satisfying workers is a win-win for both the employee and employer. This helps improve employee satisfaction and also value-add to their skill set. This makes the employee happier thereby increasing his chances of sticking with the company in the long-run.

Advantages and Disadvantages of Job Restructuring

Job restructuring is not for every business. Before one decides to implement job restructuring in the company, one should judiciously weigh the pros and cons.

Advantages of Job Restructuring

- Meeting equal employment opportunity requirements (EEO)
- Aligning with company reorganization
- Improving employee satisfaction and benefits
- Enhances quality of work life
- Increases organization's and employees' productivity
- Brings a sense of belongingness in employees
- Creates a right person-job fit.

Disadvantages of Job Restructuring

- Costs
- Spending time making adjustments (for example, spending time adjusting job descriptions and duties)
- Overlapping positions
- Employees being uncertain about their responsibilities
- Potential conflict in the workplace.

Steps for Restructuring a Job

Before restructuring a position, one must ask the following questions:

1. What are the pros and cons of job restructuring for my business?
2. Is job restructuring absolutely necessary?
3. Are there any other changes I can make before restructuring a position?
4. Will job restructuring negatively impact any employees?

If the company management decides to move forward with job restructuring, one must complete the following steps:

1. Notify the employee(s)
2. Inform necessary departments about any changes (for example, HR)
3. Have the employee fill out or sign paperwork (for example, contract or notification of changes)
4. Adjust the employee's pay (if applicable)
5. Implement job restructuring in the workplace

Changes are never easy but they are always crucial for a business. In this way, job restructuring is no different either. But, while it may be difficult, a redesign can help companies survive, compete and thrive in their domain during difficult times. It is a fact that every employer must understand this to succeed, sooner or later.

Examples of Job Restructuring

Job restructuring is a complex process, which is why it must be considered on a case-by-case basis. Listed below are some examples from the Indian corporate that created quite a flutter *vis-a-vis* quality of work life:

- An individual with epilepsy worked as a driver for a delivery service. Due to his condition, he was prohibited by law from driving a commercial vehicle. His job required him to drive a commercial vehicle but only 5% of the time.

It would have been a reasonable accommodation to restructure his job to eliminate the requirement that he drive commercial vehicles. His employer could have removed this job task by making only a few small route adjustments, which were regularly made for other reasons.

- A fire-fighter became blind in one eye. He could do his entire job except he could not drive the fire truck. His employer could have removed this job task. Driving the truck was not a specialized task and it was not a task that only a limited number of employees could perform. His job description noted that it was something he "may" need to do, not "must" need to do.
- An employee with social anxiety disorder worked as a lower division clerk in a High Court. She experienced panic, stress and extreme nervousness when working at the front desk, but she was able to do other job responsibilities. It would have been a reasonable accommodation to restructure her job to eliminate the requirement to work at the front desk because there were 30 other LDCs and fewer than 15% regularly worked the front desk and some never did at all.

The right approach would have been to show empathy towards them and involve these (and many more) employees in other productive work profiles. The organizational management should have kept in mind that job restructuring can happen on a smaller scale at department-level as well, where department managers could have reorganized their roles, priorities and department budgets.

Group Cohesiveness

Many people wonder what the team cohesion means. Group cohesiveness/Team Cohesiveness (also known as Social Cohesion) is a degree of unity of any group. Team cohesiveness is a degree to which group members are attracted or motivated by each other.

It is defined as the degree to which members are attracted to one another and share the group's goal. That is, the more the members are attracted to each other and the more the group's goals align with their individual goals, the greater the group's cohesiveness.

It is seen that members of a highly cohesive group develop some common characteristics:

- Everyone respects each other.
- They are fully committed to the decision made by the group.
- There is good accountability amongst members.

Cohesiveness is a vital aspect of any workplace for better productivity. Cohesiveness and job engagement are interchangeably used as they all belong to the category of what forms an effective and productive environment at workplace today.

Today's organizations look at people as assets, who are increasingly getting involved in complex technologies and are functioning in extreme complex economic, social and political environments. Humans have no time to interact with each other while discharging their duties, which results in stress at workplace. Their socio-cultural differences such as region, language, caste, class, religious beliefs etc are also a contributing factor in this regard.

Engagement is not a mathematical process that can be managed by the press of a button. It is a human experience that reacts to each interaction an employee may have. Our job as communicators is to lend and help our organization create positive engaging interactions.

Building cohesive teams is absolutely essential to high employee engagement levels and high performance. Employee engagement and performance can be adversely affected if the team is dysfunctional to any degree due to conflict, ambiguity or misunderstanding.

It is well known that new teams go through a natural process to start performing, which can take some time. Various programs have been designed to accelerate this process and develop high levels of team engagement quickly.

Features

Group cohesiveness is another important factor besides group norms that affect group behaviour. If group cohesion is high, interaction between its members and the degree of agreement is also high.

1. Cohesive groups have relatively few members.
2. Members have similar interests and backgrounds.
3. Group loyalty among the members is high because the group enjoys high status.
4. Members interact among themselves quite frequently and their interpersonal communication is very effective.
5. They are physically remote or isolated from other groups in the organization.
6. The group leader usually rewards cooperative behaviour.
7. Members stand united against any perceived external threats to the group.

8. They have a history of past success.
9. Members keep themselves glued to the group as they feel that their needs would be satisfied by the group.

Goals

A cohesive group alone can achieve the desired goals. Everyone in the group knows his responsibility. Goal is not simply an outcome of the work for it has to be result-oriented. This is made possible by a responsible and cohesive group.

1. *Personal Attractiveness:* Virtues and values of an individual are the basis of personal attraction between each other. These foster respect and mutual understanding. They also create confidence and trust in the members of a group, leading to personal growth and development.
2. *Independence for Cooperative Decisions:* Members of a group may have independence to perform their functions with other groups. In the modern management system, a cohesive group with a facility of cooperative decision at work place needs to be promoted.
3. *Management Behaviour:* The behaviour of management has direct effect on the cohesion of work groups. A conflict is disgusting and is considered as something resulting from inter-personnel relations rather than structural contradictions. Management has a special responsibility to obtain the consent of workers to its program of action to motivate them.
4. *Group Provides Security:* Members are provided security by the group from all external threats and pressures from other groups. In a particular situation for safeguarding individual interest, the group may forget their differences to meet threats and pressures, and protect the members.
5. *Leadership Style:* Every leader has a style of his own style to deal with inter-personal relations. An effective leader understands his subordinates as well as their needs. He integrates individuals with the organization and leads them to achieve the goal. Thus, leadership influences group cohesiveness to a large extent.

Outcomes

1. Increment in interaction of individuals
2. Cooperative behaviour
3. Satisfaction amongst group members

4. Goal orientation and success
5. Enhancement of productivity.

Relationship between Group Cohesiveness and Productivity

Evidences such as Hawthrone studies[4] indicate that highly cohesive groups are more effective than those with less cohesiveness. It is also seen that a high degree of cohesiveness is both a cause and effect of high productivity. However, the relationship between these two is moderated by the degree to which group attitudes are aligned with organizational goals.

Cohesive groups have important implications for managers mainly for two reasons. First, a cohesive group being united commands control over its members. It enables the group to command a powerful bargaining power.

Second, if the cohesive groups are not managed and motivated effectively, its productivity is sure to be low. Therefore, it is imperative for the management to work in close cooperation with cohesive groups to attain higher productivity.

Group cohesiveness and productivity shows three types of characteristics:

1. The productivity of a cohesive group members' tends to be more uniform. This is so because high group cohesiveness promotes high control over the level of production of individual members and this reduces variation among them.
2. In the group with low cohesiveness, productivity tends to show wide variation among members reflecting that the group has lower social control over its members.
3. There may be a perception that a highly cohesive group produces better results. However, this relationship is much more complex than what it appears to be. This is because the relationship is modified by the degree to which the group's attitudes align with its own goals or those of the organization of which it is a part.

Thus, the relationship of cohesiveness and productivity of a group depends on the alignment of the group's attitudes towards the organizational goals (setting performance norms). It is, therefore, safe to say that both group cohesiveness and productivity need to be high for a higher productivity.

If the performance norms are low, the group's productivity will be low inspite of high group cohesiveness. Even in the case of high performance norms, less cohesive groups may produce more as compared to highly cohesive groups because of lower impact of group on its individual members.

This relationship between group cohesiveness, group norms and productivity has important implications for management. If the management simply focuses its attention to have better cohesive groups, it may not be able to achieve high productivity unless it focuses its attention on group norms and their alignment with organizational goals.

Advantages of High Group Cohesiveness

1. Goal Achievement
2. Satisfaction
3. Quantity and Quality of Interaction
4. Group Think
5. Enhancement of Communication Skills
6. Improves coordination
7. Inspirational source
8. Saves effort and time.

Disadvantages of Low Group Cohesiveness

1. Difficulty in Achieving Goals
2. Less Interaction
3. 'I' Approach
4. Less Commitment to Group Goals.

Importance

When we talk about any organization it is important that there is team cohesion to achieve the goal. Group cohesiveness is important because of the following factors:

- *Performance:* If there is great bonding amongst the group then the performance of the group will become better. If management wants good performance it should encourage its employees towards group cohesion.
- *Satisfaction:* When there is group cohesion the performance will increase, and hence, it will bring satisfaction to the employees and they will work harder to achieve the goal.

- *Assurance Pressure:* When we talk about group cohesiveness characters, behaviour is the most important factor. When there is a great bonding between groups, it is assured that surely the task will be completed.
- *Emotional Factors:* When people work together and have strong bonding people feel emotionally attached, and hence, people will work with each other in harmony and achieve the goal together.

Managerial Actions to Increase Group Cohesiveness

A manager can adopt any one or more of the following actions to encourage group cohesiveness in their organizations:

1. Make the group smaller
2. Encourage agreement with group goals
3. Increase the time members spend together
4. Increase the status of group and the perceived difficulty of getting membership of the group
5. Stimulate competition with other groups
6. Give rewards to the group rather than to members
7. Physically isolate the group
8. Increase membership homogeneity
9. Increase interaction among members.

Managerial Actions to Decrease Group Cohesiveness

Sometimes, high group cohesiveness adversely affects the productivity. In such cases, managers have to reduce the cohesiveness of groups.

Following are some of the actions that can be initiated by managers:

1. Induce disagreement on group goals
2. Increase membership heterogeneity
3. Restrict interactions among members
4. Increase group size
5. Reduce the time members spend together
6. Allocate rewards to individuals rather than to group members
7. Remove physical isolation
8. Disband the group
9. Introduce a dominating member.

Consequences

Group cohesion has been linked to a range of positive and negative consequences. Its consequences on motivation, performance, member satisfaction, member emotional adjustment and the pressures felt by members are vital for organizational well-being.

- *Motivation:* Cohesion and motivation of team members are key factors that contribute to a company's performance. By adaptability development, self-worth and personal motivation growth, each member becomes able to feel confident and progress in the team. Social loafing is less frequent when there is cohesion in a team. The motivation of each team member is also considerably greater then.
- *Performance:* Studies have shown that cohesion can cause performance and that performance can cause cohesion. Most meta-analyses (studies that have summarized the results of many studies) have shown that there is a relationship between cohesion and performance. This is the case even when cohesion is defined in different ways.

When cohesion is defined as attraction, it is better correlated with performance. When it is defined as task commitment, it is also correlated with performance, though to a lesser degree than cohesion as attraction. Not enough studies were performed with cohesion defined as group pride. In general, cohesion defined in all these ways was positively related with performance.

However, some groups may have a stronger cohesion-performance relationship than others. Smaller groups have a better cohesion-performance relationship than larger groups. Experts are of the opinion that cohesion-performance relationships are strongest in sports teams.

From strongest to weakest, they ranked the strength of relationship in the following order:

- Sports teams
- Military squads
- Groups formed for a purpose
- Groups in experimental settings.

There is some evidence that cohesion may be more strongly related to performance for groups that have highly interdependent roles than for groups in which members are independent. In regards to group productivity, having attraction and group pride may not be enough.

It is necessary to have task commitment in order to be productive. Furthermore, groups with high performance goals were extremely productive. However, it is important to note that the link between cohesion and performance can differ depending on the nature of group that is studied.

Some studies that have focused on this relationship have led to divergent results. For example, a study conducted on the link between cohesion and performance in a governmental social service department found a low positive association between these two variables, while a separate study on groups in a Danish military unit found a high negative association between these two variables.

- *Member Satisfaction:* Studies have shown that people in cohesive groups have reported more satisfaction than members of a non-cohesive group. This is the case across many settings, including industrial, athletic, and educational settings. Members in cohesive groups also are more optimistic and suffer less from social problems than those in non-cohesive groups.

One study involved a team of masons and carpenters working on a housing development. For the first five months, their supervisor formed the groups they were to work in. These groups changed over the course of five months. This was to help the men get to know everyone working on this development project and naturally, likes and dislikes for the people around them emerged.

The experimenter then formed cohesive groups by grouping people who liked each other. It was found that masons and carpenters were more satisfied when they worked in cohesive groups. As quoted from one of the workers, "the work is more interesting when one has a buddy working along. You certainly like it a lot better anyway."

- *Emotional Adjustment:* People in cohesive groups experience better emotional adjustment. In particular, people experience less anxiety and tension. It was also found that people cope better with stress when they belong to a cohesive group.

One study showed that cohesion as task commitment can improve group decision making when the group is under stress, more than when it is not under stress. The study studied 55 three-person teams all of whom were faced with the task of selecting the best oil drilling sites based on information given to them.

The study manipulated whether or not the teams had high cohesion or low cohesion and how urgent the task was to be done. Researchers found that teams with low cohesion and high urgency performed worse than teams with high cohesion and high urgency. This indicates that cohesion can improve group decision-making in times of stress.

Attachment theory has also asserted that adolescents with behavioural problems do not have close interpersonal relationships or have superficial ones. Many studies have found that an individual without close peer relationships are at a higher risk for emotional adjustment problems currently and later in life.

While people may experience better emotional in cohesive groups, they may also face many demands on their emotions, such as those that result from scapegoating and hostility.

- *Conformity Pressures:* People in cohesive groups have greater pressure to conform than people in non-cohesive groups. The theory of groupthink suggests that pressures hinder the group from critically thinking about the decisions it is making. Social scientists have suggested that this is because people within a group frequently interact with one another and create many opportunities for influence.

It is also because a person within a group perceives other members as similar to them and are, thus, more willing to give into conformity pressures. Another reason is because people value the group and are, thus, more willing to give into conformity pressures to maintain or enhance their relationships.

Illegal activities have been stemmed from conformity pressures within a group. It was found that the degree to which a group of friends engaged in illegal activities was a predictor of an individual's participation in an illegal activity. This was even after the individual's prior behaviour was controlled for and other controls were set in place.

Furthermore, those with friends who all engaged in illegal activities were most likely to engage in illegal activities themselves. Another study found that adolescents with no friends did not engage in as many illegal activities as those with at least one friend. Other studies have produced similar results.

- *Learning:* An investigation was conducted on how group cohesiveness influenced individual learning to test whether learning would be better if children studied with peers they liked than peers they did not like. The degree of members liking was presumed to indicate group cohesiveness.

Researchers found that children with a high IQ performed better on learning tests when they learnt in high cohesive groups than low cohesive groups. For children with a low IQ, however, the cohesiveness factor made little difference.

Still, there was a slight tendency for low IQ children to perform better in high cohesive groups. The researchers believed that if children worked with other students whom they liked, they would more likely have a greater drive to learn than if they had neutral or negative attitudes towards the group.

Happiness

Positive attitudes being prominent topic of positive psychology movement has gained much attention by policy makers and researchers. This may be because positive attitudes are essential to explaining the employee's wellbeing but the causes of these attitudes are still not fully explored.

Institutions usually expect employees to be collaborative, committed and proactive to high performance standards to achieve excellence through employee productivity and effectiveness. Experts argue that each organization plays a role in the society. Universities responsible for public education and the development of communities besides countries play an important role in social development.

Happiness is a positive feeling that is vital and significant to maintain health. Even though the pursuit of happiness is as old as human history, research in this field is relatively new. It is of great importance to all professions because it helps one become altruistic, self-confident, dedicated, creative, kind, and energetic. All of these attributes are directly linked with happiness.

Occupational stress, on the other hand, undermines an employee's self-confidence and concentration, increases their irritability, results in sleep disorders and job burnout, thereby, negatively affecting their happiness and quality of life. Factors that influence happiness include positive and negative emotions, life satisfaction and personal & work-related dynamics.

Of these, research shows that physical health status, workplace dynamics, friendly relationships, satisfaction with salary, workload, quality of life, amount of work experience, satisfaction with colleagues, satisfaction with clients and their feedback, satisfaction with the conduct of management, satisfaction with the conduct and the performance of colleagues, satisfaction with welfare facilities at workplace and job satisfaction are essential.

Happiness is considered as the personal perspective about a favourable and pleasant state. Individuals with more pleasant feelings are more satisfied with their job. In fact, happy individuals evaluate their skills and abilities very positively and remember positive events more frequently than negative ones.

Therefore, they exchange positive energy with others and in their environment, improve their relationships with them, and therefore, feel more satisfied with their job, colleagues and the workplace. Job satisfaction is considered to be an important part of work dynamics as it directly or indirectly affects customer care.

Employees with a lower level of job satisfaction in an organization had the local authorities and management to blame. It is believed that job dissatisfaction usually occurs when issues of incivility with the employee, whether individually, collectively or at the organization-level, starts cropping up.

There is growing concern for job redesigning for it can provide meaning to the work for an employee, thereby, enhancing both their quality of work life and quality of life. It is now accepted that a good design of job should have certain characteristics which provide intrinsic satisfaction to human being. These have been identified as autonomy, high-level skills, leaving a high degree of self-investment in work, work offering opportunities for growth and satisfaction.

This implies that people tend to work better when they are more relaxed and happy with their work. This will, no doubt, help in bringing out greater efficiency and organizational effectiveness. Improvement in QWL is an incentive towards production, cooperation and cohesiveness among group members (organizational consequence) and general life satisfaction (personal consequences).

However, the consequences of happiness at work can be broadly classified into two categories, which are described below:

1. *Personal Consequences:* The traditional ways of organising work in industrialized society are in conflict with basic human needs related to creativity, influence and growth.

   The conflict seems to affect adversely not only work satisfaction, job and labour market behaviour but also participation in regards to non-work activities. Researchers, undoubtedly, suggest the importance of work climate and general life satisfaction due to the challenges of a variety of jobs.

2. *Organisational Consequences:* Among the various organizational consequences of better quality of work life is productivity, which is the most desirable end for industrial managers. Productivity can be increased by improving the QWL.

   Experts also believe that improved quality of work life and productivity are related. Happiness at work contributes not only to the quantity of production but it also improves the quality of work.

Happiness at work is an important variable. But the most important thing is to know about individual values. Although, they do not directly impact behaviour, values strongly influence a person's attitudes. So the knowledge of an individual's value system can provide insight into his or her attitudes.

Managers should be interested in their employees' attitudes because they influence behaviour. To keep resignations and absenteeism down of productive employees, managers must generate happiness for employees at their work place.

Happiness at Work

For humans, life is both vital and good. Happiness, with its psychological and philosophical assumptions, is being deliberated for decades. Can people be happy? How can they achieve happiness? Happiness has been termed as global judgment of a person's life, satisfaction in the life of a person, the mitigation of good emotions, and a negligible level of negative effects.

However, despite a positive work attitude it is difficult to say or define certain emotions. Happiness at Work is defined as "the feeling of happiness in the work itself, work characteristics and the entire organization". This definition clearly states that different attitudes are involved at the work place. No doubt then, job satisfaction results from positive and pleasant emotions at work.

There are three areas of focus so far as happy emotions at work are concerned. They are:

- Defining happiness at work as a sense of happiness for the work itself.
- For work including contextual characteristics.
- For the entire organization.

Happiness at Work as a Resource

This is essential to make the most of the challenges individuals face at the workplace. Keeping the resource factor in mind, the broad definition of happiness at work will now be "the motivation and satisfaction that people feel at work".

When linking happiness at work to the concept of burnout and job engagement, and arguing that dedicated employees are better able to meet their psychological needs through work, experts reason that one is happier at work as compared to exhausted employees'. It is also a broad-based concept for measuring the quality of employees' work and life.

Similarly, defining the concept as "a perception to achieve potential and maximize profit by enabling actions" and looking for a causal relationship between happiness at work and organizational outcomes, we realize that there are a number of major positive relationships such as happy employees lead to higher productivity, enhancing greater volumes of sales and bettering overall performances.

There are several merits of happiness at work such as improvement in work quality, creating better results, enhancing decision making skills & communication, enabling people to have a stronger immune system, decrease in leave taking & absenteeism, motivating employees to work more efficiently and providing customers with highly satisfactory services.

The happiness factor leads to employees' being satisfied with their jobs, workers feeling a balance between their job and personal life, opportunity & eagerness to learn new things, high job security and support from colleagues.

One must realise that happiness precedes many successful outcomes. Therefore, there is a direct relationship between happiness at work and organizational outcomes.

Happiness in the Workplace[5]

By its bare definition, 'work' does not embody something fun or something that people look forward to doing. How frequently does one deliberate on resigning from the job or perhaps feel that one is not getting paid enough for the over-the-top efforts that one puts in an organization?

Workplaces that strive to balance the everyday stresses of a job to encourage workplace happiness can enjoy strong competitive advantages.

Contentment and gratification are very peculiar concepts that tend to mean a variety of things to different people.

For some, workplace happiness can mean getting excellent pay and other incentives and benefits. For others, it is about having a good time at work and having the opportunity to socialize in an office environment. Others may see happiness in the workplace as something directly tied to the company culture. For instance, having a welcoming work setting, a fulfilling responsibility, and a collaborative work environment, and having the opportunity to give back.

While being happy at work is something extremely personal, the reality is that younger generations are placing workplace happiness high on their list when it comes to choosing between jobs, moving to a different company, or choosing a different career path. No matter what the expectations are, companies can highly benefit by having a culture that welcomes happiness, inclusivity, and openness.

Most employers seem to think that money is the most important factor in job satisfaction. After all, people work to earn a living and a competitive salary does seem like a reasonable exchange for their services. However, there is more to work than just money. There are different factors that play into workplace happiness and productivity.

In the corporate workplace culture, happiness plays a crucial role in determining the productivity and satisfaction of a workforce. It also enhances the image of a company and improves its ability to retain its employees for the long term. So, it is fair to say that happiness at work is indispensable.

Yet, the concept of happiness at work has only started to gain prominence in the past couple of decades. Before that, employers primarily focused on their business, trade relations, profits, and so on. Only until recently did researchers start realizing the benefits of fostering employee happiness and consequently, employers also started giving importance to it.

Now, numerous institutions provide "happiness" courses for people. These courses, like "The Science of Happiness" by edX, teach people how to find happiness in their lives and be happier at work and life in general.

Our culture has taught us that we must work to support ourselves financially and become a responsible member of society. That is why most people go to work because they feel obliged to do so, not because they feel happy working. However, we rarely think of workplaces as places where people go to seek happiness. Instead, we perceive them as places where we provide our skills and time in exchange for money to help us lead a comfortable life.

Humans generally pursue happiness in our personal lives, either by maintaining our relationships or fulfilling our wants and aspirations. But happiness in life also can be achieved at work. And contrary to popular belief, work doesn't have to be boring and unfulfilling.

Importance

Workplace happiness is not about playing games and practicing sports during business hours. It is also not about having your boss as your best friend. Happiness in the workplace is about people enjoying their everyday tasks, openly collaborating with their team members, feeling acknowledged and respected at work, having a healthy work-life balance, and come home fulfilled at the end of the day.

It is not just employees that benefit from being happy at work, it is also companies themselves. There is substantial research that proves that productivity is directly impacted by how happy people are performing tasks. At the same time, happy employees also mean that the employee turnover rates will diminish. Ask yourself, how likely will you be to leave your job if you enjoyed your everyday?

Consider the following statistics to re-assess the idea behind importance of happiness in the workplace:

- Happiness leads to higher retention rates: Happy employees tend to stay four times longer in their jobs than those that are not happy at work.
- Happiness directly impacts stress levels: And stress directly impacts productivity. Eliminating stress through a happy workplace leads to more productive employees.
- Openness and psychological safety: Happy employees are more likely to share information and admit mistakes. Hiding mistakes in business, as history has proven, can have terrible consequences.
- Creativity is directly ties to happiness: Happier employees mean more creative minds are put to work.
- Happy employees are willing to do more: Research has found that people who are happy at their jobs are twice as likely to spend extra hours at work, reject higher-paying jobs, and place an extra effort to reach the company's vision.

Happiness in the workplace might just be the secret ingredient missing in some organizations. Leaders that want to boost their company's productivity, psychological safety, employee turnover rates, and their workforce's creative capacity, should make workplace happiness a priority.

How Leaders can Create a Happy Workplace

Even though measuring levels of happiness can be highly subjective and impossible to make accurate, the benefits make it worth pursuing. There are specific tips that can be followed to create a happy workplace and motivate each and every team member to work even more efficiently.

1. *Host Engaging and Interactive Team-Building Events*

Nowadays, more and more companies understand the value of making time to have fun in the office and continuously hold interesting events. Hosting team-building events where employees can play together, giggle together, and resolve issues together is a great way to promote contentment and fulfilment. This brings employees together and allows for them to get to know each other in aspects other than as colleagues—building trust and connection.

Team-building activities are known for their ability to empower teams to collaborate, boost morale, improve communication, and, more importantly, bond. It is easier to create workplace happiness when employees know each other well. Some great ideas for team building activities that boost engagement and trust are:

- Scavenger hunts
- Healthy competition through fitness, sports, or arcade
- Board game tournaments
- Trivia challenges
- Room escape games

The key for team building activities to be successful is for them to be creative, authentic and interactive.

2. *Focus on Positive Aspects*

Happiness leads to positivity. Do not permit negativity to aggravate in the office. It will take blowouts like germs. Whether that is a mistake made, goals not being achieved, or just a poor-performing month, it is important to keep energy levels high. Particularly during uneasy times, it is essential for management to emphasize the good.

It is important for leaders to lead by example. Simple things such as starting the day well, greeting everyone, praising co-workers for their efforts, asking them about their day, and making them feel valued can all have a significant impact on their wellbeing.

By celebrating even the smallest of either individual or team accomplishments, leaders can help foster a happy workplace. Holding feedback sessions is a great idea to tackle workplace problems and discuss the positives. Feedback sessions are also a great strategy to limit the dangers of group think.

3. *Build a Sense of Fulfilment through a Higher Purpose*

A clear purpose is essential to keep a team focused. It can also build a sense of fulfilment within colleagues. A purpose, however, cannot be something selfish such as maximizing profits. Purpose represents something way more meaningful.

As British-American author and inspirational speaker Simon Oliver Sinek would argue, purpose refers to something more profound. It is what gives meaning to your life. Having a purpose is your answer to, "Why do I wake up every morning and why should anyone care?"

Reminding your team of the purpose behind their responsibilities will help keep everyone's motivation high. Leaders should have team members visualize how their individual contribution is part of a bigger mission. With everyone being on the same page, leaders can capitalize upon people's innate need to serve.

4. *Boost Professional Relations*

Leaders should always see their colleagues as human first, co-workers second. This means making time to build relationships, checking in, and getting to know each other better. What are your colleague's hobbies? What are their unique skills?

If we look at the current scenario, many people are comfortable working remotely. Yet, remote work often leads to employees feeling lonely. Workplace happiness can never be achieved if employees are feeling that way.

Some simple ways that company cultures can encourage happy professional relationships are:

- Come up with a mentor system
- Host simulated events and games

- Generate time blocks for virtual chit chats
- Pair new hires with experienced employees

Despite hybrid or fully remote working conditions, technology is a great way to bring people together. Yet, driving happiness in the workplace often means getting off your computer and engaging with each other in settings other than the office—whatever that looks like today.

Benefits of Promoting Happiness in the Workplace

Being happier at work is associated with improved health, increased creativity, more productivity, and lots more. Happy workers can help create a harmonious and positive work environment. Moreover, such people are more committed to work and are eager to put in effort beyond their job descriptions.

Happy workplaces enhance employees' outcomes. When the vibe is friendly, work no longer feels like a burden, but a place where to feel valued. Below are some reasons why having a happy workplace is important for any employee, employer and company:

1. *Business Success:* A happy workplace is one where employees support each other and are open about their vulnerabilities—a key component of business success. Mistakes are not being hidden and failures are often seen as opportunities. Both business and employees benefit from a happy workspace.
2. *Motivation:* More energy and optimism can be seen when employees enjoy their work. Individuals feel driven to perform their daily tasks and are open to receiving feedback. Happy employees are more likely to see feedback as an opportunity for growth and development.
3. *Health Improves:* Happiness also boosts people's immune systems. Therefore, happy employees mean it will be less likely that people will call in due to sickness. Fewer call-ins mean greater productivity and stronger financial gains.
4. *Creativity Upsurges:* People become even more creative when they are feeling happy. They will want to innovate, explore new initiatives, make their voices be heard, and give their best. It is very unlikely that something original can arise from an unhappy mental state.
5. *Teamwork:* Employees will start engaging with each other more as a team if the workplace encourages happiness. A happy workplace always denotes healthier communication. Employees will interact on a better level amongst themselves and also with customers. This is an even more important feature for salespeople.

6. *Learning from Mistakes:* Hiding mistakes often involves losing time, money, energy, and other resources. Workplace happiness is key to avoid this pitfall. Happy employees are more likely to praise each other, give feedback, and learn from the mistakes made. Unhappy employees, on the other hand, may see feedback as criticism and might end up frustrated.

Life is Too Short Not to be Happy

If one thinks about it, we spend most of our awake time in the office. Do you really want to spend most of your day miserable? Do you really want to take all the stress of your job home and to your family members and loved ones? Why not make the most of it instead? Finding happiness in the workplace, and in anything you do really, is the key to being successful.

Hacks for a Happy and High-Performance Workplace

As we embark on a new decade, this is a good time to reflect on happiness in general (and specifically, happiness at work). The trouble starts right at the very beginning, with the basic question of the definition of happiness.

1. ***Happiness is an Abstract Concept:*** Had this topic been mentioned a couple of decades back, people would have laughed and brushed it aside. Then, people were "old school" professionals from a different era who were brought up in work environments where concepts like happiness did not even occur in collective consciousness at the workplace. The message was simple—there were things to be done, often very tough and unreasonable, and one had to just plough through to get the job done.

After office, colleagues got together for some drinks, and had animated spicy storytelling sessions of the day gone by. In the process, people created their own "happiness". Those were the days before laptops, smart phones and the internet. Once an employee was out of office, it was pretty much shutters down. The common model was, you work, make money, come home or meet friends and be happy.

2. ***Happiness @ Work and Ways to Measure it:*** Prof. Edward F. Diener is an American psychologist, professor and author. He is noted for his research over the past thirty years on happiness. According to Professor Ed Diener, happiness and subjective wellbeing is defined as a person's cognitive and affective evaluation of his or her own life. It broadly means experiencing pleasant emotions, low levels of negative mood and high life satisfaction.

The outcomes of his various researches on happiness at work are as follows:

- a positive and pleasant feeling at work
- excitement at going to work
- liking the people you interact with at the workplace
- feeling safe and appreciated at the workplace
- ability to associate some meaning to our work, and
- have some fun in the process.

Lord Richard Layard is a well-known British economist. He is the founder-director of the Centre for Economic Performance, at the London School of Economics, where he is presently the program director. In 2012, he co-edited with Jeffry Sachs and John Helliwell, the World Happiness Report. For the first time, a concerted effort was made to move happiness (at work) from just being a fluffy concept to the realm of proper measurements.

The study has a couple of significant findings for happiness related to work. It revealed that a majority of the people around the globe were unhappy at work. In an interview with McKinsey in 2019, Lord Layard said, "Here is the most shocking fact that I have come across in happiness research: the time of day or the time in the week that people least enjoy is when they are with their boss."

"This says something about the management style that we have been generating in recent years. There is too much rule by the creation of anxiety and fear and not enough by motivation and enjoyment and inspiration. We need bosses who will inspire, and lead by inspiring, rather than by frightening people," he added further.

We cannot expect employees to be engaged if they don't enjoy work. This co-relates well with the many Gallup surveys over the years that a majority of employees are not fully engaged in their jobs.

On the other hand, research from Professors Ed Diener and Shigehiro Oishi in 2006 (which included about 10,000 respondents in over 40 countries) confirmed that happiness was the top goal of people globally, ahead of big (six-hundred-pound gorilla) goals like success and wealth.

If you put together these studies, the picture that emerges is not pretty. It clearly shows that our work is not aligned and congruent to our life's top goal and in fact one can argue that it works actively against our highest stated goal. This effect seems graver when you take the perspective that we spend more than a third of our waking life at work.

3. *Need to be Happy at Work*

(a) *Higher Productivity:* A study at Oxford University has clearly established what people have long suspected—happier employees are on average more productive. This six-month study of 1,800 sales and call centre workers at British telecom firm BT found a clear causal effect of happiness on productivity.

The workers were asked to rate their happiness each week via an email survey comprising five emoji buttons, from very sad to very happy. Happy employees not only worked faster, making more calls per hour, but also achieved 13% higher sales than their unhappy colleagues.

(b) *Better Team Players and Co-workers:* According to Prof Rajagopal Raghunathan of McComb's Business School at UT Austin, a leading researcher and author on happiness, happy employees:

- Are more collegial, better team players
- Have better health and energy—take less sick leave, and
- Are more helpful to co-workers.

(c) *More Creative and Innovative:* In her seminal and interesting study, called "Broaden and Build", Prof Barbara Fredrickson of the University of North Carolina, Chapel Hill, has elegantly shown that even small positive emotions (a good indicator of happiness), broaden our awareness and create a kind of expansiveness.

As humans, we are almost hardwired for this expansiveness. It is like opening an aperture, which in turn, creates more resourcefulness, innovation and creativity.

(d) *Lower Attrition and Higher Customer Loyalty:* Other significant benefits include lower employee turnover, better customer satisfaction and loyalty. The single most important reason for employee turnover globally is the relationship with their manager. Happy employees usually have a better relationship with their managers and more importantly, happier managers have a better relationship with their subordinates.

We all know the cost of employee turnover to companies is quite high. It increases talent acquisition cost and time, training cost, time to market and significantly lowers productivity overall. A happy employee also serves a customer better, increasing customer satisfaction and loyalty.

Customer satisfaction and loyalty are pillars of business strategies and many companies like Zappos and Southwest Airlines have built their entire business model on customer obsession.

(e) *Makes us Human (and Moral):* The economic benefits of the happy employee for the company are clear. What I think is even more important is the negative effects of an unhappy and dissatisfied workforce. Job dissatisfaction is strongly correlated to mental health issues.

According to Lord Layard, one in six people in the work force are facing mental challenges and one in three will face them at some point in their careers. This is a problem of almost epidemic proportions. It then becomes a business, societal and moral imperative that companies create environments to promote employee wellbeing.

(f) *Facilitating happiness at work:* There are several things that one can do to increase our happiness at work. We can broadly divide these into two categories. One is personal, things that the employee can do themselves, irrespective of the employer and two, things the manager, employer or the company can do to promote wellbeing.

(g) *Five Actions that An Employee Can take*

- Increase attention and focus: Paying attention is difficult and has become more so with all the global digital products competing for our attention. This has placed a huge premium on our ability to pay attention and stay focused. There is a myriad of ways to be distracted today at work.

Prof Cal Newport has written a book on this subject called "Deep Work". In this book, he recommends that we block and schedule certain times of the day daily as uninterrupted time. Experts have consistently said that it must be like a habit rather than dependent on our will power. **The cognitive cost of "attention residue" that is created even by small switching of context is not trivial.**

- ***Mind Training:*** Emotional Intelligence Guru, Daniel Goleman and a few others, have shown that even a few minutes of paying attention to our breathing or meditating helps us to de-clutter the mind and increase focus, a fundamental prerequisite for happiness.
- ***Manage Your Energies, and Not Time:*** It is super difficult to be happy if you are sick and lack energy. A commitment to a regular exercise regimen can go a long way in being happier.

During a seminar, the key insight of Tony Schwartz, CEO of the Energy Project, a high-performance coach who has coached many elite athletes and CEOs, was that for high performance in any field, we need to manage energy and engagement and not necessarily time. Tony suggests that the foundation to managing energy starts with physical health.

- ***Make Social Connections:*** Having a close buddy at work is one the biggest determinants of happiness at work. Prof Raj Raghunathan, esteemed professor of marketing at the University of Texas at Austin and author of "If You're So Smart, Why Aren't You Happy?" says it really helps to have a very close friend at work and this belongingness is key to workplace happiness.

An Inc magazine article mentions a study on the impact of work friendships and found strong evidence that close friendships at work are essential to personal happiness and career success: 70% of employees said friendships at work are the most crucial element to a happy working life.

- *Create Your Own Challenges (and Meaning):* Prof Adam Grant at the Wharton Business School along with Amy Wrzesniewski at the Yale School of Management and Jane Dutton at the Michigan's Ross School of Business, talk about a concept called **'Job Crafting'. It is a** set of techniques for helping you reconfigure the elements of your job to spark greater engagement and meaning. The forms of job crafting are Task Crafting, Relational Crafting and Cognitive Crafting.

For example, a corporate attorney with a passion for teaching could start an intern program (task crafting), get her colleagues involved in the program (relational crafting), and mentally frame the program as an opportunity to fulfil and spread her passion for teaching (cognitive crafting).

That does not mean advocating for doing whatever you want at work. **Instead, pitch your boss a meaningful side project that will take up about 10 per cent of your time at the office.**

1. *Always Smile:* Whenever you talk with or come across someone at work, greet them with a warm smile. According to a paper published in the Psychological Bulletin, smiling can make people happier. So, remember to smile whenever you get an opportunity to do so.
2. *Be Grateful:* Be grateful and appreciative to everyone you meet at work, whether it's your co-worker or your boss. Expressing gratitude can help improve relationships and help people increase positive feelings towards each other.
3. *Engage with Other Departments:* Get out of your workspace and connect with other teams and departments in your office. Doing so will help create better relations with them, and you might also learn new skills that might increase your worth for the company.
4. *Keep Your Workspace Clean and Organized:* Always keep your workspace neat and tidy. A clean and organized workspace can

create a positive vibe and increase motivation and productivity. It will also keep your mind fresh and leave you feeling good throughout the day.

5. *Go on a Vacation:* Long hours at work day in and day out can take a toll on anyone. If all else fails and you feel that your productivity has hit rock-bottom, and then it may be time for a vacation. Taking a vacation can result in greater success and more happiness at work.
6. *Help Others:* Come forward and help your colleagues whenever they need assistance. Helping and supporting people in their time of need can make you feel better about yourself and the level of happiness it provides is unparalleled by anything else.
7. *Focus on One Task at One Time:* Focusing on more than one task at a particular time can increase stress and be a cause of unhappiness. Prioritizing your tasks according to their importance will help you combat this and keep you focused at work.
8. *Meditate Regularly:* People around the world are realizing the benefits of regular meditation and implementing it in their lives. So, jump on the bandwagon and practice mindful meditation regularly to de-clutter your mind and feel energized, refreshed, and happy.
9. *Eat Healthy:* Proper nutrition is essential for staying healthy and happy. It plays a crucial role in how we function physically and mentally. So, avoid unhealthy food items and eat healthily to keep health problems at bay and stay happy.
10. *Socialize at Work:* Humans are social beings, and we need socialization to function correctly. As you spend most of the time of your day at work, it's a good idea to have good relationships with everyone at work. Talk to your co-workers at work and connect with them on a personal level.
11. *Ask for Feedback:* Feedback from your employer or your co-workers can help you realize your drawbacks and work on improving them. Being able to take feedback and criticism positively is one of the critical factors of being happy and successful in life.
12. *Exercise Regularly:* Besides keeping you fit and healthy, regular physical exercise can go a long way in eliminating stress and uplifting your mood. It also helps increase self-confidence and boost morale. So, start exercising regularly and reap the benefits it provides.
13. *Set a Goal or Purpose:* Having a goal or a sense of purpose is very beneficial for our overall well-being. It can positively affect our abilities to think and combat stress. Determine what your purpose is

and work towards achieving it. It will help you become more satisfied and happier in life.

14. *Sleep is Important:* Make sure you get enough sleep every night. Sleep is essential for functioning optimally and getting sufficient sleep increases our resilience to stress and illnesses. Aim for at least 7-8 hours of sleep every night to make sure that you are functioning to the best of your abilities.
15. *Take Breaks:* Sitting on your chair and working non-stop for long hours can cause serious repercussions in your life. Take short breaks at work frequently and go for a walk or maybe socialize with your colleagues. Taking breaks can increase happiness, productivity and make you more focused at work.
16. *Read about Happiness and Feeling Better:* Many books describe the concept of happiness and the different factors affecting it. For example, "The Happiness Advantage" by Shawn Achor describes in detail the principles of positive psychology which affect work performance and success. Get your hands on one it will help you to stay happy in all situations.
17. *Value Yourself:* Never forget what your real worth is. Always take a moment now and then to appreciate and value yourself. Remind yourself of your abilities and your past achievements. Doing so can make sure you find happiness and satisfaction at work and in life in general.

Five Actions that a Manager, Employer and Company can take

- Communicate a Clear Purpose: We should regularly communicate a clear purpose and tie our employee/team member's work to that purpose. For example, if call center salespeople who are calling for donations from alumni are told that the donations that they are collecting are ultimately funding the education of underprivileged students, the performance of the team goes up significantly.

In some other cases, the company has clearly defined its purpose and that can be communicated to teams consistently. For example, Southwest Airlines' purpose is "To connect people to what's important in their lives through friendly, reliable, and low-cost air travel."

- *Team Performance Instead of Individual Performance:* This is the idea that the whole is greater than the sum of its parts. By measuring individual performance, we pit one against the other in a race. This is inherently anxiety-producing to team members. Instead, if we can look at the entire team's performance, that can promote a healthy culture of trust, helpfulness and cooperation.

Dan Coyle, a New York Times bestseller author of "Culture Code", mentions that (team) interactions are as important as individual skills. Bad team culture is often caused by certain group members being focused on their place in the group, everything becomes personal and the focus sways away from the task at hand to personal egos. Good teams and managers build a psychological safe environment that helps create a "band of brothers" kind of camaraderie.

- *Promote Mastery:* It can immensely help if mastery goals (rather than only performance goals) are set up for team members. With mastery goals, individuals can reappraise identity threatening situations in more positive ways, which can affect how they feel and act.

Specifically, when individuals actively change their mindset to construe an identity threat as a learning experience (rather than a time to perform at one's best or avoid errors), it allows them to feel challenged, engaged and ultimately perform well.

- *Create Conditions of Flow:* Create goals that are a little harder/ challenging than what the person is used to. If the goals are too hard, the person will burnout and lose confidence. If the goals are easily achieved, it creates boredom.

Also, it is long acknowledged that for significant or challenging work to happen, one needs uninterrupted time. Our days are peppered with multiple interruptions—unscheduled meetings, managers wanting some information immediately, open office clutter and noise, and so on and so forth. Managers should make concerted effort to reduce this clutter for their team members.

- *Give Greater Autonomy:* Managers must give their teams more autonomy and stay away from their tendency to micromanage. This is easier said than done. A careful balance needs to be struck between providing autonomy and creating chaos.

In an HBR article, Prof Deborah Anacona and Dr Kate Issacs have suggested that organizations can achieve this balance by adopting one or more of the following:

(a) Cultivating a Strategic Mindset (b) Implement Simple Rules (c) Funnelling (d) Distributed Risk Mitigation.

- *Provide Constructive Feedback:* Feedback can help an individual improve his skills and become more satisfied in life. Organize daily scrums at work where you can acknowledge the hard work of your employees and give them the necessary feedback and suggestions. Doing so can make your employees feel appreciated and create a happier workforce.

- *Brainstorming Sessions:* Conduct brainstorming sessions among your employees to increase creativity and innovation. Brainstorming sessions will also help them interact and collaborate. Furthermore, the work environment will improve, and employees will feel motivated to work.
- *Provide Wellness Programs and Challenges:* Wellness and challenges come with various benefits for employers and employees alike. They are an effective and proven way to increase employee engagement and improve employee health. Creating wellness initiatives like a step or fitness challenge, or maybe a cycle to work scheme can significantly benefit your workplace as a whole. It can do wonders for the company culture and employee happiness and satisfaction.
- *Create a Room only for Recreation:* Every company should have a place explicitly dedicated for recreation and refreshment where employees can take a short break from their work, rewind, and have some fun. If your workplace doesn't have one, providing one can make a difference in the happiness of your workforce.
- *Conduct Office Events:* Office events provide perfect opportunities for employers to get their employees together and help them bond with each other. They can double as amazing team-building activities which increase employee engagement and improve team morale. Celebrate holidays and festivals with your employees and create an enjoyable environment at work.
- *Take Your Employees Out on Outings:* If you want to create a work environment where everyone is engaged, satisfied, and happy, then take your employees out on a team outing. A team outing will foster unity and solidarity among your workforce. Most importantly, your employees will love it, and it will do great to increase happiness at work.
- *Office Decor and Ergonomics are Essential:* Office decor and workplace ergonomics play an important role in determining employee creativity and productivity. Brightly painted walls, comfortable chairs, inspirational quotes and images on the walls, etc. can all help you create a sense of motivation and happiness in your workplace.
- *Offer Free Healthy Snacks and Lunches:* The availability of fresh and healthy snacks and lunches at work will make sure your employees

avoid junk food items at work. Moreover, everybody will be happy at the thought of getting free food.

- *Provide Flexible Hours to Your Employees:* Be open to providing flexible work hours and remote options for your employees. Flexible schedules significantly increase employee productivity and morale. They allow a level of freedom to create their work schedules and achieve work-life balance. Also, by offering such options, you can attract and retain better talent to work for your company.
- *Provide Training and Mentoring Sessions:* Offer training programs and mentoring sessions in your workplace. They will help to make your employees more motivated and make sure they give their best effort at work. Your employees will also be able to improve their skills and feel more confident in their jobs.

Quality of Life (QoL)

The meaning and nature of Quality of Life (QoL) can be simply states as "the individual's achievement of a satisfactory social situation within the limits of perceived physical capacity." But it can also be defined in much simpler terms as "the possession of resources necessary for the satisfaction of individual needs, wants and desires, participation in activities enabling personal development and self-actualization & satisfactory comparison between oneself and others".

More recently, the World Health Organization (WHO) defined QoL as "including the individual's perception of his or her position in the context of culture and value systems in which they live in relation to goals". Various definitions reveal not only the complexity of this concept but the very real differences in opinion as to the nature of Quality of Life[6].

Quality of life is an area of study that has attracted an ever increasing amount of interest. Its conceptual models and instruments for research, evaluation and assessment have been developed since the middle of the last century. However, Greek philosophers spent centuries searching for meaning of life which could help people look for a higher existential level of their life.

In the past century, QoL was determined to be material welfare or wealth. Of course, interest in quality of life is not a recent phenomenon. Ancient Greeks were much taxed by notions of happiness and good life. Aristippus, a philosopher of the 4th century BC, taught that the goal of life is to experience maximum amount of pleasure, and that happiness is the sum total of hedonic episodes.

Others in the hedonic tradition argued that happiness lies in the pursuit and fulfilment of human appetites while some said the pursuit of pleasure and sensation is the ultimate goal in life. On their part, psychologists said that hedonism includes the pleasure and preferences of the mind as well as of the body.

Arostotle believed that hedonic happiness was a vulgar ideal and argued that true happiness is found in what is worth doing. The term 'eudaimonia' (daimon = true self) refers to this type of wellbeing. Eudaimonia occurs when activities are congruent with deeply held values and are holistically engaged.

The debate between hedonic and eudaimonic theorists continue to exert an influence on conceptions of wellbeing. However, what appears to have transpired over the last 20 years is a move away from the measures of, as well as interest in, the construct of wellbeing to discourse about the quality of life.

First, in medicine there was a need to recognize that many treatments and interventions could not cure disease but could best control unpleasant symptoms. For example, coronary artery bypass surgery could not cure heart disease, nor could it necessarily prevent a heart attack, but it could reduce the pain associated with angina.

In other words, patients would be happier, not only because of a reduction in unpleasant events but because they could engage in activities leading to self-actualization. However, an increase in happiness is a less scientific health-related outcome while improved QoL is a more objective outcome measure when assessing the impact of treatment and intervention.

Not only did quality of life appear to be an outcome with more scientific nuances, it was and perhaps still widely is, believed to be something that can be assessed by others rather than relying on the subjective views of the patients.

A second factor contributing to the shift from a research interest in wellbeing to quality of life in the past two decades is a growing interest in inequalities in health, social exclusion and government policies that might disadvantage large sections of the population.

Governments do not, on the whole, view themselves as responsible for individual happiness, but have come to acknowledge that there are things that governments can do to affect the quality of housing, work, neighbourhood environments and other things outside family and private life.

Thus, QoL came to prominence as a concept as government departments set out a program evaluation. As in medicine, quality of life proved to be a useful concept in that governments were unlikely to 'cure' many of the problems besetting society, but might be able to make improvements of one's QoL in the general population.

Although it is widely acknowledged that there is no definition of QoL, what seems to be clear is that there is a general reluctance to suggest that the quality of life is identical to hedonic happiness or eudaimonia. This may be due to a growing body of literature suggesting that happiness and psychological wellbeing are related to personality characteristics which are not only stable across life spans but are biologically determined.

Since it seems that personality traits influence levels of subjective wellbeing, there is little, or certainly less, that governments can do to increase happiness. Hence, the interest in QoL construct rather than happiness or psychological wellbeing.

What can, however, be hoped for by policy makers is that policies can alter the environment, service provision, distribution of wealth etc and that such factors will influence quality of life perceptions.

The personality characteristics most consistently and strongly related to subjective well-being are extroversion and neuroticism. Optimism and self-esteem are also correlated with subjective wellbeing, though the direction of causality has not been determined. Physical health will have a major impact on QoL perceptions.

However, an argument has risen in recent years that government policies have a major impact on the likelihood of poor health. It is through their influence on levels of poverty and the distribution of wealth & status that government policies can influence health.

When reviewing the relationship between money and happiness, happiness depends less on exterior factors then might be expected. Indeed, several studies have indicated that the more individuals focus on financial and materialistic goals, the lower their wellbeing.

In addition, the belief shared by most industrial psychologists is that work should be morally desirable so that people enjoy it, that everybody concerned with the world of work should be taking more active and vigorous steps than at present to make work more likeable for those who have to do it.

Therefore, the task of making work more likeable has increasingly been discussed within the points of reference supplied by the phrase, quality of work life. In order to have QWL, it is not enough to have a job that generates labour satisfaction. There are several other factors involved such as the physical conditions of workplace, which contribute to a better or worse QWL.

One factor is satisfaction with one's work but other relevant factors are levels of stress, fatigue & overcrowding and weekend work schedules. All these factors contribute to determine the quality of life at work that an individual experiences. Besides, relations that the worker maintains with others at the workplace also have an influencing impact.

From an organizational psychological perspective, QWL involves a hierarchy of concepts that includes life satisfaction, job satisfaction and work-specific facet satisfaction such as satisfaction with pay, co-workers and supervisor among others.

Evaluation of QoL

Evaluation of the quality of life must encompass all the above elements. QWL includes such areas as workers health and wellbeing, guarantee of employment, career planning, competence development, life and work balance and other. The evaluation of QWL factors could be a possibility for the establishment, implementation and development of social programs in organizations, at national and international-levels.

Given the lack of consensus concerning the solutions that have been developed to date, a new definition of QWL is suggested. This was inspired by research on a related concept of the Quality of Life which has faced the same conceptualization and definition challenges as the quality of work life.

Connection between QWL and QoL

When we use the concept of work life, we do not exclude life. When we show our preference for quality of work life, we include quality. By implication then we accept that there is teleological justification for quality of life. It is by no means surprising that social scientists, who are not directly or immediately concerned with work redesign, socio-technical systems or the quality of work life devoted to an organizational setting alone, describe their concern for the future of work on a more comprehensive framework that the applied behavioural scientists do.

The following characteristics clearly bring out the connection between quality of work life and quality of life:

- There is scope for extending critical consciousness of the members from work place to their immediate environmental context within the organisation itself. There are examples in support of this proposition. Workers at grassroots, participating in work system redesign, picking key lessons from their experience, showed interest in the company-run school system for children so that educational quality can improve. A large number of welfare services, healthcare, food supply, immediate environment and worker's residential colonies could be looked upon with a new perspective.
- There is also an array of examples in Norway, Edinburgh, Spain, Canada and the United States where there have been productive spill-over of interest to the community life by employees who started redefining role as actively involved citizens of the community. There is a message of hope for extension possibility.
- Employees of a productive organisation can increasingly influence qualitative decision making, plan processes and implement machinery with their productive intervention. It is possible for the members of productive organization to put across alternatives that exist in the style of functioning of the ruling party elites or the government of the day, in order that a sick social system including its economic parameters can reach the viable alternatives.
- The quality of work life in micro organisations can derive its substance and broaden its horizon by drawing upon the insights of QoL movements. The popular Chipko movement in Garhwal region to revive decimated forestry, the resurrection of Jamestown urban area by collective citizen effort in New York State, the Rost Island upswing in Norway and by now the well-acknowledged Mondragon comprehensive cooperative coverage in the Basque country in Spain provide discernible lessons on building blocks for laying firm footholds for newer designs of human organisations that can set to course the knowledge-based applied behavioural science interventions in micro economic organisations.
- Need to perceive the life-sized burning problems which cast deepening shadow of threats upon quality of life and work. Though slated in the end, we emphatically maintain that this proposition is of utmost urgency to the contemporary world. The contexts of the globalisation of economic, political and cultural malaise can no longer remain unquestioned and unexamined.
- The global economic crises are sought to be overcome by taking recourse to such technological marvels as chips, robots and artificial

intelligence to name a few. But at the end of it all, human labour is compelled to yield grounds for organizational survival. This is a harsh reality even if it tramples the right to work and human dignity. Misery of labour at work is giving way to elimination of employees.

What we have to ask is where in do we pitch our values and canons of quality of life and work in these contexts? Do they call for reappraisal simultaneously in the conclaves of organizations and communities? Whatever is our approach in specific situations, the survival of life and work demands a fresh look and reformulation of our concepts and tools.

QWL's QoL Perspective

While an economic orientation may remain a necessity for business organizations, it need not preclude a focus on overall employee wellbeing. QWL programs are organizational development efforts that result not only in job satisfaction but also life satisfaction. People segment their feelings or compensate for divergent affective reactions across life domains (work life, family life, social life etc).

Also, people experience reciprocal spill-over between job satisfaction and life satisfaction. Research has shown that the spill-over from one's experience in a particular life domain to one's satisfaction/dissatisfaction with life in general may be affected by a variety of moderators such as organizational commitment. That is, employees who have a higher level of organizational commitment tend to experience a greater spill-over effect than those who expressed lower levels of commitment.

Interestingly, both job and life satisfactions share a substantial dispositional component. A top-down approach to the study of job and life satisfaction suggests that common traits (such as positive and negative affectivity) influence both. In fact, although personality removes a huge chunk of the variance from job-life satisfaction relationship, the link still remains.

Such traits may gauge the broader construct of life satisfaction, which is a higher order concept that encompasses domain satisfactions. It is interesting to note that situational influences on reports of life satisfaction—the bottom-up approach to the study of life satisfaction—have been found to account for a significant amount of variance in life satisfaction.

The QWL research based on the QoL perspective has indicated that a number of organizational factors can explain the job-life satisfaction link.

One such factor is organizational structure. Bureaucratization is associated with an increase in job dissatisfaction and life dissatisfaction. That is, workers in a decentralized bureaucracy experience a greater spill-over between job satisfaction and life satisfaction than workers in a centralized bureaucracy.

Fostering decentralized bureaucracies allows workers to enjoy greater work discretion and lesser immediate supervision. Work discretion and lower levels of supervision reduce work role stress, which in turn reduces negative affect and dissatisfaction in work life. This reduction of negative affect and dissatisfaction in the work domain serves to decrease negative effect in overall life through spill-over thereby contributing to life satisfaction.

Another factor moderating the job-life satisfaction link is occupational status. Social psychologists argue that different jobs carry different levels of social status, with clerical and sales scoring moderate in both social status and job satisfaction and unskilled workers scoring lowest in both social status and job satisfaction. Spill-over occurs between job satisfaction and life satisfaction moderated by occupational prestige.

Specifically, occupational prestige is a poor predictor of both job and life satisfaction except for the highest status occupations. Higher prestige jobs often nourish self-esteem and generate positive affective experience (that is, job satisfaction and life satisfaction), which is not generated by lower prestige jobs.

Research continues in the context of both study programs: QWL from a management development perspective and from a QoL perspective[7]. Much more is needed to study the various QWL programs to better understand their effects not only on job performance and job satisfaction but also on life satisfaction.

Different QWL programs tend to affect different role identities in various ways. Some are effective in generating more resources to facilitate the realization of role expectations.

Others are effective in reducing conflict within a specific role identity or between two or more role identities. Some programs are designed to clarify and articulate role expectations to match work and non-work demands.

UNIT–III

Models and Measurement

Quality of work life describes a person's broader employment-related experience. Various authors and researchers have proposed QWL models[1]—also referred to as the quality of work life—which include a wide range of factors, sometimes classified as "motivator factors", which if present can make the job experience a positive one, and "hygiene factors", which if lacking are more associated with dissatisfaction.

So far as models are concerned, authors differ in their views on the types of models and core constituents of the quality of work life.

It has generally been agreed, however, that the quality of work life is conceptually similar to well-being of employees but differs from job satisfaction which solely represents the workplace domain.

Quality of work life is not a unitary concept, but has been seen as incorporating a hierarchy of perspectives that not only include work-based factors such as job satisfaction, satisfaction with pay and relationships with colleagues, but also factors that broadly reflect life satisfaction and general feelings of well-being.

More recently, work-related stress and the relationship between work and non-work life domains have also been identified as factors that should conceptually be included in quality of work life.

Models and Components

1. *Hackman and Oldham (1976):* With their model, they drew attention to what they described as psychological growth needs as relevant to the consideration of quality of work life. Several such needs were identified that are as follows:
    - Task Identity
    - Task Significance
    - Autonomy
    - Feedback

    The duo suggested that such needs have to be addressed if employees are to experience high quality of work life.

2. *Cooper and Mumford (1979):* In contrast to such theory-based models, these two more pragmatically identified the essential components of quality of work life as basic extrinsic job factors of wages, hours and working conditions and the intrinsic job notions of the nature of work itself. They suggested that a number of other aspects could be added including:
   - Individual Power
   - Employee Participation in Management
   - Fairness and Equity
   - Social Support
   - Use of One's Present Skills
   - Self-Development
   - Meaningful Future at Work
   - Social Relevance of Work or Product
   - Effect on Extra Work Activities.

   Cooper and Mumford suggested that relevant quality of work life concepts may vary according to organization and employee group.
3. *Warr and Colleagues (1979):* In an investigation of quality of work life, Warr *et al.* Considered a range of apparently relevant factors including:
   - Work Involvement
   - Intrinsic Job Motivation
   - Higher Order Need Strength
   - Perceived Intrinsic Job Characteristics
   - Job Satisfaction
   - Life Satisfaction
   - Happiness
   - Self-related Anxiety.

   They discussed a range of correlations derived from work such as those between work involvement and job satisfaction, intrinsic job motivation and job satisfaction and perceived intrinsic job characteristics and job satisfaction.

   In particular, Warr *et al.* found evidence for a moderate association between total job satisfaction & total life satisfaction and happiness, with a less strong but significant association with self-rated anxiety.

   Thus, while some authors have emphasised the workplace aspects in quality of work life, others have identified the relevance of personality factors, psychological well-being and broader concepts of happiness and life satisfaction.

Factors more obviously and directly affecting work has, however, served as the main focus of attention, as researchers have tried to shed light on the important influences on quality of work life in the workplace.

4. *Mirvis and Lawler (1984):* They suggested that quality of work life was associated with satisfaction with wages, hours and working conditions, describing the "basic elements of a good quality of work life" as:
   - Safe Work Environment
   - Equitable Wages
   - Equal Employment Opportunities
   - Opportunities for Advancement
   - Opportunities to Learn and Grow
   - Protection of Individual Rights.
5. *Baba and Jamal (1991):* The duo listed what they described as typical indicators of quality of working life including:
   - Job Involvement
   - Work Role Ambiguity
   - Work Role Conflict
   - Work Role Overload
   - Job Stress
   - Organizational Commitment
   - Turn-over Intentions.

   They also explored routinization of job content suggesting that this facet should be investigated as part of the concept of quality of work life.
6. *Ellis and Pompli (2000):* Some have argued that the quality of work life might vary between groups of workers. For example, Ellis and Pompli identified a number of factors contributing to job dissatisfaction and QWL in nurses including:
   - Resident Aggression
   - Workload, Inability to Deliver Quality of Care Preferred
   - Balance of Work and Family
   - Shift Work
   - Lack of Involvement in Decision Making
   - Professional Isolation
   - Lack of Recognition
   - Poor Relationships with Supervisor/Peers
   - Role Conflict
   - Lack of Opportunity to Learn New Skills

7. *Sirgy and Colleagues (2001):* They suggested the quality of work life as a second-order factor with seven first-order dimensions:
   - Health and Safety Needs
   - Economic and Family Needs
   - Social Needs
   - Esteem Needs
   - Actualization Needs
   - Knowledge Needs
   - Aesthetic Needs.

   They defined quality of work life as satisfaction of these key needs through resources, activities and outcomes stemming from participation in the workplace.

   Needs as defined by psychologist Abraham Maslow were seen as relevant in underpinning this model, covering health & safety, economic, family, social, esteem, actualization, knowledge and aesthetics, although the relevance of non-work aspects is played down as attention is focussed on quality of work life rather than the broader concept of quality of life.

   These attempts at defining quality of work life have included theoretical approaches, lists of identified factors, co-relational analyses, with opinions varying as to whether such definitions and explanations can be both global, or need to be specific to each work setting.
8. *Bearfield (2003):* He used 16 questions to examine quality of working life and distinguished between causes of dissatisfaction in professionals, intermediate clerical, sales and service workers, indicating that different concerns might have to be addressed for different groups.
9. *Herzberg and Colleagues (1959):* The distinction made between job satisfaction and dissatisfaction in quality of work life reflects the influence of job satisfaction theories. Herzberg *et al.* used "hygiene factors" and "motivator factors" to distinguish between the separate causes of job satisfaction and job dissatisfaction.

   It has been suggested that motivator factors are intrinsic to the job, that is, job content, the work itself, responsibility and advancement. Meanwhile, hygiene factors or dissatisfaction-avoidance factors include aspects of the job environment such as interpersonal relationships, salary, working conditions and security.

Of these the latter are the most common cause of job dissatisfaction can be company policy and administration, whilst achievement can be the greatest source of extreme satisfaction.

10. *Nanjundeswaraswamy and Swamy (2013):* They used nine components to measure quality of work life of employees in private technical institutions:
    - Work Environment
    - Organization Culture and Climate
    - Relation and Cooperation
    - Training and Development
    - Compensation and Rewards
    - Facilities
    - Job Satisfaction and Job Security
    - Autonomy of Work
    - Adequacy of Resources.

    Their research revealed that adequacy of resources is more correlated and training and development are less correlated with people perception towards quality of work life. Meanwhile, compensation and rewards are more correlated and work environment are less correlated with QWL.

11. *Lawler and Porter (1966):* An individual's experience of satisfaction or dissatisfaction can be substantially rooted in their perception rather than simply reflecting their "real world".

    Further, an individual's perception can be affected by relative comparison—am I paid as much as that person—and comparisons of internalised ideals, aspirations and expectations, for example, with the individual's current state.

QoL and QWL Relationship

In conjunction with clarifying the theoretical questions relating to the subjective nature and holistic integration of the main actors in QWL, in the 1970s researchers gradually turned their attention to the potential influence of work on a person's other spheres of life. Some theoretical models were proposed in this regard, which include a wide range of factors. Selected models are reviewed below:

Integration Model: As early as 1975, Seashore conceptualized QWL as being based on three levels of actors involved in the work environment. They are the employee, the company and the community respectively.

This approach differs from the concept of quality of work life that had hereto been reserved for employees at the bottom of the pyramid.

According to this model, the domains constituting QWL differ from the perspective of employee, company and community, which contributes to the confusion surrounding the construct.

Ten years later, the concern for integration initiated by Seashore (1975) resurfaced with a more holistic view of the role of the three structures involved. This integrative perspective considered QWL as a social movement with repercussions that extend beyond the strictly organizational framework.

Moreover, many authors have noted that workers are becoming better educated and that they now consider work as a tool for personal growth and social support rather than merely a means of achieving financial independence.

The Quality of Work Life, therefore, becomes an integral part of people's overall Quality of Life (QoL). Social scientists consider this model of the quality of work life to be the most complex and the most contemporary developed to date.

Transfer Model (or Spill-over Effect): Job satisfaction affects other areas of life and vice versa. Many authors conclude that there is a positive correlation between work and areas of life outside of work.

However, a motley few add certain nuances to this observation. Following an in-depth analysis of the research, experts conclude that only certain spheres of work life are positively correlated with other spheres outside work.

In support of this hypothesis, social scientists claim that the transfer model does not apply to all kinds of jobs. Jobs with extreme characteristics (prolonged solitude, oppressive physical requirements, etc) fit better with the compensation model.

Many experts add that the spill-over effect between job satisfaction and personal life may be either direct or indirect. A direct effect can be observed when an objective condition of either one's working or personal life (change of workplace, arrival of a new baby etc) influences the environment without an individual's subjective perception being involved. An indirect effect results from the individual's perception of an objective condition as creating either stress or satisfaction.

Compensation Model: This model assumes that when a person is not satisfied at work, they will try to correct this situation through stimulating activities outside work. Studies have shown that this analysis tends to confirm the compensation model in certain circumstances and shows that certain spheres of work life correlate negatively with areas outside work.

For example, workers who have physically demanding jobs generally tend to seek out non-tiring leisure activities so that they can recuperate better. The main criticism various authors have concerning the compensation model is that, taken to the limit, this model predicts an inverse relation between job satisfaction and satisfaction outside work.

Segmentation Model: This model assumes that life at work and life outside work does not influence each other. Social scientists are of the view that the state that characterizes a person who makes this kind of segmentation may be qualified as psychological disengagement in the face of life or work domain that is divested.

According to the Stressor-Health Path Analysis Model, which identified a similar relationship between job and life satisfaction, projected that a clear separation of job and life dimensions creates balance, whereas a spill-over of work-related feelings detrimentally affects life satisfaction.

While describing the uniqueness of work and non-work demands, experts hold the opinion that an active role is often required to maintain a separation between roles. This model stressed the importance of boundary creation between these two roles in order to maintain equilibrium.

Leakages can develop between role boundaries as responsibilities in one area spill-over to others. When workers are unable to maintain a balanced, separate role and responsibilities between work and family, likelihood for conflict between the two role areas increases. Research shows that spill-over and stress can adversely affect mental health.

Accommodation Model: This model consists of voluntarily reducing one's investment in one sphere of activity in order to more adequately respond to the demands of another. This way of reconciling work life and life outside work is particularly common among mothers of young children.

However, considering the importance recently given to "work life - family life" conciliation, this model will probably be suitable for more categories of workers, either men or women. Research has shown that none of the first three models described above have been universally accepted.

The most solid support for any of the models comes in the form of who confirms the existence of a relationship between job satisfaction and life satisfaction. However, results have shown that the present qualify the adoption of any of the models and suggest that they should be applied based on the spheres and jobs studied.

Along the same lines, it was also attempted to define the relationship between general quality of life and quality of work life. In their efforts to clarify the situation, researchers formulated a conceptual system in the shape of a cone, with QoL at the base of the cone and QWL at the apex.

In this model, job satisfaction, life satisfaction and perceived quality of work performance are located between the extremities of the cone. The interpretation was that the quality of work performance is affected by both QoL and QWL. Thus, to evaluate the total impact of role of work for an individual, it is important to consider the work aspects likely to influence their life away from work.

Based on the model of general Quality of Living (QoL), the appropriate definition of Quality of Work Life (QWL) is as follows:

Quality of Work Life, at a given time, corresponds to a condition experienced by the individual in his or her dynamic pursuit of his or her hierarchically organized goals within work domains where the reduction of gap separating the individual from these goals is reflected by a positive impact on the individual's general quality of life, organizational performance, and consequently, the overall functioning of society.

It is, therefore, evident that there are a number of models that relate to the quality of work life. Managers can administer these measures to employees through a confidential and anonymous process that can reveal strategic gaps in the organization's work environment, job requirement, supervisory behaviour and ancillary programs.

Walton's QWL Model[2]

The Walton Model of quality of work life deals with compensation, welfare measures, development and career growth of employees, social integration in the work force, constitutionalism, work and quality of life and social relevance.

He said that these eleven criteria or characteristics influence the quality of work life. They are described as follows:

1. *Compensation:* It includes salary and wages, fringe benefits and welfare activities. Compensation plays a vital role in employee satisfaction.

2. *Safe and Healthy Working Conditions:* This parameter comprises statutory safety provisions, insurance, production and productivity, delegation of authority and reward system.
3. *Opportunity to Develop Human Capacities:* It refers to training and development of employees.
4. *Opportunity for Career Growth:* The employee seeks career growth and they drift from a job which does not ensure career growth. Prolonged employment in the same position may cause stress to the employees.
5. *Work and Quality of Life:* Challenging work can influence the employees' QWL immensely. In order to motivate the work force, due importance has to be attached to job design techniques such as job rotation, job enlargement and job enrichment.
6. *Constitutionalism:* Manipulative attitude, improper grievance handling and ineffective career counselling among others temper the constitutionalism of an organization. Absence of constitutionalism may have adverse effect on employees. Counselling and Grievance Redressal Committees are the measures to promise in the maintaining of constitutionalism.
7. *Social Integration in the Workforce:* Freedom from prejudices, egalitarianism, upward mobility, supportive work groups, sharing of feelings and openness are required to create a progressive environment for industrial democracy.
8. *Social Relevance of Work:* An organization's management must take substantial steps for the welfare of society.

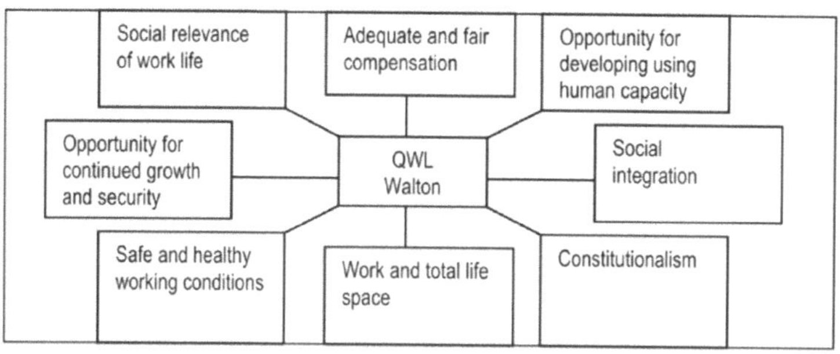

The Eight Dimensional Constructs of Walton's QWL
Source: (Kanten and Sadullah, 2012).

Determinants

An examination of what is involved in psychological growth, of what it is that distinguishes this condition from others, leads one to a consideration of the so-called dimensions or determinants of QWL. In effect, what is being proposed is a set of yardsticks which could be used to assess QWL.

It should be clear that these determinants must both include those that have been set down by each of the previous reform movements as well as the more recent ones concerned with job satisfaction namely effective performance, mental health and psychological growth.

The focus should be on adequate and fair compensation, safe and healthy working conditions, immediate opportunity to use and developing human capacities, future opportunity for continued growth and security, social integration in work, constitutionalism in work organization, work and total life space and the social relevance of work life.

Criticism

Ever since it first appeared, the theoretical evolution of the construct of quality of work life has been subject to an ongoing conceptualization effort. The presumed goal of this exercise is, above all, to develop a definition capable of giving rise to an operational strategy (evaluation method, measuring instrument, etc.) that will make it possible to adequately measure the construct.

Consequently, the assessment focuses on two aspects of past publications on the definition of QWL. First is the lack of precision of theoretical models underlying the currently existing definitions in literature and the second is the confusion created by the use of QWL components to mitigate the weaknesses in current definitions.

Though QWL emphasizes the dynamism of employee and organization welfare, it is described as a process experiencing constant change. Unfortunately, the superimposition of the concepts of goal and process make it, to all intents and purposes, impossible to operationalize in a measuring instrument.

When defining QWL as a 'way of thinking', the approach adequately integrates the three QWL constituents but its main weakness lies in attempting to define a complex subjective construct by means of an equally complex and subjective notion.

Nevertheless, this theoretical approach has the advantage of taking account of the vibrant nature of QWL. In a recently published validation of a QWL questionnaire based on a definition that returns to the concept of satisfaction as an underlying theoretical model, the quality of work life is still being defined in terms of satisfaction.

The difficulty of defining QWL represents a sizable obstacle to the further development of research in this field. If this criticism is justified, an examination of work on QWL should confirm the difficulty of creating a link between the state of theoretical knowledge and its application in research.

Measurement

The basic premise of the quality of work life construct and measure is that workers bring a cluster of their needs to their employing organization and are likely to enjoy a sense of QWL to the extent that these needs are satisfied through work in that organization. The satisfaction of health and safety needs involve three need dimensions:

- Protection from ill health and injury at work (that is, safety at work).
- Protection from ill health and injury outside of work (that is, job-related health benefits.
- Enhancement of good health (that is, encouragement at work of preventative measures of health care).

Experts further go on to say that any method for measuring QWL must respect four characteristics:

1. First of all, it must be valid, that is, it must measure the important aspects of QWL.
2. It must also have sufficient face validity in the eyes of anyone likely to use it.
3. It must be objective and, consequently, verifiable, without any possibility of being manipulated.
4. It must be capable of distinguishing between individual differences within the same work environment.

Recognized Instruments

There are few recognised measures of the quality of work life. Of those that exist, few have evidence of validity and reliability, although both the Brief Index of Affective Job Satisfaction and the Quality of Work Life Scale[3] have been systematically developed to be reliable and is rigorously psychometrically validated.

- The Brief Index of Affective Job Satisfaction (BIAFJS) is a 4-item, purely affective as opposed to cognitive, measure of overall affective job satisfaction that reflects quality of work life.

The BIAJS differs from other job satisfaction measures in being comprehensively validated not just for internal consistency reliability, temporal stability, convergent and criterion-related validities, but also for cross-population invariance by nationality, job level, and job type.

- The six psycho-social factors contributing to overall quality of work life are measured by the Work-Related Quality of Life Scale (WRQoL). It provides support for the psychometric structure of this instrument. This conceptual model, as measured by WRQoL scale, incorporates a six factor structure.

WRQoL Sub-Scales

The six sub-scales of WRQoL are—General Well-Being (GWB) scale, Home-Work Interface (HWI) scale, Job and Career Satisfaction (JCS) scale, Control at Work (CAW) scale, Working Conditions (WCS) scale and Stress at Work (SAW) scale.

- The Job & Career Satisfaction (JCS) scale of the Work-Related Quality of Life scale (WRQoL) is said to reflect an employee's feelings about, or evaluation of, their satisfaction or contentment with their job & career and the training they receive to do it.
- Within the WRQoL measure, JCS is reflected by questions asking how satisfied people feel about their work. It has been proposed that this Positive Job Satisfaction factor is influenced by various issues including clarity of goals and role ambiguity, appraisal, recognition and reward, personal development career benefits and enhancement and training needs.
- The General Well-Being (GWB) scale of the Work-Related Quality of Life scale (WRQoL) aims to assess the extent to which an individual feels good or content in themselves, in a way which may be independent of their work situation. It is suggested that general wellbeing both influences and is influenced by work.
- Mental health problems, predominantly depression and anxiety disorders, are common, and may have a major impact on the general wellbeing of the population. The WRQoL-GWB factor assesses issues of mood, depression and anxiety, life satisfaction, general quality of life, optimism and happiness.
- The WRQoL Stress at Work sub-scale (SAW) reflects the extent to which an individual perceives they have excessive pressures, and feel stressed at work. The WRQoL-SAW factor is assessed through items

dealing with demand and perception of stress and actual demand overload. Whilst it is possible to be pressured at work and not be stressed at work, in general, high stress is associated with high pressure.

- The Control at Work (CAW) sub-scale of the WRQoL scale addresses how much employees feel they can control their work through the freedom to express their opinions and being involved in decisions at work.
- Perceived control at work as measured by the Work-Related Quality of Life scale (WRQoL) is recognized as a central concept in the understanding of relationships between stressful experiences, behaviour and health. Control at work, within the theoretical model underpinning the WRQoL, is influenced by issues of communication at work, decision making and decision control.
- The WRQoL Home-Work Interface scale (HWI) measures the extent to which an employer is perceived to support the family and home life of employees. This factor explores the interrelationship between home and work life domains. Issues that appear to influence employee HWI include adequate facilities at work, flexible working hours and the understanding of managers.
- The Working Conditions scale of the WRQoL assesses the extent to which the employee is satisfied with the fundamental resources, working conditions and security necessary to do their job effectively. Physical working conditions influence employee health and safety, and thus, employee quality of work life. This scale also taps into satisfaction with the resources provided to help people do their jobs.

Other Measures[4]

Besides the more popular ones, there are various other QWL scales that are mentioned as follows:

- Many other measures are being used to determine QWL including the Michigan Quality of Work Program which measures various work-related concerns and the Michigan Organizational Assessment Questionnaire (MOAQ) for measurement of group processes, supervisor behaviours etc.
- Social psychologists believe that diary studies can be powerful in the examination of terms of technological stressors and certain temporal issues. Diary studies ask people to keep track of work-related events on a frequent basis. The frequency of measurement varies from hourly to daily to weekly, and can be used to examine fluctuations of work stressors.

- Based on two leading models in occupational stress research, the Job Demand Control-Support Model and the Michigan Model, a comprehensive quality of work questionnaire, was constructed as the Leiden Quality of Work Questionnaire.

  It measures the key components of psychological demands, skill discretion, decision authority and social support from supervisor and co-workers. Furthermore, it also measures physical exertion, hazardous conditions and toxic exposure, job insecurity and the outcome variable of job satisfaction.
- The questionnaire for organizational stress, which assesses key concepts of the Michigan Model, includes items on overload, role ambiguity, responsibility, role conflict, restrict place, lack of decision authority, lack of meaningfulness of the insecurity. Items on moderators, support from supervisor, support from co-workers and outcome variable, lack of job satisfaction etc are also included in it.
- The wellness of work method is used o measure interview content and organization of work.

From the above-mentioned, it is evident that many attempts have been made to measure QWL. Definitions of what criteria are relevant differ from the point of view of individuals, organizations or society at large.

Needless to say, the measures to be included in a QWL index are not without controversy. In addition, there remain significant methodological challenges to overcome in constructing robust measures that can operationalize the indicators effectively.

Scale Means and Norm Tables

Norm tables allow the scores on a scale achieved by one sample group (or individual) to be indexed against the scores achieved by a known or representative sample group. Norm tables allow the researcher or user to determine the percentile of distribution that the new sample score is equivalent to.

For example, the Job-Career Satisfaction score of a group of university professors may be found to be equivalent to the 80th percentile of a general sample of professors—indicating that their average JCS score was equal or higher than that of 80% of general teachers. Norm tables are produced for summative scales (that is, those scales whose values are expected to make sense when added together).

Summative scales may be derived from simple summation (for example, question 3 score + question 4 score + question 5 score), or some form of transformed item scores.

Improvement on Previous Measures

A new measure builds on the previous Need Satisfaction Questionnaire (NSQ)[5], developed in the 1960s, in a way that it employs a comparable taxonomy of needs in an organizational context. Experts believe this new measure is significantly better than the previous measurement on several grounds.

First, it does not only capture need satisfaction per se but also employees' perceptions of organizational sources of need satisfaction stemming from work environment, job requirement, supervisory behaviour and ancillary programs.

Thus, this measurement may have better diagnostic value for management action. Managers can administer this measure to their employees (through a confidential and anonymous survey), and the survey results should reveal strategic gaps in the characteristics mentioned above.

Second, the validity of measurement is not only tested through traditional tests of convergence and discrimination validity but also tested through specific hypotheses logically deduced from spill-over theory and to a lesser extent need satisfaction theory.

Off course, QWL's need-based theories have been criticized in relation to the need pre-potency notion, that is, the assumption that lower order needs have a stronger pre-potency than higher-order needs. It should be noted that the QWL measure is partly based on Maslow's taxonomy of needs, not his notion of need pre-potency.

Third, the measure does not rely on computing a difference score between "actual states" and "need levels." Such difference scores have been criticized by many methodologists.

In particular, measures based on difference scores have been criticized as being potentially unreliable, having systematic correlations with their components, having spurious correlations with other variables, having questionable construct validity, and restricting variance.

Disagreement on Interpretation

Social psychologists opine that the diversity in QWL's definition generates widespread disagreement about its measurement and interpretation. The point of view from which the construct is defined will determine which determinants/dimensions are relevant in its evaluation.

This will then also have an effect in a manner in which the research on QWL will be approached, as well as the selection of appropriate data gathering instruments. While working with their definitions of the quality of work life, researchers have decided on who would constitute an appropriate survey population.

Subsequently, many scientific instruments and tools have been developed. A few have contested that that the approach taken to QWL measurement varies along a continuum from completely quantitative to completely qualitative methodologies, with many variations between.

Since a dominant theme of much of QWL research is the assumption that individuals' experiences of satisfaction or dissatisfaction define the quality of their work life, many quality of work life surveys typically measure the job-related perceptions and attitudes of individuals such as job satisfaction, job involvement, work commitment and organizational commitment. Of these, job satisfaction is studied most often.

This approach measures the overall job satisfaction an individual is experiencing or specific facets of job satisfaction such as pay, benefits, working conditions, changes for advancement, job security, co-workers, physical resources and equipment, chances to develop skills, supervision, opportunity for personal growth and development.

Those who approach the quality of work life from a Socio-Technical Systems (STS) theory perspective usually reduce the measurement of QWL to work content and job characteristics, and the consequences that these have on internal labour relations. Characteristics such as skill variety, task identity, task significance, autonomy, speed of working and feedback are evaluated.

Job characteristics measures differ from job satisfaction measures in that the former scales are primarily descriptive rather than evaluative. Therefore, instead of assessing respondents' reactions to their jobs, items assess the extent to which various characteristics are descriptive of their jobs.

A QWL survey is distinguished from other standard surveys of employee satisfaction in that it is more comprehensive. The survey should include, at a minimum, the measure of overall job satisfaction, job characteristics and job involvement.

It might also include a dispositional measure, thus, allowing individual dispositional characteristics such as differences in abilities, values, expectations, personality, perceptions and needs to be considered as a moderating variable.

Subjective opinions such as perceptions held by an individual employee may play an important role in their decision to enter, stay with or even leave an organization. It seems as if a long-standing debate has been centred on this question of whether personal factors or structural factors (job characteristics) are the principal determinants of perceived QWL.

The basic assumption of dispositional approach is that personal attributes such as dispositional tendencies are the primary influence on the quality of work life. Meanwhile, the structural approach assumes that situational variables, such as characteristics of the job, have the greatest effect on QWL.

Advocates of the dispositional position argue that individuals tend to be consistent in their job attitudes over time and that enduring dispositional attributes exert as strong an influence on job attitudes as objective job characteristics.

It is, therefore, suggested that dispositional variables probably have a greater impact and are more relevant for managers seeking to improve the QWL of their workers.

In the structural approach, high QWL is defined by the existence of a certain set of organizational conditions and practices. High QWL is assumed to occur when jobs are enriched, supervision is democratic, employees are involved in their jobs and the work environment is safe.

A third approach, based on expectancy theories, suggests the possibility that individuals come to the work place with different goals and needs that they seek to fulfil their work as well as different perceptions of job characteristics. Although individuals' particular needs, values and dispositions shape their work attitudes, this approach recognize that a single, pervasive need structure cannot be assumed.

Differences in needs are, therefore, assumed to account for variation in work attitudes among employees in same jobs. Those in favour of a more integrated approach focus on the interaction of structural and personal influences, with quality of work life determined by the degree to which the full range of human needs are met.

This approach acknowledges aspects such as democratic decision-making and enriched jobs are not desirable or important to everyone. Individuals bring different needs to the workplace and are likely to experience the extent that these needs are satisfied. Therefore, some researchers make use of the discrepancy theory of satisfaction to explain their results.

Some see the goals of QWL surveys as the study of workplace experiences, the work itself, and the world of work, in order to suggest aspects of the workplace or work that could be modified so that the employees and organization reach their goals simultaneously. This approach measures QWL in terms of extrinsic, intrinsic or prior traits.

Extrinsic traits are salaries and other tangible benefits. Intrinsic traits include skill levels, authority and challenge while prior traits are those of the individuals involved, such as their gender or employment status.

In terms of the development and construction of measuring instruments, some researchers base the development of their QWL survey instruments on general topic areas of QWL, as identified through a literature review, such as co-worker and supervisor support, team work and communications, staff training and development and compensation and benefits.

Others base the construction of their questionnaires on specific theoretical models such as occupational stress models or need satisfaction and spill-over theories. Often researchers design questionnaires by borrowing and combining items from different questionnaires such as job satisfaction, job characteristics, work involvement, work stress, wellness at work and other questionnaires.

Cultural Variations

It has been argued that organizational stress can best be understood in the context of an individual's cultural values. While work overload and lack of autonomy were the main sources of stress and strain in the United States, lack of role clarity was the key issue for workers in India.

Research based in Taiwan concluded that lack of managerial role clarity and poor recognition by managers were the two main sources of stress, whilst relationships and organizational climate, whereas personal responsibility appeared to be key source of stress and strain in the United Kingdom.

One of the social Dutch management researcher, Geert Hofstede in 1980s developed the model of cultural dimension that cultural difference in attitude can affect perception of quality of work life and in turn productivity of the employees.

Power Distance Index

It refers the extent to which inequality and power are tolerated. High power distance index represents a culture that accepts inequity and power differences while low power distance indicates organizational structures and decentralized decision-making responsibility.

Individualism vs Collectivism

This dimension suggests the degree to which societies are integrated into groups and their perceived obligations and dependence on groups. Individualism indicates that more emphasis is given on achieving personal goals i.e., "I". On the other hand collectivism signifies greater importance on the well-being of the TEAM i.e., "We".

Uncertainty Avoidance Index

It is the extent to which uncertainty and ambiguity are tolerated. This dimension considers how uncertain situations and unpredictable events are dealt with. A high uncertainty avoidance index indicates a low tolerance for uncertainty and low risk-taking. The uncertain is dealt strictly through policies and regulations, etc. On the other hand low uncertainty avoidance index indicates a high tolerance for uncertainty and high and risk-taking behaviours. The unknown is more openly accepted, and rules and regulations are not very stringent.

Masculinity vs Femininity

This dimension is also referred as "tough vs tender", and considers the preference of society for achievement, attitude towards sexuality equality, behavior, etc.

- Masculinity emphasizes more on distinct gender roles, assertiveness and is more focused on materialistic pleasures and wealth-building. On the other hand femininity is characterized by fluid gender roles, socialization and quality of life.

Long-Term Orientation vs Short-Term Orientation

This dimension considers the time horizon viewed by the society. Long-term orientation lays emphasis on the future and is characterized by persistence, perseverance, and long-term growth. On the other hand short-term orientation lays emphasis on the present and expects quick results and respect for tradition.

Indulgence vs Restraint

This dimension considers the extent to which a society has the tendency to fulfill its desires and can control their impulses and desires.

- Indulgence indicates that a society allows gratification and is more fun loving and allows the people to enjoy life. On the other hand restraint indicates that a society suppresses gratification and regulates the needs of the people by following social norms.

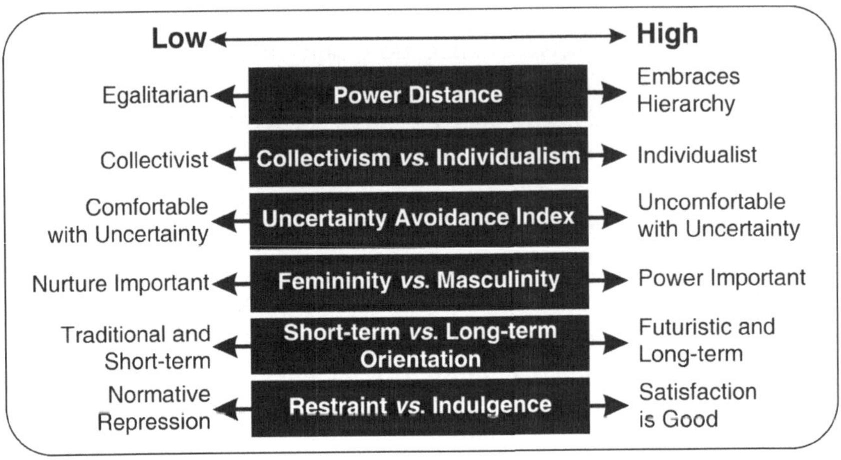

Hofstede's Six Dimensions of Culture across Countries

Countries	Power Distance	Individualism	Uncertainty Avoidance	Masculinity
Australia	Low	High	Low	High
Canada	Low	High	Low	High
China	High	Low	Medium	Medium
Germany	Low	High	Medium	High
Mexico	High	Medium	High	High
France	High	High	High	Low
Spain	Medium	Medium	High	Low
Greece	Medium	Medium	High	Medium
Denmark	Low	High	Low	Low
Finland	Low	High	Medium	Low
Brazil	High	Medium	Medium	Medium
India	High	Medium	Low	Medium
Japan	Low	Medium	High	High
U.K.	Low	High	Low	High
U.S.A	Low	High	Low	High

Inevitably, generalizations about culture and work were challenged. This led to an alternative set of seven culture-level value types:

1. Conservatism (the degree to which a culture or society places importance on the maintenance of status-quo.
2. Intellectual autonomy (the degree to which individuals are seen as entitled to pursue their own intellectual interests and desires).

3. Affective autonomy (attitude towards the pursuit of hedonism, personal interests and desires and other examples).
4. Hierarchy (the degree to which hierarchical structures and roles are legitimised).
5. Mastery (attitude towards concepts such as mastery of social environment and focus on promoting competition between individuals).
6. Egalitarian commitment (attitude towards self-interest).
7. Harmony (attitude towards harmony with nature).

Across cultures, there has been little agreement in what makes up the key aspects of an individual's quality of work life. It is, therefore, proposed that the relationship between stress and strain is broadly common to various cultures, but suggest that sources of work stress differ across cultures.

Application

Regular assessment of the quality of work life can potentially provides organisations with important information about the welfare of their employees, such as job satisfaction, general wellbeing, work-related stress and the home-work interface. Studies at the UK University have shown that a valid measure of the quality of work life exists and can be used as a basis for effective interventions.

Critics point out that a low-level of wellbeing at work is estimated to cost about 5–10 per cent of gross national product per annum. Yet, the quality of work life as a theoretical construct remains relatively unexplored and unexplained within the organizational psychology research literature.

A publication of the National Institute of Clinical Excellence (NICE) emphasizes the core role of assessment and understanding of the way working environments pose risks for psychological wellbeing through lack of control and excessive demand.

The emphasis placed by NICE on assessment and monitoring wellbeing springs from the fact that these processes are the key first step in identifying areas for improving the quality of work life and addressing risks at work.

Development of Scale

With the quality of work life drawing more importance globally, organizations are facing many issues related to human resource of which, employee stability is one of the major problems and addressing it is a top most priority. Amongst various reasons for employee stability, QWL is one among them. The quality of work life is a multi-dimensional construct and it has been influenced by many variables.

An elaborate survey conducted with the use of a well-defined questionnaire identified nine significant dimensions based on factor analysis, which are stated below:

1. Work Environment
2. Organization Culture and Climate
3. Relation and Cooperation
4. Training and Development
5. Compensation and Rewards
6. Facilities
7. Job Satisfaction and Job Security
8. Autonomy of Work and Adequacy of Resources.

Scale Validation

The validity of a psychometric scale can be assessed in a number of ways. For example, the factors generated based on items given to a particular organization should also give rise to the same factors when given to another organisation.

The construct validity of a scale is concerned with the idea that if a number of scales are given to the same sample, then scales measuring related constructs should correlate with each other (convergent validity) and not correlate with each other if they measure theoretically unrelated constructs (discriminant validity).

It is, therefore, reasonable to assume that if the WRQoL scale is a good measure of the broad definition of quality of working life then the same factors should be generated in any organization, that scores on the scale should be highly correlated with, for example, scores on a jobs satisfaction scale and on a general well-being scale, but be unrelated to say, scores on attitudes to recycling.

However, sections test the validity of WRQoL scale on each of these concepts as well as for test-retest reliability which is also a required property for a valid scale.

Strategies for Improvement

QWL is the shared responsibility not only of the management and workers but also of union leaders, government officials and behavioural scientists. Experts outline six strategies which can be used for improving QWL in organizations. They are:

1. *Development of Careers and Career Paths:* Career refers to a sequence of positions occupied by an individual during the course of a lifetime. Exploration, establishment, mid-career and later career are the four stages in an individual's career. From the management's point of view, the process of development of careers and career paths forms a means to improve and sustain employees' productivity to prepare them for changing work situations in the organizational setting.

   It involves aspects such as career counselling, charting career paths, career information systems, human resource planning, periodic skill assessment, training and help for disadvantaged groups. Three conditions are needed for effective performance of activities *vis-a-vis* development of career paths of employees in organizations. It comprises three important dimensions:

   (a) Coordination of these activities with other activities in HR management.
   (b) Active involvement of line supervisors in designing and implementing them.
   (c) Provision for equal access to the benefit of all employees.

2. *Work Design:* It influences employee satisfaction, motivation and productivity. In order to improve quality of work life, work design must consider factors that moderate employees' reactions to their work. These factors relate to individual differences and inter-personal and organizational factors. As there is no universally good work design, there are varied job-design options to improve QWL.

   Depending upon situational requirement, management may choose relevant strategies for specific design alternatives. Whatever work design options management uses, following strategies for planned personal and organizational change seem to be relevant for effective introduction of QWL through work redesign in organizational settings:

   (a) Diffusing knowledge about work redesign theory and practice.
   (b) Disseminating work redesign innovations.
   (c) Paying more attention to jobs of first-level managers.
   (d) Paying more attention to role of unions in work redesign efforts.

3. *Organizational Reward System:* The reward systems motivate employees in organizations. Workers do what satisfy their needs.

Before doing anything, they look for the reward in terms of salary increases, benefits, desirable job assignments etc that organizations control.

These organizational rewards may be direct or indirect, financial or non-financial and distributed on individual or group basis. Whatever the type of rewards, they influence every other aspect of the organization and must be used as an integral part of any program of organization at change.

4. *Design and Maintenance of Group and Inter-group Relationships:* There exists group dynamics in formal and informal situations. In conjunction with different characteristics of intra-group behaviour there are systematic characteristics of inter-group relationships in organizations. There arises a complex set of behaviours, emotions, attitudes and beliefs when groups tend to have interdependent relationships.

   As a strategy to improve QWL, efforts may be made to take into account the dynamics of intra-group and inter-group relations in designing and maintaining them in organizations. Different behavioural science interventions can be applied to reduce the destructive effects of inter-groups conflict and improve the quality of work life.

   Such interventions aim to increase communications and interactions between work-related groups, reduce the amount of dysfunctional competition and replace a parochial, independent point of view with an awareness of the necessity for interdependence of action calling on best efforts of these groups.

5. *Managerial Practices:* The prevailing management practices in an organization influence the quality of work life in it. Specifically, the role of supervision and management is of utmost significance in improving the quality of work culture. The supervisor influences employees' productive behaviour through his treatment of individuals, his influence on job designs, management influences through reward systems and the development of team work.

6. *Internal and External Strategies for Change:* A set of internal and external strategies is used to introduce five strategies aimed at improvement of QWL in an organization. Before sticking to this set of strategies, there is a need to make a number of choices between centralized-decentralized strategies, power-based and collaborative strategies, fast and slow-paced strategies, and individual & structure-oriented strategies.

Often, three general strategies are used to introduce QWL programs, which are:

(a) Strategies arising internally in organization such as management and union strategies.
(b) Strategies originating with political and special interest groups such as community action approaches.
(c) Societal level strategies such as use of legislation involving integration of internal and external programs.

Some of the factors used to measure the quality of work culture pick up on things that don't actually make people feel good but which seem to make people feel bad about work if those things are absent.

For example, if the place where someone works is too noisy, they might get frequent headaches or find they cannot concentrate, and thus, feel dissatisfied. But when it is quiet enough they don't feel pleased or happy—they just don't feel bad. This can apply to a range of factors that affect someone's working conditions.

Guidelines for Best Results

A quality of work life assessment and intervention programs are particularly successful where careful attention is given to the detail of the whole process. An effective program will be based on the idea that optimising staff QWL in an organization is an ongoing process of continuous improvement and not just about conducting a survey.

To help one get best out of a QWL survey, the following observations can be adopted by organizations:

1. Programs tend to be less successful if there is insufficient senior management commitment.
2. Preparation is paramount.
3. Programs are less likely to be successful if the project group making the decisions do not understand QWL and other issues involved.
4. Programs are not very successful if a survey is carried out without prior communication with staff.
5. Program work can be linked to other methods of information gathering.
6. Programs can benefit from benchmarking.
7. Programs are less likely to be successful if the results of surveys are not communicated effectively to staff.

8. Programs are more likely to be successful when a constructive and positive approach is taken to the use of survey results.
9. Programs are less likely to be successful if solutions to problems are determined by senior management with no input from staff.
10. Programs are most likely to be successful if decisions and policies are first tested on pilot groups.
11. Programs are more likely to be successful if support is in place before introducing a process to improve QWL.
12. Programs are less likely to be successful if attention is only paid to educating the individual.

Newer strategies for attracting and retaining skilled workforce require organizations to better evaluate their employees' quality of work life. The need of the hour, therefore, is for more precise and more complete measurement instruments.

UNIT–IV

Mental Health in the Workplace

All of us have the right to decent and productive work in conditions of freedom, equity, security and human dignity. For persons with mental health problems achieving this right are particularly challenging.

The International Labour Organisation (ILO) has long recognized the importance of documenting the extent of disabilities among the labour force and setting up effective preventive and rehabilitative programmes. ILO's activities promote the inclusion of individuals with disabilities in mainstream training and employment structures.

The importance of addressing specific issues related to the employment of persons with mental health problems has also been recognized. ILO promotes increased investment in human resource development, particularly the human resource needs of vulnerable groups, including persons with mental health problems.

Employees' mental health problems and their impact on an enterprise's productivity and disability/medical costs are critical human resource issues. Increasingly, employers' organizations, trade unions and government policy-makers are realizing that the social and economic costs of mental health problems in the workplace cannot be ignored.

Because of the extent and pervasiveness of mental health problems, the World Health Organization (WHO) recognizes mental health as a top priority. Using instruments that allow us to see not how people die but rather how they live, we now know that the problems of mental illness loom large not just in India but around the world. It accounts for 12% of all disability-adjusted life-years (DALYs) and 23% in high-income countries.

Five of the 10 leading causes of disability are mental problems (major depression, schizophrenia, bipolar disorders, alcohol use and obsessive-compulsive disorders).

These disorders—together with anxiety, depression and stress—have a definitive impact on any working population and should be addressed within that context. They may also develop into long-term disorders with accompanying forms of disability.

Given the fact that numerous affordable interventions exist, the time has come to challenge both the low priority given to mental health and the stigma that those with mental ill-health still endure around the world. We now know that when essential drugs, if needed, are made available and access is offered to a psychosocial rehabilitation programme (including the access to meaningful and realistic employment) many persons will be able to lead more socially and personally satisfying lives.

Given the multifaceted nature of the factors that contribute to good mental health, the Government of India is ever mindful of the need to highlight activities that foster good practices in mental health.

I am, especially, interested in the importance of mental health in the workplace in general, and will suggest appropriate management for workers with mental health problems. In addition, it takes a practical look at strategies to promote and sustain good mental health while highlighting examples of good practices.

It is hoped that this important document will assist employers and employees in raising awareness of the benefits of good mental health practices and encourage the implementation of strategies to maintain a healthy working environment.

Scope

There is growing evidence of the impact of mental illness. Mental health problems are among the most important contributors to the burden of disease and disability worldwide. Five of the 10 leading causes of disability are mental health problems. Furthermore, trends (especially in the post-pandemic era) indicate that the future will see a dramatic increase in mental health problems.

The burden of mental health disorders on health and productivity has long been underestimated. The National Mental Health Program (NHMP) has estimated that 15-20% people will experience some form of mental health problem during their working lives. In fact, mental health problems are a leading cause of illness and disability in the country.

The European Mental Health Agenda of the European Union (EU) has recognized the prevalence and impact of mental health disorders in the workplace in EU countries. It has been estimated that 20% of the adult working population has some type of mental health problem at any given time.[1]

In the USA, it is estimated that more than 40 million people have some type of mental health disorder and, of that number, 4–5 million adults are considered seriously mentally ill.[2] Depressive disorders, for example, represent one of the most common health problems of adults in the United States workforce.

The impact of mental health problems in the workplace has serious consequences not only for the individual but also for the productivity of the enterprise. Employee performance, rates of illness, absenteeism, accidents and staff turnover is affected by employees' mental health status.

In the United Kingdom, for example, 80 million days are lost every year due to mental illnesses, costing employers £1–2 billion each year.[3] In the United States, estimates for national spending on depression alone are US$ 30–40 billion, with an estimated 200 million days lost from work each year.[4]

Mental Health Causes Disability

As illustrated in this monograph, mental health problems affect functional and working capacity in numerous ways. Depending on the age of onset of a mental health disorder, an individual's working capacity may be significantly reduced. Mental disorders are usually one of the three leading causes of disability, together with cardiovascular disease and musculo-skeletal disorders.

The cost to society of excluding people with disabilities from taking an active part in community life is high. This exclusion often leads to diminished productivity and losses in human potential. The United Nations estimates that 25% of the world's population is adversely affected in one way or another as a result of disabilities. The cost of disability has three components:

- Direct cost of welfare services and treatment including the costs of disability benefits, travel and access, possible medication etc.
- Indirect cost to those who are not directly affected (carers).
- Opportunity costs of income foregone as a result of incapacity.

People with disabilities, particularly psychiatric disabilities, face numerous barriers in obtaining equal opportunities—environmental, access, legal, institutional and attitudinal barriers which cause social exclusion. For people with mental illness, social exclusion is often the hardest barrier to overcome and is usually associated with feelings of shame, fear and rejection.

Mental illness imposes a heavy burden in terms of human suffering, social exclusion, stigmatization of the mentally ill and their families and economic costs. Unfortunately, the burden is likely to grow over time as a result of ageing of the global population and stresses resulting from social problems and unrest, including violence, conflict and natural disasters.

Using the Workplace for Referral and Rehabilitation

Globalization and interdependence have opened new opportunities for the growth of the world economy and development. While globalization has been a powerful and dynamic force for growth, work conditions and the labour market have changed dramatically during the last two decades. The key elements in these changes are increased automation and the rapid implementation of information technology.

Workers, especially in the post-pandemic era, confront as never before an array of new organizational structures and processes—downsizing, contingent employment and increased workload. Employers have tended to take the view that work and/or the workplace are not etiological factors in mental health problems.

However, whatever the causal factors, the prevalence of mental health problems in employees makes mental health a pressing issue in its own right[5]. Although, effective mental health services are multidimensional, the workplace is an appropriate environment in which to educate individuals about, and raise their awareness of, mental health problems.

For example, the workplace can promote good mental health practices and provide tools for recognition and early identification of mental health problems, and can establish links with local mental health services for referral, treatment and rehabilitation. Ultimately, these efforts will benefit all by reducing the social and economic costs to society of mental health problems.

For people with mental health problems, finding work in the open labour market or returning to work and retaining a job after treatment is often a challenge. Stigma surrounds those with mental illness and the recovery process is often misunderstood.

This provides a practical guide and resource for human resource managers, mental health professionals, rehabilitation workers, policy-makers, trade unionists and other authorities' concerned.

The central themes of this unit are:

- To examine the importance of mental health problems in the workplace.
- To consider the role of workplace in promoting good mental health practices for employees.
- To examine the importance of work for persons with mental health problems.
- To discuss different vocational strategies and programmes for persons with mental health problems.
- To provide examples of good practices. These examples illustrate:
    - (a) Good mental health promotional practices in the workplace by employers
    - (b) How to handle an employee who becomes ill with a mental health problem, such as depression
    - (c) Vocational rehabilitation models/programs for persons with long-term mental health problems.

Workplace Mental Wellbeing

The workplace is one of the key environments that affect our mental wellbeing and health. There is an acknowledgement and growing awareness of the role of work in promoting or hindering mental wellness and its corollary—mental illness. Although it is difficult to quantify the impact of work alone on personal identity, self-esteem and social recognition, most mental health professionals agree that the workplace environment can have a significant impact on an individual's mental well-being.

Organizations are affected by employee mental health problems in the form of absenteeism, poor work habits, low job satisfaction, interpersonal conflict and indecisiveness. It has been found that executives are suffering from poor mental health due to high levels of stress. Warr (1990) gave two separate dimensions, pleasure and arousal for affective well-being. High or low level of arousal may accompany a particular level of pleasure and a particular level of arousal may be either pleasurable or displeasurable. A feeling of affective well-being is derived from both the dimensions. This is the most general aspect of mental health, which relates to the overall feeling of good or bad that can be associated with the feelings of happiness and cheerfulness. While good mental heath is generally associated with the quadrants 1 and 2, mentally healthy individuals will also experience the affect in quadrants 3 and 4

(Exhibit 1). But the most distinguishing feature between the mentally healthy and unhealthy is the length of the time they spend in various quadrants.

It is not so that a mentally healthy individual will not experience tension/gloom but it will not exist for a long time. On the other hand, the individual with poor mental health experiences negative states most of the times. According to Warr (1990), a mentally healthy individual sees a relationship among all the four components of mental health. Mentally healthy individual is balanced and is in harmony with the environment and other individuals. Jahoda (1958) emphasized that a mentally healthy individual is one who is consistent in character, has a unified outlook of life and is able to accept and resolve the mental conflicts.

Exhibit 1: Affective Well-Being and Mental Health

Aroused			Surprised
Alarmed			Full of Energy
Tense			Cheerful
Uneasy			Happy
Discontented	4	1	Pleased
Dejected	3	2	Contented
Depressed			Comfortable
Sad			Relaxed
Lacking Energy			Tranquil
Bored			Sluggish

Source: Warr, P. (1990). The Measurement of Affective Well-Being and other Aspects of Mental Health. New Jersy: Erlbaum

Integrated functioning is sometimes considered in relation to the balance which an individual finds between different aspects of life. Workaholic who can only find time to work cannot be considered to exhibit good mental health. In fact, for good mental health one has to have a balance between work and family relation, social circles and the whole environment. The concept of mental health differs with respect to cultural and social norms even though, Dalal (2001) holds the view that mental health can be socially constructed.

Warr Vitamin Model of Mental Health

Warr (1990) explained environmental features of work which affect mental health in a vitamin model. This model represents nine features of work, which are considered to be necessary contributors to mental health just as each vitamin is necessary contributor to the physical health.

Deficiency in the environmental feature will impair the mental health, and an increase in that feature beyond the required level will lead to no further improvement. For some of the features, an addition beyond the required level will lead to reduction in mental health, while for others any addition will have no effect. The analogy being that too much of certain vitamins (A and D) will result in toxic poisoning which leads to reduction in mental health. On the contrary, once the required level is reached for other vitamins (C and E), any additional intake will have no adverse or positive effect.

A/D vitamin operation comprises externally generated goals, variety, environment clarity, opportunity of control, skill use and interpersonal features. If they have a low presence, they will impair mental health, but if present in over-abundance their effect will be over-damaging. On the other hand, C/E vitamin operation comprises availability of money, physical security and valued social position as the environmental features of work where mental health is unlikely to be affected by having too much of them. Only a deprivation of these essential features will impair mental health.

Optimal quantity of all these environmental features will vary as individuals differ in what they need, their level of skill, experience and their perception as well as their ability. These nine features overlap to a considerable degree, but Warr argues that inclusion of all of them provides a more comprehensive treatment of the environment. There is also a clear overlap with latent and manifest functions of work (Jahoda, 1958) with the vitamin model expanding some of these functions. The importance of such models is that they provide the starting point for considering the impact of the job on an individual's mental health. To improve mental health in work, it will be necessary to improve the extent to which the job incorporates these features. The need for job variety can be seen as deriving from the importance of competence and aspiration to good mental health. Conversely, too much variety is likely to be perceived as threat, which ultimately leads to development of ill mental health. Nine environmental features of work are:

- ***Opportunity for control:*** Jobs vary in degree to which they enable the individual to control the activities and events. Researches have revealed that lack of control is an important causal factor of stress. Jobs which do not allow the worker much or any control over the outcome of actions will be detrimental to mental health.
- ***Opportunity for skill use:*** Opportunity for using the skills and developing new skills has been assumed to have a positive impact on mental health as it enables an individual to achieve one's goals and aspirations.
- ***Externally generated goals:*** Individuals in work occupy roles and a set of normative expectations about how the role occupant should behave in particular situations. Requirements of a role allow an individual to focus on the attainments of the goal, which has positive impact on mental health.
- ***Variety:*** In some jobs task requirements are repetitive and the individual stays in one place doing the same thing over and over again. The monotony of repeating same job can promote poor mental health.
- ***Environmental Clarity:*** Environmental clarity is the degree to which job environment provides feedback to an individual about his performance. Feedback enables the individual to know the consequences of the action taken, to predict the outcomes in advance and to take the steps to avert negative consequences. It also relates to role expectation clarity accepted in the individual's role set. Thus, more clarity will lead to improved mental health.
- ***Availability of money:*** Job differs in financial rewards. This may not directly affect the mental health but the absence of money may be restricting an individual in many ways. This can affect the mental and physical health by inducing stress and frustration in the individual.
- ***Physical security:*** Job environments that involve adverse physical conditions such as cold, danger, lack of space, physiological security and even the non-permanent jobs may pose threat to the individual which in turn can affect mental health.
- ***Opportunity for interpersonal contact:*** Interpersonal contact provides opportunity for interaction and social affiliation which is responsible for a strong human need for survival. A job environment which

restricts access to interpersonal contacts can affect mental health adversely.

- *Valued Social Positions:* Jobs differ in the degree of status attached to them depending upon the value attributed to activities associated with the roles. Individuals who hold a valued social position may be able to maintain higher levels of self-esteem and confidence, which is an important aspect of mental health.

While considering different organizational approaches for improving health and reducing stress at work, it is necessary to consider how far, if at all, they actually change the job environment to incorporate more of the vitamins. The main criticism against the stress and resilience techniques is that they focus on helping the individual to cope up with the stress, rather than actually attempting to change the environment per se. The vitamin model would suggest that this could only be a short-term solution, as it does not attempt to change the environment.

Categories of Psychological Experience

Employment provides five categories of psychological experience that promote mental well-being:

- Time structure (an absence of time structure can be a major psychological burden).
- Social contact.
- Collective effort and purpose (employment offers a social context outside the family).
- Social identity (employment is an important element in defining oneself)
- Regular activity (organizing one's daily life).

Many large companies now realize that their employees' productivity is connected to their health and well-being. However, more emphasis has traditionally been placed on physical health than on mental health and well-being. Several factors at a workplace can promote employees' psychosocial well-being and mental health.

Especially important in this respect is the opportunity to be included in planning and carrying out activities and events in the workplace (for example, opportunity to decide and act in one's chosen way and the potential to predict the consequences of one's action).

A related feature is the degree to which the environment encourages or inhibits the utilization or development of skills. Physical security, opportunity for interpersonal contact, and equitable pay are also important.

Promotion of Mental Health at Workplace

Notions of mental health at work tend to focus on the individual rather than the organization. A comprehensive policy of mental health at work includes, however, an assessment of the mental health of the organization itself. The gain to both individuals and the organization from promoting good mental health at work is reflected in increased presence, well-being and production.

The constant and unremitting rate of change that affects all businesses today is increasingly motivating employers to address the health of their staff. Moreover, it is taking its toll on employees, some of whom fail to cope with the changes and need support to help them avoid under-performance and absenteeism.

The global marketplace is forcing organizations to upgrade their efficiency and this, in turn, is encouraging employers to seek ways of enhancing the performance of employees and to avoid losses associated with health and safety.

Job Stress at Work

Job stress can be defined as the harmful physical and emotional response that occurs when the requirements of job do not match the capabilities, resources or needs of the worker.[6] Job stress can cause poor health and can increase rates of work-related injuries and accidents.

Some potential causes of work-related stress are over-work, lack of clear instructions, unrealistic deadlines, lack of decision-making, job insecurity, isolated working conditions, surveillance, and inadequate child-care arrangements.

Although sexual harassment and discrimination are often excluded from lists of traditional job stressors, they must be included in any comprehensive analysis of the causes of workplace stress.

Sexual harassment is a stressor for women in the workplace, and discrimination is a stronger predictor of health outcomes, including mental ill-health, for ethnic minorities than traditional job stressors. Some of the many effects of stress include numerous physical ailments as well as mental health problems such as depression and increased rates of suicide.

Workplace Activities for Mental Health, United Kingdom

A Good Practice Initiative #1

A large international retailer with 696 stores in many parts of the world including North America, Asia and Europe employs some 56,000 people. Over 52,000 of these are employed in stores. Eighty three percent of the workforce is female and 62% of these are part-time. Their stated policy is to take the mental health of its workforce seriously: "We realize that in ensuring the mental well-being of staff we benefit from an individual and company point of view," is the standard company policy.

Strategy for Health Promotion

The strategy for overall health promotion, which includes mental health, is based on the following:

- Health education to raise awareness of factors affecting health and well-being
- Screening programmes to detect risk factors or early signs of disease
- Action programmes to do something about them.

Role of Occupational Health Service

The occupational health service works closely with personnel and line management regarding all aspects of mental and physical health of employees. The occupational health team is available to look at the effects of health on work, to discuss with staff any health problems they may have and to promote good health through health education, screening and action programmes.

The company believes that an occupational health service can play a major role in helping:

- To identify work problems caused by mental ill-health.
- To take action to improve the health of employees.
- To assist employers in modifying the work and work environment.
- To enable employees to remain at work rather than withdraw.

The organization assists in preventing mental ill-health by giving people a good working environment and a clearly defined job.

Following absence, it is often essential to be able to modify working hours during the rehabilitation period and to provide a gradual return to usual working practices through a good sick pay scheme.

Financial support at this time allays anxiety and encourages a speedier return to work. Regular honest appraisals are important and problems in performance should be discussed when they occur, with an opportunity to follow up and review progress.

People should feel able to contribute to their development and feel accountable for their jobs. On-site counselling facilities from personnel or health professionals are available, reducing time away from work.[7]

In India, there is increasing concern regarding the health impact of job stress. For example, an increased risk of work-related illnesses and accidents has been observed with rapid industrialization. Though, there was no specific legislation addressing the impact of job stress in the past, quite some standards for safety and health features exist at the workplace now.

However, these standards tend to focus on the physical aspects of the workplace and do not explicitly include the psychological and/or mental health aspects of working conditions. Notable exceptions include the Tata, Wipro, Infosys and other such enterprises.

Consequences of Mental Health in the Workplace

The consequences of mental health problems in the workplace can be summarized as follows.

Absenteeism

- Increase in overall sickness absence, particularly frequent short periods of absence.
- Poor health (depression, stress, burnout).
- Physical conditions (high blood pressure, heart disease, ulcers, sleeping disorders, skin rashes, headache, neck & backache, low resistance to infections).

Work Performance

- Reduction in productivity and output.
- Increase in error rates.
- Increased amount of accidents.

- Poor decision-making.
- Deterioration in planning and control of work.

Staff Attitude and Behaviour

- Loss of motivation and commitment
- Burnout
- Staff working increasingly long hours but for diminishing returns
- Poor timekeeping
- Labour turnover (particularly expensive for companies at top levels of management).

Relationships at Work

- Tension and conflicts between colleagues
- Poor relationships with clients
- Increase in disciplinary problems.

Workers' health is a separate goal in its own right. Addressing mental health issues in the workplace means incorporating social responsibility in a firm's everyday practices and routines.

Mental Health and Unemployment

Re-employment has been shown to be one of the most effective ways of promoting the mental health of the unemployed.[8] A review of studies of the mental and physical health effects of unemployment and the mechanisms by which unemployment causes adverse health outcomes reveals a complex relationship. There has been a serious debate about the direction of causality.

Does unemployment cause deterioration in health, both mental and physical? Are the sick more likely to become unemployed? In a study reported in the Journal of Community Psychology,[9] an analysis of employed respondents revealed that those who became unemployed had over twice the risk of increased depressive symptoms and diagnosis of clinical depression than those who remained employed.

Furthermore, the data did not support any relationship between clinical depression and becoming unemployed. In the respondents' community at the time of the study, depression was not a causal factor for the unemployment rate. The incidence and prevalence of depression increased once individuals became unemployed.

Table 1: Successful Characteristics at Work

This is the consensus from literature outlining nine different characteristics of jobs, work environment and organizations that are hazardous:

Work Characteristics	*Condition Defining Hazard (Demands, Control and Support)*
CONTEXT	
Organizational Function and Culture	1. Poor task environment and lack of definition of objective. 2. Poor problem solving environment. 3. Poor development environment. 4. Poor communication. 5. Non-supportive culture.
Role in Organization	1. Role ambiguity. 2. Role conflict. 3. High responsibility for people.
Career Development	1. Career uncertainty. 2. Career stagnation. 3. Poor status or status incongruity. 4. Poor pay. 5. Job insecurity and redundancy. 6. Low social value to work.
Decision Latitude/Control	1. Low participation in decision-making. 2. Lack of control over work. 3. Little decision making in work.
Interpersonal Relationships at Work	1. Social or physical isolation. 2. Poor relationships with supervisors. 3. Interpersonal conflict and violence. 4. Lack of social or practical support at home. 5. Dual career problems.
CONTENT	
Task Design	1. Ill-defined work. 2. High uncertainty in work. 3. Lack of variety of short work cycles. 4. Fragmented or meaningless work. 5. Under-utilization of skill. 6. Continual exposure of client/customer groups.

Work Characteristics	*Condition Defining Hazard (Demands, Control and Support)*
Workload/Work Pace	1. Lack of control over pacing.
Quantities and Quality	1. Work overload or underload. 2. High levels of pacing or time pressure.
Work Schedule	1. Shift working. 2. Inflexible work schedule. 3. Unpredictable working hours. 4. Long or unsociable working hours.

Source: HSE Contract Research Report No. 61/1993. Cox T. Stress Research and Stress Management: Putting Theory to Work.

Issues Facing Employers and Managers

Although our knowledge of mental health issues has increased over the past few decades, employers and enterprises have lagged behind in their understanding and acceptance of the pervasiveness, treatment and impact of mental health problems on organizational life.

Most human resource management and public administration training programs do not cover adequately the area of mental health and employment. Recognition of mental illness in the workplace is often difficult for there is often a psychological component to physical symptoms and physical ailments may be present in some mental disorders.

Whatever the original cause, employers and managers are faced with three main issues as they attempt to address the mental health needs of their employees:

1. *Recognition and acceptance of mental health as a legitimate concern of organizations:* There is a need among employers to recognize mental health issues as a legitimate workplace concern. As disability costs and absenteeism increase in the workplace due to mental ill-health (whatever the precipitating factors), more and more employers are faced with the challenge of developing policies and guidelines to address these issues.
2. *Effective implementation of anti-discrimination provisions:* The last decade has seen a significant increase in anti-discrimination legislation specific to employment for people with disabilities. Although many of these laws and statutes have weak enforcement mechanisms, there is an increasing need for employers and their human resource managers to understand how these laws affect their company's employment policies.

3. *Preventive, treatment and rehabilitation programs that address employees' mental health needs:* The development of appropriate prevention and mental health promotion policies in the workplace is an increasing concern for many employers. Understanding the need for early intervention and treatment, as well as reintegrating an employee into the work environment, is also a critical challenge.

Outstanding Workplace

Finland has one of the best mental health workplace programs in the world. Measures most commonly taken at the Finnish workplace aim to:

- Improve work environment (for example, enhancing occupational safety and ergonomics, communication, clear goals, independence at work).

Total Wellness Program, Finland

A Good Practice Initiative #2

One of the world's leading wireless and wireline telecommunications firms runs a total wellness program, which includes mental health issues for its employees. The program's purpose is to create an efficient and healthy workplace and health promoting working conditions.

This company's human resources and occupational medicine departments are responsible for workplace health promotion and prevention programs. The Total Wellness Programme was developed in collaboration with the Finnish Institute of Occupational Health.

To plan its health promotion activities, the company uses its own statistics on working days lost due to illness, industrial accidents and occupational diseases, as well as data on staff satisfaction and the health of employees. The occupational medicine department organizes medical examinations and assessments of the need for rehabilitation.

As part of the fitness survey, employees are assessed on a scale of one to five on health-related issues such as work, physical condition and ability to cope with stress, family life, social contacts and hobbies. Receiving the lowest score in any of these sections prompts quick intervention to determine how the situation can be improved.

Participation in the program is evaluated on a regular basis. Work stressors, health and career development are part of the agenda of annual development discussions between employees and their superiors. The company places great emphasis on continuing professional education. It has established its own global learning centre network.

- Provide further training and learning opportunities (for example, improving occupational skills and team work or promoting independent studying).
- Promote health (for example, promoting physical activities, healthy lifestyle, offering rehabilitation and preventing substance abuse).

The Finnish Institute of Occupational Health recommends the following means to promote mental health in work organizations:10

- To implement models of good workplace practices and disseminate this information in the community.
- To increase the cooperation of mental health and occupational health professionals in promoting mental health activities at the workplace.
- To train occupational health care professionals in mental health issues and mental health professionals in work-life issues.
- To increase the general knowledge of the whole population regarding preconditions for and value of good mental health in working life, and develop self-help skills for creating satisfactory working conditions.

Action needed by Employer

An employer can take the following specific steps to help an employee return to work after treatment for a mental health problem such as depression.

1. Inform the attending physician or appropriate mental health professional of exact duties of job before the physician makes a final decision on return to work.
2. In consultation with the individual's physician or other mental health professional, encourage an early to return to work. The longer an employee is out of work due to treatment, the more he/she will worry about losing the job. Furthermore, the longer a person is away from the job, the more mentally detached he/she will become.
3. Consider gradual return to work. Allowing part-time work for several weeks may help reduce stress, leave time for additional medical counselling and allow the worker to quickly get back into a normal routine. Flexitime, temporarily changed duties that involve less job-related stress or other flexible arrangements may be useful.

   However, there should be a clear understanding between the employee and the employer as to the details of the return-to-work programme: the expected length of time for which special accommodations will be granted, what day-to-day flexibility is allowed, the exact duties of the employee and who will supervise the work.

4. Other possible stress-reducing accommodations include:
   - Altering the pace of work
   - Lowering the noise level of work
   - Providing water, tea or soda and crushed ice to combat a dry mouth caused by some medications
   - Extra encouragement and praise of job performance, but only if warranted and not obviously excessive
   - While taking steps to reduce stress, avoidance of over-protection of the employee
   - Making sure the employee is treated as a member of the team and not excluded from social events, business meetings or other activities relevant to the job.

Employee Assistance Programs

Employee Assistance Programs (EAPs) are company-sponsored programs designed to alleviate and assist in eliminating workplace problems caused by personal problems. These programs typically provide supportive, diagnostic, referral and counselling treatment services.

Many EAPs began as occupational alcoholism programmes and gradually evolved into broader-based efforts as employers recognized that alcoholism was not the only problem that could negatively affect job performance.

Although some EAPs continue to focus only on identifying and assisting workers who are substance abusers, most now offer a wide range of other services to help employees resolve personal and work-related problems.

These services may include:

- On-site and telephone counselling
- Referral for psychological symptoms or mental health disorders (such as, depression, stress, anxiety)
- Marital or family-related issues
- Legal and financial problems
- Catastrophic medical problems (such as AIDS, cancer)
- Pre-retirement planning needs
- Career-related difficulties.

Many EAPs have been affected by changes in national and state-level legislation. As an employer develops programs to respond to national policies as well as legislation, EAP professionals have had to become knowledgeable about the statutes and how they affect their company's employees and policies.

Use of Group Process to Facilitate Work Reintegration of Employees with Mental Health Problems in Canada

A Good Practice Initiative #3

A 12-week program was created to bring about a "synergetic partnership" and a dynamic alliance between employee, employer, health professionals, unions and insurance companies. The program, offered to no more than 12 individuals at any one time, combines group intervention and an individual action plan.

It is action-oriented and centred on the regaining of power for the person. First, the programme aims at:

- Identifying and resolving collective and individual problems
- Reviewing vocational skills and interpersonal relationships
- Consolidating job skills.

Secondly, the employee is accompanied in the negotiation of his/her progressive return to work. A joint supervisory process (involving the employee, the vocational consultant and the employer) takes place on the job scene. This serves to give confidence to the employee while at the same "sensitizing" other workers.

Thirdly, in order to avoid relapses and to consolidate job stability, the individual is followed up for 6 months and as needed thereafter.

Results: After 2 years, 85% of the employees who took the program have returned to their jobs and are still in them.

Cost: The program costs 2600 Canadian Dollars (US$ 1700) for 12 weeks.

Source: Charbonneau, C.: Accès Cible S.M.T. Dix ans à faire renaître la confiance. November 1998.

Suggestions for Small Businesses

Often the smaller employer (with fewer than 25 employees) cannot afford to have a specific EAP or medical and rehabilitation experts on the staff. However, the model that is often used by many large employers can be adapted to a small setting in the following manner as well:

- The personnel or human resource director or other appropriate officer of the company should visit the employee who is on a medical/ disability leave as soon as possible to demonstrate concern and to encourage an early return to work.
- Always try to return the worker to his or her old job, even if an accommodation or flexible work time is required. This minimizes complications to the employee, reduces stress which may trigger a reoccurrence of depressive symptoms, and maximizes the company's advantage of having a trained employee.
- Use community resources. Local rehabilitation agencies and support groups may aid in a successful return to work with minimal or no expense to the business.
- Make a special effort to inform the employee's physician or mental health professional regarding the requirements of the job and possible changes and accommodations.

Employee Assistance Program, USA

A Good Practice Initiative #4

The psychiatric disability case of a large diversified health care company with more than 54,000 employees illustrates the benefits of an effective workplace program to manage mental health problems.

An office assistant in her early thirties was a divorced single mother with two children. Her manager, having observed her recent problems with concentration and productivity, referred her to the company's EAP. Due to the severity of the employee's condition, the EAP recommended that she be placed on medical leave.

The employee, who had a history of childhood abuse and symptoms of depression, had been under the care of a psychiatrist and therapist. These providers were not responsive to the EAP's request for additional evaluation and more intensive out-patient treatment.

Therefore, with the employee's agreement, she was referred to in-network providers, a psychiatrist and psychologist team, who quickly determined that she needed more and timely intensive care. Her medications were modified and she began partial hospitalization treatment.

The EAP case manager also arranged for the employee to receive financial assistance through a company program, which helped to reduce her level of stress. After seven weeks, the woman had stabilized and was returned to work. However, shortly thereafter she had a relationship break-up and quickly slipped back into crisis mode, including suicide ideation.

The employee was again placed on medical leave and her providers admitted her to an inpatient program. After a few days in the hospital, the employee stabilized again, returned to partial hospitalization and began attending a depression support group. Within six weeks, the employee returned to work for a second time.

This time, she was eased back into the work routine, beginning on a part-time basis and slowly increasing her work hours. Within a month, she returned to full-time work. The EAP case manager maintained contact with her after the return to work, and also worked with the employee's manager to ensure a successful transition back to work.

The employee has since demonstrated positive progress with a good prognosis. Over a 10-month period, the EAP had made a total of 163 contacts with the employee, providers and company personnel. This investment in support has enabled an employee who had been a probable candidate for long-term disability to remain productive.[11]

Reintegration Mechanism

According to the World Health Organization (WHO), more than 500 million people around the world are afflicted with serious mental illness, alcoholism and/or drug addiction. Expressed differently, 1.5–2% of the population of each country has to face this issue.

According to the International Labour Organization (ILO), mental illness hits more human lives and gives rise to a greater waste of human resources than all other forms of disability. The unemployment rate of this group is around 90% in contrast to that of persons with physical or sensorial disabilities, which is approximately 50%.

Again, expressed differently, only 10% of persons with a serious psychiatric background who wish to work and are judged capable of working are in fact working. Women fare less well than men. It has long been known that severe mental illness often impairs dramatically one's capacity to work and to earn a living.

It can lead to impoverishment, which in turn may worsen the illness. Thus, all efforts to find employment for these persons are essential since they improve quality of life and reduce both impoverishment and the high service and welfare costs engendered by this group.

Developing Work Skills

While our focus is on access to paid employment, we know that a majority of persons with severe mental health problems have been exposed to programs that focus more on developing work skills than on actual paid work.

These programs are summarized briefly as:

- *Hospital-based programs of training and work integration:* These are less used now than in the past. Their aim is to increase self-confidence and general functioning and the type of activities that one finds in such programmes include food distribution, gardening, running a small store, etc. While participants tend to have reduced numbers of days of hospitalization, it appears that few obtain successful permanent employment.
- *Sheltered Workshops:*This is another traditional approach where sub-contract work is used. It is felt that this type of work does not prepare very well for remunerative employment and that the person tends to remain in a patient role. However, 10-15% of participants have been found capable of moving to more intensive programs.
- *Training in Community Living:*These programs have been developed through the pioneering efforts of Stein, Test & Marx.[12] They attend to basic needs and feature strong individual management as well as a global approach. While participation in such programmes reduces hospitalization and increases independent living, it has not been found to have a great impact on keeping a permanent job.
- *Programs of Assertive Community Treatment (PACT):* These programs were also developed by Stein, Test & Marx in response to the growing need for community-based services for persons with severe mental illness. The focus has been on recovery from illness and enhanced quality of life. This training has been implemented in Canada and in several areas of the United States.

PACT is an inter-disciplinary team approach including a psychiatrist, registered nurses, peer specialists, vocational specialists, an addiction specialist and a program administrator. Crisis care is available 24 hours a day. This integrated, community-based model provides "the treatment, rehabilitation and support services that persons with severe mental illness need to live successfully in the community".[13]

In part, the clinical principles of treatment include:

1. An assertive approach to keeping individuals involved
2. Continuous monitoring to maintain current knowledge of their functioning and to facilitate intervention when necessary, and
3. Individually tailored treatment and rehabilitation programmes.

Current Context—Changes in the Nature of Work

Obtaining competitively paid employment for a person with a background of serious mental illness remains a challenge at the best of times. It is even more difficult in periods of high unemployment when the availability of non-disabled workers is plentiful.

Globalization, technological development, post-pandemic and changes in the organization of work are having an impact worldwide. In the country's manufacturing sector, employment of unskilled labourers has fallen by 20% and there is a definitive trend towards the hiring of highly-skilled workers.

Important changes have taken place in the very nature and organization of work—the free market economy which predominates, is often accompanied by downsizing of human resources and increased loss of job security.

Moreover, various state governments, in order to balance their budgets, have felt the need to reduce their social costs from which persons with serious mental illness traditionally get support. The conditions of eligibility have been made stricter and the duration of the support program often shorter.

With respect to the near future, there seem to be two schools of thought—one pessimistic and the other more optimistic.

The pessimist's viewpoint, as represented by sociologist Jeremy Rifkin, states that we are nearing the "end of work". The recent technological advances have resulted in a sharp reduction of new jobs in the industrial sector and he predicts that, with the assistance of computer technology, the reduction will be even greater in the services sector.

The optimists, as represented by Charles Goldfinger, are of the opinion that "each time a new technology is developed, it brings not a decrease, but an increase in job opportunities, albeit, not necessarily of the same kind as before". The new economy contains huge pools of new jobs that can more than make up for the inevitable loss of traditional jobs."[14]

Supporters of both viewpoints seem to agree that the organization of work is becoming more intangible and that regular 8 to 5 jobs may be less common, to be replaced by 'flexible schedule, increased part-time work, short-time contracts, often done in the employee's own home.'

There seems to be agreement that the newer jobs will be in the following sectors:

- Handling Information and Knowledge
- Information Technology
- Health Sector
- Leisure Economy

Whenever they have been successful in finding a paid job in the past, persons with a background of serious mental illness tended to work either in the traditional industrial sector or in service areas that did not require high technological capacity.

While it is too early to predict what will happen in the post-pandemic era, it is obvious that work programs for these persons will have to take into account the changes in nature of work. This will include the need for a better education and the development of professional skills in keeping with the requirements of new jobs.

Barriers

The six principal barriers to the employment of individuals with severe mental illness are as follows:

1. Lack of choice in employment services and providers.
2. Inadequate work opportunities.
3. Complexity of the existing work incentive systems.
4. Financial penalties of working.
5. Stigma and discrimination, and
6. Loss of health benefits.

Overcoming Obstacles Affecting People's Ability to Access Work

Individuals with mental illness want to work but are often discouraged by many barriers in the current public system. A recent survey in the country showed that 72% of unemployed people with disabilities, including people with severe mental illness have a strong desire to work.

Several recent surveys have found this rate to be as high as 80% for adults with mental illnesses.[15] Employment is an essential part of recovery for people with mental illnesses and recent advances in treatment services and medications have increased the capacity of people with mental illnesses to join the mainstream and live independently.

A) *Overcoming Obstacles Linked to the Illness*

A substantial majority of persons with serious mental illness take medication. When appropriately prescribed and monitored, these medications, especially the newer molecules, not only control the positive symptoms of illness (agitation, restlessness etc.), but also have a significant impact on negative symptoms such as apathy, passivity and social withdrawal as well as interpersonal relationships.

All in all, 60-80% of persons with serious mental illness can be substantially helped with a well monitored medication regime and an appropriate psychosocial management and support programme.

It remains essential for persons with serious mental illness to have access to (and be able to afford) both appropriate medication and a psychosocial programme that will focus on the person's living conditions, his/her ability to relate to others, and his/her willingness and capacity to work. In all instances the person's choices must be sought and taken into account.

There is still a debate as to how much an employer should (or wants to) know concerning an employee's psychiatric background. In all modern legislation, disability cannot be sufficient grounds to refuse employment if otherwise the person can do the job.

The assurance that there will be a quick and easy access to appropriate medical and psychological help has been found to influence very positively the willingness of employers to offer jobs to persons with mental health problems.

In the past, and still today, many persons with psychiatric backgrounds have had to lie to a potential employer about their illness. Some of the most successful programmes are those where a mutual trusting and respectful attitude has been developed so that issues that may arise are easier to address.

B) *Overcoming Obstacles Linked to Lack of Educational Training and Work Experience*

Mental illness can strike at any age of life. Some of the most severe forms begin in the late teens and early twenties and usually prevent the person from completing secondary education, college and/or university. This renders the person ill-equipped to face the requirements of a job, especially in today's world.

Other forms of illnesses start in the late twenties and early thirties while the person is already working. The work milieu is often intolerant of a colleague suffering from mental illness. The first episode may result in a demotion or a change of job, if not an outright firing. The impact on the person's self-esteem is usually very negative. The loss of one's remuneration brings with it economic hardship notwithstanding the various aid programs.

Research has shown a constant positive relationship between the skills of a client and his/her vocational outcome and that people with severe psychiatric disability can indeed learn new skills. With the ever-increasing importance of technology, we find that the "low-tech jobs" to which many persons with serious mental illness had access in the past are no longer available, at least in developed countries.

There is need to develop training programs that take into account the requirements of persons with mental health problems as well as the requirements of potential employers. It makes eminent sense to encourage someone whose academic career was interrupted by mental illness to go back to school, college or university, in order to complete a qualification and therefore have access to a much wider choice of jobs and opportunities.

Whereas government programs have traditionally supported direct employment, there now exists' a number of support programs that will allow one to return to school.

Supported Education in Boston—Choose/Get/Keep

A Good Practice Initiative #5

As part of its array of rehabilitation services, a University-based Centre for Psychiatric Rehabilitation has developed an extensive program of "supported education".

The centre applied a basic model[16] called "Choose/Get/Keep" which was initially developed for persons seeking a return to employment. Supported education has been defined as the provision of post-secondary education in integrated educational settings for people with psychiatric disabilities whose education has been interrupted.

The program utilizes supported learning specialists with a Masters degree in Psychiatric Rehabilitation (Practitioners) who assist and accompany the person with a former psychiatric disability throughout the three phases of the program.

The guiding principle is to focus on participant process rather than on practitioner activity.

- In the 'choosing' phase, a participant is helped in describing why he/she wishes to go back to school and in making an enlightened choice as to the type of environment which suits his/her needs, as well as in making a choice as to which school might meet expectations.

The eliciting of educational goals, the assessment of personal criteria, and the realistic objective evaluation of the student's abilities are paramount in facilitating the decision-making process. Part of this phase also involves the identification and securing of other sources of support for the student, including family and friends.

- In the 'getting' phase, a decision is made by the practitioner and the student concerning the assignment of responsibility for getting enrolled in the academic facility chosen, including obtaining the financial support needed.

A decision has to be made concerning the amount of information which the student may wish (or may not wish) to disclose concerning the psychiatric disability.

- In the 'keeping' phase, efforts are made to continue to support students in enrolment and in academic success. The practitioner needs to provide the teaching of special skills which the student might need to pursue the program. Coordination also applies to those facets of academic life with which the students might encounter some difficulties.

Experience has shown that the need for greater support arises during stressful periods such as examinations. All in all, the relationship established between the practitioner and the participant (student) is a crucial factor. It has to be egalitarian, continuous and very flexible.

As with other successful rehabilitation programs, the outcome has an impact on the person's illness. There tend to be fewer re-hospitalizations and a need for lower doses of medication (occasionally the need for medication may disappear) for persons involved in the program.

C) *Overcoming Obstacles Linked to Prejudice and Stigma*

Stigma is basically an attitude that aims at marginalizing and ostracizing someone because that person has a mental health problem. While the stigma can be quite overt, it tends nowadays to be more subtle. For instance, a person may find it very difficult to obtain appropriate lodging or to join a social club. It may include fears of violent behaviour on the part of the person with the mental health problems.

While violence attributable to mental illness exists, it is very low when compared to other forms of violence. The risk of violence is much greater when severe mental illness is associated with alcoholism & drug abuse and when there is a past history of violent behaviour.

In its most advanced forms, stigma leads to exclusion of the person from several spheres of social functioning. Stigma may have disastrous consequences when a person with a mental health problem starts believing that he/she deserves to be treated in such a way. Stigma can also manifest itself in the 'denial' of the person's competence, ability and potential.

The best way to fight stigma is through appropriate education and information. This may include a public information campaign, courses, conferences, etc. It is important to delineate very precisely what component of 'general stigma' one wants to address and to develop a specific plan of action for it. The mass media often portray persons with mental illness in a most unfavourable light.

Since the media play a crucial role in filtering information that reaches the public, it is obvious that all efforts should be made by mental health professionals to work closely with them and to correct the misconceptions which they may harbour.

Recently, advocates in the mental health/illness field have made progress with the mass media, stirring up interest and controversy at both the international and national levels.

In general, there has been more widespread discussion in the press and on television regarding the situation of this traditionally overlooked disability group and more in-depth presentations about some of the political and professional issues in this field.

Today, advocates are more successful at working with the press and on the Internet to bring mental health/illness issues both into the mainstream of the disability rights movement and to the attention of the public.

At the international level, advocates are combining three themes to attract media coverage:

1. Redefining the bottom line as a universal human rights issue.
2. Subjecting residential institutions to worldwide exposure, and
3. Building support for community based services.

Ultimately, this type of advocacy can ameliorate negative myths and stereotypes and, in turn, can impact and influence work opportunities for individuals with mental health problems. Another important way to fight stigma is to inform the community of 'good practices' and of programs that work.

Myths about Mental Illness and the Workplace

The following are major myths and facts regarding the impact of mental illness on the workplace:[17]

- *Myth 1:* Mental illness is the same as mental retardation.

  Facts: These are two distinct disorders. A diagnosis of mental retardation is chiefly characterized by limitation in intellectual functioning as well as difficulties with certain daily living skills. In contrast, among persons with psychiatric disabilities, intellectual functioning varies as it does across the general population.

- *Myth 2:* Recovery from mental illness is not possible.

  Facts: Long-term studies have shown that the majority of people with mental illnesses show genuine improvement over time and lead stable, productive lives. For many decades mental illness was thought to be permanent and untreatable.

  People with mental illness were separated from the rest of society through institutionalization in mental hospitals. As medications were discovered which helped to alleviate the symptoms of mental illness, there was a gradual evolution towards the provision of treatment and rehabilitation services in the community.

- *Myth 3:* Mentally ill and mentally restored employees (the term denotes when the disorder is effectively treated) tend to be second-rate workers.

  Facts: Employers who have hired these individuals report that they are higher than average in attendance and punctuality and are as good if not better than other employees in motivation, quality of work and job tenure. Studies reported by the National Institute of Mental health and Neuro Sciences (NIMHANS) states that there are no differences in productivity when compared to other employees.

- *Myth 4:* People with psychiatric disabilities cannot tolerate stress on the job.

  Facts: This oversimplifies the complex human response to stress. People with a variety of medical conditions, such as cardiovascular disease, multiple sclerosis and psychiatric disorders, may find their symptoms exacerbated by high levels of stress. However, the source of personal and job-related stress varies substantially between individuals.

Some people find an unstructured schedule to be very stressful while others struggle with a regimented workflow. Some people thrive on public visibility or high levels of social contact, while others require minimal interaction in order to focus and complete tasks.

Workers with psychiatric disabilities vary in their response to stressors on the job. In essence, all jobs are stressful to some extent. Productivity is maximized when there is a good match between the employee's needs and working conditions, whether or not the individual has a psychiatric disability.

- *Myth 5:* Mentally ill and mentally restored individuals are unpredictable, violent and dangerous.

  Facts: The vast majority of these individuals are not dangerous or violent. Upon learning that an applicant has a mental illness, some employers may expect that the individual is likely to become violent.

  This myth is reinforced by portrayals in the media of people with mental illnesses as frequently and randomly violent. Although, stigma and shame are still the dominant attitudes towards mental health and mental illness, there has been a dramatic shift in perception during the last 10 years.

  Advancement and improvements in the legal system have had a positive impact on attitudes and knowledge relating to all disabilities and to mental illness in particular. This has, in turn, created a greater openness towards all mental health issues.

  Additional contributing factors include public and professional awareness that prolonged hospital stays can be disabling, advances in pharmacology, and a shift in focus from pathology to strengths and abilities.

(D) *Overcoming Obstacles Linked to Government Policy:* While there exists a number of programs to help disabled unemployed persons (unemployment insurance, income support, job training, job search clubs, subsidies to employers etc.), each program has its set of fairly complicated rules and it becomes apparent that the philosophy underlying such programs was not conceived for persons with mental health problems in mind.

The programs are either too short in duration or have requirement of rigid working hours or high output which persons with serious mental illness cannot be expected to fulfil, at least initially.

A cursory look at existing programs reveals that, notwithstanding the fact that persons with mental illness may represent a majority of those with a disability, only a very small number of structured programs exist and are adapted to the needs of this group, as compared to programs for physical or sensorial disabilities.

In some countries, a paradoxical situation exists. The disability benefits paid to someone officially classified as a 'person with a disability' and without any obligation to work may be very close to the minimum wage which the same person would earn if working. To compound the problem, the person may also lose an entitlement to free medication, to transportation subsidies, or other social benefits by accepting the status of employee.

This often constitutes a powerful disincentive for a person with a disability to join the labour force. The impact of welfare reform on the employment of people with psychiatric disabilities is an issue worth noting.

Many of the problems associated with welfare reforms as it concerns people with mental illness are not unique to India, particularly as many developed European countries are trying to decrease their social welfare costs.

By focusing on the importance of work and training, the current national trend in welfare reforms has the potential to expand employment opportunities for people with psychiatric disabilities. However, many mental health experts express concern about this impact. The reasons cited for concern are:

- Increased competition for employment from welfare recipients entering the job market could crowd out people with psychiatric disabilities.
- Employment and training programmes designed for general welfare population are unlikely to address the special needs of people with psychiatric disabilities.
- Disincentives to work inherent in many government benefit programs can make it difficult for persons with psychiatric disabilities to enter and remain in the workforce.

Despite these concerns, many mental health advocates hope that welfare reform will encourage state and local mental health agencies to adopt more innovative and effective strategies to help people with psychiatric disabilities to enter or re-enter the workforce.

It is hoped that welfare reform will create an environment that encourages state and local agencies to work together in new ways to address the issue of employment and training.

In addition, welfare reforms offer an opportunity for the mental health system to contribute its considerable expertise and experience to promoting and supporting employment in the effort to assist welfare recipients to enter the world of work.

(E) *Overcoming Obstacles Linked to the Labour Market*

Previous successful work history has traditionally been mentioned as a key factor in predicting successful return to employment. This obviously puts persons with a background of serious mental illness at a disadvantage.

With a few exceptions (notably the United States of America), unemployment rates in many countries are around 10%. Changes in the labour structure mean that there are fewer low-tech jobs available. Training may be needed to acquire the competence which newer jobs may demand.

Perspective of International Agencies

1. *United Nations Organization (UNO)*

The United Nations, which proclaimed the International Year of Disabled Persons in 1991, adopted the World Programme of Action concerning Disabled Persons in 1992. This emphasized the right of persons with disabilities to 'the same opportunities as other citizens and to an equal share in the improvements in living conditions resulting from economic and social development'.

On the same occasion, it defined 'handicap' as a function of the relationship between persons with disabilities and their environment. In 1994, the United Nations published the "Standard Rules on the Equalization of Opportunities for Persons with Disabilities".[18]

The term 'equalization of opportunities' means the process through which the various systems of society and the environment such as services, activities, information and documentation are made available to all, particularly persons with disabilities.

Persons with disabilities are members of society which have the right to remain within their local communities. They should receive the support they need within the ordinary structures of education, health, employment and social services.

Article 7 deals specifically with employment. It mentions that "States should recognize the principle that persons with disabilities must be empowered to exercise their human rights particularly in the field of employment. In both rural and urban areas they must have equal opportunities for productive and gainful employment in the labour market."

Sub-article 2 mentions that "States should actively support the integration of persons with disabilities into open employment. This active support could occur through a variety of measures, such as vocational training, incentive-oriented quota schemes, reserve or designated employment, loans or grants for small business, exclusive contracts or priority production rights, tax concessions, contract compliance or other technical financial assistance to enterprises employing workers with disabilities. States should also encourage employers to make reasonable adjustments to accommodate persons with disabilities."

Article 7 also proposes that public awareness-raising campaigns and further mentions that the goal should always be for persons with disabilities to obtain employment in the open labour market. However, for those whose needs cannot be met in open employment, "small units of sheltered or supported employment may be an alternative."

The World Health Organization's Mental Health Policy and Service Development Team's objectives and strategies are as follows.

- To strengthen mental health policies, legislation and plans.
  - (a) Increasing awareness of the burden associated with mental health problems and the commitment of governments to reduce this burden.
  - (b) Helping to build up the technical capacity of countries to create, review and develop mental health policies, legislation and plans
  - (c) Developing and disseminating advocacy and policy resources.
- To improve the planning and development of services for mental health.
  - (a) Strengthening the technical capacity of countries to plan and develop services.
  - (b) Supporting demonstration projects for mental health best practices.
  - (c) Encouraging operational research related to service delivery, and
  - (d) Developing and disseminating resources related to service development and delivery.

2. *World Bank and the Harvard Report*

With few exceptions, severe mental illness does not represent an immediate threat to life. Therefore, mortality rates are of little use to measure the true impact of mental illness on an individual, family or society as a whole.

To address this issue, the World Bank has introduced[19] the concept of Disability-Adjusted Life Years (DALYs): this is a measure that combines healthy life years lost because of both premature mortality and losses resulting from disability.

The sum of DALYs is referred to as the Global Burden of Disease (GBD). The seminal 1995 Harvard Report on World Mental Health: Problems and Priorities in Low-Income Countries points out that whereas there have been, over the last 50 years, marked improvements in the physical health there (owing among other things to better control of fertility rates, improved pre-natal care and prevention and treatment of several infectious diseases, resulting in reduced mortality rates), on the other hand the mental health of these populations has either remained stagnant or has decreased.

According to The World Health Report 1999, neuropsychiatric disorders account for 11.5% of the burden of disease worldwide—as measured by DALYs—which is more than the proportion of the burden imposed by respiratory infections and diseases (10.7%), cardiovascular diseases (10.3%) or malignant neo-plasma (5.8%).

It has been reported[20] that for the USA, the United Kingdom and Australia, 43% of DALYs are traceable to mental disorders and that the latter account for 22% of the GBD. The much higher percentages in developed countries reflect the fact that pre-natal death and disability from infectious disease are much lower than in developing countries.

3. *International Labour Organization (ILO)*

ILO generally agrees with WHO estimates that more than 500 million people, or 7–10% of the world's population, are disabled. ILO also feels that this number is increasing owing to greater longevity and the physical and psychological ravages of wars.

Today, ILO has a new organizational structure in which the disability program is part of the Employment Sector which reflects the principle of mainstreaming. The Employment Sector is responsible for developing and promoting employment strategies, job creation programs & human resources development policies and for initiating actions to respond rapidly to economic crisis in conflict countries and to the needs of those devastated by natural disasters.

Within the Employment Sector, the disability programme has been integrated into a broader unit (Target Groups Unit of the InFocus Programme on Skills, Knowledge and Employability).

The aim behind the establishment of this new unit is to enhance synergy between the ILO's different programs targeting disadvantaged groups such as youth, older workers, displaced workers and people with disabilities which include mental health disorders.

ILO recommendations on vocational rehabilitation and employment opportunities stress the following:

- Disabled persons should enjoy equality of opportunity and treatment in respect of access to, retention of and advancement in employment which, whenever possible, corresponds to their own choice and takes account of their individual suitability for such employment.
- Measures for disabled persons should conform to employment and salary standards applicable to workers generally.
- Measures which are recommended include:
  - (a) Measures to create job opportunities on the open labour market
  - (b) Appropriate government support for the establishment of various types of sheltered employment for disabled persons for whom access to open employment is not practicable
  - (c) Appropriate government support for vocational training and vocational guidance, placement services
  - (d) Encouragement of the establishment and development of cooperatives by and for disabled persons
  - (e) Elimination by stages if necessary of physical, communication and architectural barriers and obstacles
  - (f) Non-discrimination and information on successful instances of integration
  - (g) Research on various types of disability.

Measures should be taken to ensure, as far as practicable, that policies and programs concerning vocational rehabilitation are coordinated with policies and programs of social and economic development (including scientific research and advanced technology) affecting labour administration, general employment policy and promotion, vocational training, social integration, social security, cooperatives, rural development, small-scale industry and crafts, safety and health at work, adaptation of methods and organization of work to the needs of the individual and the improvement of working conditions.

4. *World Health Organization (WHO)*

The WHO was founded in 1948 as the main international organization to oversee the issue of world health. Its constitution[21] gives the organization and member countries the objective of the attainment by all people of the highest possible level of health. It further states that the enjoyment of the highest standard of health is one of the fundamental rights of every human being.

In 1977, the World Health Assembly expressed this as "Health for all by the year 2000".[22] The 9th General Program of Work of WHO establishes the global health policy framework for action by the world health community (international organizations of the United Nations system, including WHO, non-governmental organizations, bilateral and multilateral donor and development agencies, banks and countries themselves).

In 1981, the World Health Organization adopted primary health care as the way to achieve the goal of health for all. As a strategy, primary health care seeks reorientation of health systems to enable the whole population to have effective and essential care and to promote individual and community involvement in health, as well as inter-sectoral collaboration.

Appropriate treatment of common diseases and injuries and mental health care are integral components of primary health care. Much of the attention of the World Health Organization's Department of Mental Health and Substance Abuse is focused on the most effective ways to ensure the highest quality of life for persons with serious mental health problems. Several projects deal specifically with rehabilitation issues, including access to employment.

Throughout the 9th General Programme of Work there is a constant reference to the necessity to improve the quality of life of people and to integrate health and human development in public policies. The World Health Report 1998 has the theme "Life in the 21st Century: A Vision for All".

The report states that there is increasing life expectancy due mainly to a reduction in premature death and a steady reduction in major infectious diseases. The report identifies as major problems the HIV epidemic and the enormous rise in violent death and injuries from violence.

On the issue of work, the report states that "more working days are lost as a result of mental disorders than physical conditions". It also recognizes that, whereas mental disorders contribute little to mortality, they make a huge contribution to the Global Burden of Disease.

5. *Non-governmental Organizations*

There are perhaps thousands of consumer and professional groups for individuals with mental health disabilities and their families in many countries of the world. These groups have had a vital role in raising the awareness of mental health issues, reducing stigma and discrimination, and advocating for appropriate legislation.

Jobs and other meaningful activities are important for a person to be included in the social and economic mainstream. Recently, there has been impetus by some NGOs to frame the discussion and advocacy of mental health issues within a "human rights" perspective.

Often NGOs work closely with government agencies, business groups, corporate sponsors and community-based mental health services. They are an important source of expertise and provide opportunities to reach people with mental health problems. They serve as a policy monitor and a catalyst for change.

6. *Overseeing Training and Employment of Persons with Disabilities*

In a recent worldwide survey undertaken by ILO,[23] it was found that the "organization" of vocational rehabilitation is very diverse and occasionally quite diffused in many countries. There is often an obvious lack of communication between the different agencies responsible for policies and programming.

Over the last two decades, the "users" (or "survivors") movement in mental health has grown very significantly and has become an increasingly powerful lobby group, especially in more economically advanced countries.

It is making good use of the ever-increasing knowledge that we have of the biological and genetic components of most major mental illnesses to challenge the stigma that is still too often associated with these illnesses.

Vocational Rehabilitation for Individuals with Psychiatric Disability

A Good Practice Initiative #6

The Australian National Employment and Psychological Services (NEPS) centre was founded in 1992. It operates in both Victoria and Queensland. NEPS has employment services, a work crew and two commercial businesses. Most of their clients (85%) have a psychiatric disability.

The centre also has a secondary focus on people from non-English speaking background. The following example illustrates "good practices" that have been effective in assisting people with mental illness obtain and maintain employment. The main features are that this programme is consumer-driven and fully integrated into the community.

According to centre assistant director Leonie Exel, "Our staff and clients have been through many an exponential learning curve in the last few years, particularly as we are among the first wave of specialist providers in Australia. Nowadays, we can define some of the service features which are likely to assist our clients to find and maintain relevant jobs."

"Our knowledge has come from a combination of research, hard work and sometimes painful trial and error. Our experience has taught us that many or most successful factors in our agency can be attributed to plain and simple, garden variety common sense," he adds further.

The primary factors which ensure that NEPS clients obtain and maintain relevant employment are:

- High levels of client (consumer) participation
- Client-driven processes, goal-setting and methodology
- An empowerment focus
- Flexibility in service delivery schedules and service re-entry processes
- Strong policies of non-disclosure and confidentiality
- Staff personalization of service delivery.

Implementing these factors involves the following strategies:

(a) Clients (consumers) are highly involved in the design, management and implementation of vocational services.

(b) Clients do what they choose to do ("we don't do things" for people and "we don't chose their goals).

(c) Clients choose the manner in which they are assisted (in group work, one-to-one, or via peer consultancy services).

(d) Clients fail, succeed, try again, and test the jobs, vocations, careers and periods of unemployment until they decide what they would like to do.

Clients can keep their personal lives private from other people if they want to. Service delivery phases are as follows:

- Substantial time is spent working with the client on pre-vocational factors such as medication and illness management in the workplace.
- Substantial time is spent on vocational counselling and developing community, social and service provider networks for vocational support.
- Substantial time is spent talking with other service providers trying largely to increase their optimism about the client's chance of finding and keeping work in the hope that they will be supportive throughout what can be a difficult process for the job-seeker.
- An emphasis is placed on the staff's own mental health in the workplace with a very strong sense of community and mutual support and emphasis on training and further education for staff.

Source: Exel L. Vocational Rehabilitation of People who have a Psychiatric Disability: The Australian Experience. Proceedings of Asia and Pacific Regional Conference Campaign'98 for Asia and Pacific Decade of Disabled Persons 1993–2000, Hong Kong, 23–28 August 1998.

Indian Context

Chronic mental illness is ubiquitous. With understaffed mental health services, a paucity of structured programs & case managers and very high rates of unemployment, it becomes much more difficult to find a paid job for someone with serious mental illness in the country.

Effective action to promote the availability of employment for people with mental health problems has been hindered by the difficult conditions in the labour market. The transformation of the economic system has included a massive effort to create new jobs for society and has required individuals to acquire new vocational skills.

There have been insufficient resources available to assist individuals with psychiatric disabilities in vocational rehabilitation efforts so they may compete and succeed in the job market.

In rural areas, for economic and pragmatic reasons, there are strong pressures to involve the mentally ill individual in the "field". If community leaders have been sensitized and the individual receives adequate medication and support, this may lead to quite productive employment.

In rural Northeast India, there are a few examples of women being involved in cultivating rice after discharge from the psychiatric hospital. This was not systematically used, but was always more successful when the local people committee representatives were involved in the process.[24]

There are some examples of 'psychiatric villages' where many former patients live with members of their families. In these enclaves, which are quite well accepted by the community at large, former patients can be reintegrated to a useful role and involved in the production of goods which are then purchased by the community at large.

In the rural and tribal belt of Odisha, former patients have been making and selling candles for a reasonable profit from which they derive much of their subsistence. In large, fast-moving urban areas, with crowded living space and no alternative accommodations available, the situation is often quite difficult. However, success stories, nevertheless, exist.

Drawing inspiration from Finland and other such highly effective international models, the workplace mental health well-being best practices that has been developed and is now being practised within the country is as follows:

1. Raise awareness about the importance of mental health and well-being.
2. Manage psycho-social risks related to work, environment and culture.
    - Employee Involvement
    - Employee Recognition
    - Employee Growth and Development
    - Work Life Integration
    - Healthy Work Environment
    - Health and Psychological Safety.
3. Assess mental health, well-being needs and measure intervention impact.
4. Provide and promote access to evidence-based, high-quality mental healthcare.
    - Promote mental healthcare access options
    - Increase equitable and timely access to evidence-based mental health care.
5. Integrate mental health and well-being into a comprehensive wellness program inclusive of:
    - Emotional Wellness
    - Spiritual Wellness
    - Intellectual Wellness
    - Physical Wellness
    - Environmental Wellness
    - Financial Wellness

- Occupational Wellness
- Social Wellness.

6. Partner with local and national organizations to extend and share mental health and well-being practices.

Working with Employers to Set Up Effective Programs

The corporate sector needs to be at the forefront of India's efforts to help employers build effective, science-based workplace health programs for their employees. They should develop such as workplace health model, which is a comprehensive approach that addresses multiple risk factors and health conditions at the same time.

Workplace health programs are coordinated strategies that include programs, policies, benefits and environmental supports to keep all employees healthy and safe. They can include health education classes, access to local fitness facilities, policies that promote healthy foods or tobacco-free workplaces and insurance coverage for preventive screenings.

The workplace is an optimal setting to create a culture of health because:

- Communication structures are already in place.
- Programs and policies come from one central team.
- Social support networks are available.
- Employers can offer incentives to reinforce healthy behaviours.
- Employers can use data to track progress and measure the effects.

Action steps employers can take include:

- Make mental health self-assessment tools available to all employees.
- Offer free or subsidized clinical screenings for depression from a qualified mental health professional, followed by directed feedback and clinical referral when appropriate.
- Offer health insurance with no or low out-of-pocket costs for depression medications and mental health counselling.
- Provide free or subsidized lifestyle coaching, counselling, or self-management programs.
- Distribute materials, such as brochures, fliers, and videos, to all employees about the signs and symptoms of poor mental health and opportunities for treatment.

- Host seminars or workshops that address depression and stress management techniques, like mindfulness, breathing exercises, and meditation, to help employees reduce anxiety and stress and improve focus and motivation.
- Create and maintain dedicated, quiet spaces for relaxation activities.
- Provide managers with training to help them recognize the signs and symptoms of stress and depression in team members and encourage them to seek help from qualified mental health professionals.
- Give employees opportunities to participate in decisions about issues that affect job stress.

Workplace stress remains an often-neglected aspect across different industries and countries, including India. Some key factors that cause increased stress at workplace are workload (both excessive and insufficient work), lack of participation and control in the workplace, monotonous or unpleasant tasks, role ambiguity or conflict, lack of recognition at work, inequity, poor interpersonal relationships, poor working conditions, poor leadership and communication and conflicting home and work demands.

While research has established the two-way link between stress and these physical disorders, organizations need to realize this and encourage staff to maintain a good work-life balance and have guidelines about working hours based on good industrial practices and take measures to enforce these routinely.

Sexual harassment and bullying at workplace is another workplace-related stress that can happen at any organization. Both genders could be affected by these, but often women and those lower in the hierarchy are at increased risk.

Brouwers conducted a cross-sectional study across 35 countries including India and reported that about two-third of employees who had suffered from depression either faced discrimination at work or faced discrimination while applying for new jobs. Both perceived and anticipated discrimination are major causes for people suffering silently at the workplace and not seeking proper care.

In India, there are specific legal provisions to ensure safety at workplace and there are specific laws to prevent sexual harassment of women. Strict guidelines and processes need to be advocated, and every organization should have identified committees to handle any issues of discrimination, harassment and bullying.

Corporate India's Mental Health Crisis

There have been many suicides by managers and employees in corporate India but it took the death of Cafe Coffee Day owner-promoter VG Siddhartha on 29 July, 2019 to focus national attention on the pressures and tribulations of business leaders.

The press and public speculated not only on the myriad tensions he experienced but on why he did not seek help from family, friends or mental health professionals to find a less tragic resolution to his problems.

While there is no doubt that people at the apex of the corporate pyramid face a unique set of anxieties, there is no reason to believe that employees in less exalted positions find their problems any less terrifying and for many of whom asking for help is as unthinkable as it was for the ill-fated Siddhartha.

"A 2016 study involving over 6,000 employees in multiple cities in India found that 80 percent of the respondents exhibited symptoms of anxiety while 55 percent had symptoms of depression. Another bigger worry was that between 2008 and 2016, the risk of suicidal behaviour in India has nearly quadrupled—from 2.1 out of 10 employees to 8.21.

"Mental health is the single most important health issue in the workplace. This is not only because mental health problems, including substance abuse, are a leading cause of lost productivity and sickness, but because workplace practices can worsen or enhance the mental health of workers," says Vikram Patel, Professor and research fellow, Department of Global Health and Social Medicine, Harvard Medical School."

The problem of mental illness in corporate India is rapidly growing to crisis proportions and the reasons it is likely to be immune to our existing cures. We shall then look at some newer tech solutions as well as suggest how a few, long-underutilized remedies can be deployed in new ways to address this growing menace.

Causes and Aggravators

Several of the mental health problems associated with work have been with us at least since the time mass production became the preferred technology for high-volume manufacturing and some even go back to the industrial revolution itself. Who can forget the twitching malaise and the nervous breakdown that afflicted the tramp (played by Charlie Chaplin) in Modern Times?

The sad fact is that a hundred years later, with all the advances in management theory and work psychology, we have come no closer to finding answers to the mental devastation caused by deadening work.

Not only have we continued to allot repetitive work to the majority of the operatives in the remaining non-automated shop floors in India, the other jobs we have created in high numbers (for example the delivery staff for e-tailers) are no less routine and even more stressful.

If we could have ever taken solace in the fact that soul-destroying work was the lot of those who neglected to educate themselves adequately, the last couple of decades have seen unedifying spectacles such as the mass underutilization of hundreds of thousands of people qualified as engineers, being subjected to the drudgery of routine coding by our software majors.

At forums where HR practitioners need to impress each other, we extensively expound the benefits of 'flow'. We would do well to remember that 'anti-flow' is an equal reality: one predominantly caused by repetitive work that uses substantially less than the full potential of a human being.

Going further back, industrialization itself brought much mental maladjustment some of which are evident even today. The crop of mental maladies harvested by the first waves of people moving from the relative self-regulation of agricultural work to the regimen demanded by factory jobs tended to become less acute in a generation or two.

On the other hand, psychological ailments brought on by the uncertainties surrounding progression, earnings and even tenure, were hardier plants and have occupied even larger parts of the work landscape in recent times. Impermanency of tenure, in particular, has received a hugely ruinous fillip with the growing contractualization of work.

Unlike physical ailments and disabilities, which employees rarely expend too much effort in concealing because they are generally received with sympathy and helpfulness from colleagues and supervisors, mental illnesses are hidden away for the justifiable fear of the reactions they elicit in the workplace.

Another causal factor aggravated considerably nowadays is what is frequently referred to as 'burnout', which is supposed to be an acceptable (and sometimes even desirable) term for describing mental health problems at middle and senior levels in organizations.

The 70-80 hour workweeks, impossible job demands and terrifying supervisors that are prime predictors of 'burnout' were very much present in the seventies when some of us started our careers.

What saved us and our predecessor executives were our spouses, who took on less demanding jobs than they were fully capable of doing and managed domestic affairs so well that we scarcely had had to deal with any significant demands from that front. Gender opportunities have rightly become more (if not yet fully) equal since those thoughtless days.

Not only does this put an additional demand on men to give priority to home and family matters (which people of my generation had blithely ignored), but is even more taxing for women seeking to make careers because (even if their spouses are more understanding) society still puts the prime onus for home management on them. It is not surprising 'burnout' rates have been creeping up steadily.

Women face one more source of mental stress and consequent trigger for mental illness. Particularly those who break any glass ceiling for the first time have to cope with closed clubs, snide comments and having to deliver twice as much as the dominant population in order to be accepted.

Some take solace from comparing the fire they draw to Nelson's Redoubtable as it revolutionized naval tactics by heading the column of British ships against the Franco-Spanish line at Trafalgar. Others are sobered by thoughts of being kissed by Hardy at the end of the proceedings.

Jokes apart, women are only the first exemplars of the discriminatory pressures every outgroup faces, particularly when its numbers are too small to find companionship and support from similar others. The tragedy of Payal Tadvi at Nair Hospital in early 2019 is a sad case in point of the mental stress that can be caused by dominant group exclusionary pressures.

The last major source of mental illness at the workplace, which earlier generations did not have to cope with, is brought on by technology and particularly the social media. "Numerous studies identify connections between social media use and negative outcomes such as increased depression, anxiety, compulsive behaviour, loneliness and narcissism."

There are many interpretations of the causal linkage between social media use and the form of mental illness it accentuates but no one (other than Zuckerberg, perhaps) doubts the beginning and end point.

Particularly in the younger generation, it is not only the aberrations directly caused by social media that can be damaging. It is equally worrisome that a large range of mentally, physically and socially rejuvenating activities is crowded out by the solipsistic, cloud-based confinement imposed by (over)smart devices.

A Problem with no Name

A single word captures the reason mental illness is among the least tractable problems for corporate to solve or even ameliorate. Stigma, unlike physical ailments and disabilities, which employees rarely expend too much effort in concealing because they are generally received with sympathy and helpfulness from colleagues and supervisors, mental illnesses are hidden away for the justifiable fear of the reactions they elicit in the workplace.

"Persons with mental illness often have to struggle with a double problem. First, they have to cope with the symptoms of the disease itself. Second, the misunderstandings of society about the various mental disorders result in stigma. As a further complication, some people with mental illness may accept the common prejudices about mental illness turn them against themselves and lose self-confidence. The latter is referred to as 'self-stigma'.

When persons suffering from anxiety, depression or even more serious mental health problems cannot admit even to them that they need help, it is extremely unlikely that they will turn to their friends, leave aside the counsellors and other organizational support options provided by progressive corporate.

Before blaming the afflicted with cowardice or worse for not facing up to their problems and seeking readily available help, let us look at the rational reasons that justify such concealment.

I personally know cases where supposedly closest friends started distancing themselves from the individuals who made the mistake of revealing their condition or whose symptoms could no longer be concealed. The reactions of those in arm's length working relationships, with no affect capital to dissipate in the first place, are far crueller.

Mentally ill people can, if anything, be even more sensitive to and less capable of coping with the malicious humour that roasts them behind their backs but ultimately trickles back to them through tattlers whose intentions may be bona or mala-fide but whose impact is invariably devastating.

Worse still are the unfeeling office comedians who think their innuendos and jibes in the presence of the persons concerned will not be picked up by the latter or who could not care if they are.

HR and Senior Managers

Of course, they pay lip service to progressive views, line up counselling services and sometimes even extend medical insurance cover for mental illness treatments. But ask them, if a choice has to be made between two people for a top role and one of them has been availing of the company's progressive mental health counselling program, which of the two will be picked for the prized position?

The only way to resolve this problem is to provide an avenue that guarantees absolute anonymity to the persons who need such assistance.

Tech to the Rescue

Ubiquity, round-the-clock presence and self-image seesaws imposed by tech (particularly social media) take a heavy toll on a person's mental health. Fortunately, recent tech breakthroughs also provide the means to break through the stigma that impedes us in tackling mental illness substantively and on a large scale.

With rapid improvements in Artificial Intelligence (AI), each passing day brings more sophisticated and convenient apps for both diagnosis and preliminary treatment of mental illnesses. A considerable body of research is already available in support of the efficacy and ease of dissemination of this delivery mode.

While lowering of costs and helping to cope with the shortage of mental health specialists are obvious advantages, from our point of view, assured anonymity is the biggest breakthrough bot-based diagnosis and basic therapy brings to employee wellness programs.

Here is one model for putting these technological advances to work. Each organization would need to provide access to a mental health platform for all employees, regardless of level and type of contract. Under conditions of total anonymity, the platform would provide the following five services:

1. A diagnostics module that would help an employee figure out whether she/he has a mental health issue, how serious it is and its tentative classification.

2. A preliminary guidance module which would provide AI-based suggestions of simple dos and don'ts as well suggest activities which can give relief to the specific types of disturbance the diagnostic module reveals. The next section suggests the kind of therapeutically useful activities organizations can consider providing.
3. An inter-phase bridge to an array of telephonic counselling services from which one or two would be recommended for the individual based on the diagnostic outcome. In terms of sequencing, this may precede or substitute the preliminary guidance module.
4. An inter-phase bridge to a panel of clinical psychologists and psychiatrists. While it would theoretically be possible to trigger this bridge immediately after the AI diagnostic, it would more usually be preceded by the telephonic counselling bridge.
5. A module for following up therapy sessions and providing on-line exercises for ongoing low-intensity support.

Apart from the platform itself ensuring anonymity, it is important that the bridges (especially 3 and 4) do not yield employee identities or individual diagnoses to the company (for the collective data could be useful for remedial policy initiation).

Hence, the algorithm built into the platform would need to be able to assign telephonic counsellors or psychotherapists based on the monetary limits and other guidelines adopted by the company for which the individual works. Since most health insurance schemes do not cover mental illnesses, the complication of bringing insurance companies into the workflow would probably be avoided.

Since most health insurance schemes do not cover mental illnesses, complication of bringing insurance companies into the workflow would probably be avoided. The platform requirement would essentially be the same for all companies, bar the cost parameters that might be differently specified for the bridge interfaces to counsellors and therapists.

As such, it would be pointless and inefficient to incur the platform development cost separately in each company. Moreover, a platform hosted outside the company would further assure employees that the information they put into it or the treatments they derive through its agency will remain confidential.

Until Indian industry shakes off its addiction to the excessive use of contract labour, HR managers will have to share the guilt for the inescapable mental trauma suffered by huge swathes of the Indian working population.

Promoting Mental Health

The Indian corporate needs to concentrically widen set of employment-related stressors, starting from repetitive, distasteful and hazardous work, progressing through toxic supervisors, peers and team members (who are extra-lethal for disadvantaged groups), with a way-point at unreasonably pressured targets with the bell-from-hell to toll the demise of laggards and culminating with zero-privacy (for example, fish-bowl open offices) or extremely isolated (including overmuch working from home) working environments.

None of these are individually sufficient to disturb the mental balance of all employees—otherwise we would have no sane ones left. However, what is equally incontrovertible is the mental havoc these factors can play in combination with the equanimity of those employees who are already high-strung, anxious, depressed or undergoing familial and other strains.

Making substantial improvements in all of these mental health hazards is highly desirable but may not be easy of achievement—at least in the short run. Hence, it becomes all the more important to provide a sense of corporate purpose and belongingness, remove the most noxious supervisors and create spaces where social interactions can relieve work-environment handicaps.

In the last resort, HR can also seek to doctor recruitment profiles to choose people whose personality-skins are thick enough to withstand the particular malaise which that organization or job particularly causes. There is one super-stressor, however, which no palliative measure can remedy—the one caused by insecure and contingent employment.

The greatest benefit of tackling the mental health impairments that have so far been resistant to corporate ministrations may not come simply from making a large number of sub-performers deliver adequately.

There are also positive steps HR can take to ameliorate work stress and provide non-stigmatized therapeutic activities. There was a time when most large corporate houses in the country ran hobby centres, dramatics societies and adventure clubs, without realizing the mental health benefits these provided.

In our heedless efforts to prune expenses that could not be convincingly allocated and explained as individual CTC, these fell by the wayside or became ill-funded ghosts of their former selves. Many of these will have to be revived in more modern avatars if we are to provide cost-effective and stigma-free therapeutic options on a mass scale.

There is now research-based evidence to show how, apart from the activities mentioned earlier, art, dance, meditation, exercise (though there is an unhealthy form of excessive exercise that needs to be guarded against), expressive writing and volunteering can, very economically, prevent mental illness or aid in recovery from it.

Freeing Beautiful Minds

The greatest benefit of tackling the mental health impairments that have so far been resistant to corporate ministrations may not come simply from making a large number of sub-performers deliver adequately. It will be the result of freeing the most brilliant minds that have been shackled by their mental fears and dark moods from giving their best at work.

The John Nashes may be far and few between but each organization has its share of geniuses, many of whom are held back by some or other kind of mental block for which they are too petrified to seek help. After all, as Aristotle wrote, "No great mind has ever existed without a touch of madness."

Research and Interventions to Reduce Workplace Stress

There has been previous research done on interventions to reduce workplace stress and International laws have been in force for many decades to protect human rights of employees at workplace, but the execution of policies is variable and often suboptimal.

Some interventions that were specifically found to be useful in reducing workplace stress were enhancing employee control, promoting physical activity, cognitive behaviour therapy for stress management and problem-focused return to work programs.

On the contrary, counselling and debriefing following trauma were not effective and any exposure to trauma should be followed by provision of psychological first aid and formal psychological support by trained professionals.

Workplace screening for mental disorders followed by access to basic mental health services has been found to be effective, but could lead to a potential increase in anxiety levels in those who are screened as false positives, so routine screening at workplace is not recommended.

While extant research has tended to focus on alleviation of symptoms and risk factors associated with workplace-related stress, less emphasis has been placed on gathering evidence on how mental disorders affect performance and absenteeism and how interventions have resulted in improvement of work performance and absenteeism.

Thus, more research is needed to gather evidence on the cost-effectiveness of interventions and the cost of mental disorder-related loss of productivity on the larger community. Some additional needs are:

1. Conduct basic epidemiological studies to understand the prevalence of workplace-related mental disorders and specific risk factors associated with different employment sectors,
2. Understand what kind of systems are being put in place by different sectors to manage workplace stress, and
3. To what degree are existing laws being followed and implemented, and what organizational restructuring is needed to improve the situation?

Tackling Workplace Stress at Organizational and National-level

Some policy guidelines from WHO to tackle work stress and improve workplace culture are:

1. ***Analysing the Mental Health Issues:***As a first step, it is essential to have a clear understanding of not only the prevalence/incidence and risk factors associated with workplace stress, but also a better knowledge about the cost implications to an organization in terms of lost productivity. This is an exercise that can be done at individual organizations, at specific employment sector level in specific regions or across regions.
2. ***Developing the Policy:*** A policy can be developed once the initial knowledge gained through the first step is available. The primary objective of such a policy should be to address concerns of all stakeholders and adhere to the organizations vision and mission. This should involve multiple meetings with different stakeholders to identify key components that need to be addressed. This engagement should be a continuous process throughout the development and execution of the policy.
3. ***Developing Strategies to Implement the Policy:*** While implementing the policies, care should be taken to identify the key strategies that need to be implemented, the processes that need to be in place to implement such strategies, targets to be achieved and timelines that need to be adhered to while implementing the strategies. Finally,

any additional budgetary allocations or training required to implement the policies, need to be made available.

4. ***Implementing and Evaluating the Policy:*** The implementation of any strategy will need collaboration and clear buy-in from all stakeholders. For some strategies, one might need to have a small demonstration project to start off, and based on the results tweak the strategies and then scale it up to a larger forum.

Before implementing a policy, information should be disseminated widely either through a formal launch meeting or individual organizations' dissemination network. For example, major government level policies that impact large number of employees or employers could have a launch meeting, whereas policies affecting only one organization with limited staff could be disseminated through office emails.

This would enable everyone to be aware of the policies. One major drawback of many policies is that they lack a formal evaluation. This should be built into the system and appropriately funded from the outset. Specific guidelines about how to monitor and evaluate the policies should be in place at the time of the launch of the policies and conducted as per agreed timelines.

A Cotton Factory in India

A Good Practice Initiative #7

A trend among industrial labourers of India in urban areas was for someone to join a factory and to stay in the same employment more or less for life. The employer was responsible not only for providing a salary as well as living accommodation, but also for the rehabilitation of employees back to their job in cases of serious physical or mental illness.

One of the country's largest cotton factories, which employed hundreds of labourers, had a 140-bed hospital and two schools. A 29-year-old woman who had been diagnosed as suffering from schizophrenia and had been hospitalized for a year.

On leaving the hospital (where she had been visited regularly by factory workers and managers), she returned to her apartment and to her former job on the "cotton chain" with full pay. After one month, she could not keep the pace of her co-workers in the assembly line and had to be transferred to an office job.

There is little doubt that without a legal obligation on the part of the employer to take her back, she would be unemployed.

The government should play a key role in ensuring that policies are in place that addresses workplace stress. Not only should the government identify vulnerable populations such as women, children, persons with disability at different workplaces, but also ensure that every sector has appropriate safeguards to protect the rights of all employees including vulnerable populations.

The government should also monitor how different sectors are performing with respect to workplace stress and have additional strategies in place to address issues related to sectors which have specifically higher level of physical or psychological stress such as mines, factories, health sector, among others.

All workplaces in India are seen as a fair and non-discriminatory zone as far as stress and mental ill-health are concerned. External stigma often involves negative opinions, judgements, comments, and assumptions made by others; internal stigma can take place when the person affected by mental illness internalises these negative messages.

A study by ASSOCHAM showed that nearly 43 per cent of employees in the private sector in India suffer from mental health issues at work. Also, a WHO report in 2017 found out that 18 per cent of global depression cases originate from India.

While mental health issues in the workplace are a reality for most companies, the stigma associated with mental health problems often prevents people from seeking help. Stigma is the result of negative perceptions and stereotypes and reflects a lack of understanding about mental health issues.

External stigma often involves negative opinions, judgements, comments, and assumptions made by others; internal stigma can take place when the person affected by mental illness internalises these negative messages.

Why Stigma is a Major Problem?

Though most mental health problems are common and treatable, the stigma or negative stereotypes associated with mental illness often forces employees to not talk about the issue. Even in workplaces that are quite progressive, several employees keep their mental health issues under wraps fearing that being open to talk about them will hurt their reputation, compromise work relationships, or even put their job at risk.

Employees with untreated mental health issues tend to have more serious and costly health issues in general. For instance, their risk of heart attacks and strokes is twice as high, and people with mental health issues are twice as likely to develop type 2 diabetes. This all adds up to missed work days and a loss in productivity that can significantly affect the performance of organisations.

How Can Organizations Remove Stigma from Workplaces?

Helping to improve mental health and well-being at work is not only beneficial to employees but also the company and society at large. Here are some ways organisations can remove the stigma surrounding mental health:

Awareness and Open Discussions

The more people are aware of mental health issues and the challenges faced by people with mental health problems, the less powerful stigma becomes. Through education on mental health, companies can reduce stigma, discrimination, negative stereotypes, and fear in the workplace.

Also, it is essential to create safe spaces for employees to talk about their own challenges without the fear of being "judged". Employees shouldn't fear that they will be excluded if they open up in this way. Leaders can set the tone for this by sharing their own experiences.

More Attention Towards Language

It is common practice across different organisations to address people with mental health disorders with words like "Downy", "Scary" and "Schizo". This can contribute significantly towards stigmatising mental health conditions. It is time to put an end to such practice and adopt practices that reduce prejudice, discrimination, and stigma against people suffering from mental health issues.

Increasing Access to Resources and Programs

Many organisations use Employee Assistance Programs (EAP) to support workplace mental health. Some employees may be reluctant to use this resource due to shame and lack of understanding, but they can go a long way in creating a workplace that values every individual equally and creates no discrimination or stigma. Companies can also provide direct access to mental health resources, apps, and even mental health professionals that can make employees feel supported and cared for.

Mental Health Training

It is crucial for every company to promote a culture that values every employee and understands that it's normal to suffer from mental health conditions. Mental health training for employees can help them recognise the signs of someone who may be struggling with mental health challenges and connect them to support resources. Through plays and other activities, they can offer guidance on how to listen non-judgmentally, offer reassurance, and assess the risk of suicide or self-harm.

Making mental health stigma a thing of the past is the need of the hour for organisations. The common human connection that every person shares with another person is more important than what separates us. Everyone struggles with doubt and anxiety. However, empathy is vital to see that common ground and build on it to create opportunity and hope for all.

Employee Engagement

The Covid-19 pandemic has intensified the already dwindling scenario of workplace mental health challenges, forcing employees to take a sharp look towards a holistic and methodical approach to workplace mental health.

The discussion and debates around the need for conversations, resources, and policies around Mental Health are stronger than ever. The pandemic has done its bit to help people focus on the urgent need to talk about the much stigmatized topic and also help break the stigma to a certain extent for people to actually go ahead and get the necessary treatment for their specific mental health issues.

It is highly likely that there is one person in your team who is living with a mental illness right now, perhaps without being aware of it themselves. While it is important to understand that one's struggle with their mental health is a personal one, the impact of mental illnesses transcends beyond personal and dives deep into the professional arena (illness + absenteeism) too leading organizations to bear huge costs for the same. According to the WHO the lack of treatment of depression and anxiety disorders alone would amount to a total loss of 12 billion workdays by 2030.

A study reported in the Economic Times (2018) states that 42.5% of the employees in corporate India (private sector) experience mental health issues such as depression or some form of anxiety disorder. Moreover, the pandemic has exacerbated this given that household responsibilities are shouldered by women and have increased two-fold ever since.

This reinforces the emphasis on formulating mental health policies in the workplace and the health of your organization is determined by the health of your employees. Few ways by which you can make your organization more employee-friendly and normalize conversations around mental health are:

1. *Collecting and Analyzing Data from Within the Organization*

Conduct monthly or annual studies on the employees to understand their mental health status. It can be as simple as filling out anonymous surveys which will provide insight on how healthy the work culture is and how healthy your employees are feeling.

Doing this will show them you care as an organization that prioritizes its employees. Anonymous surveys may provide a safe space for the employees to speak up about issues they are otherwise uncomfortable or hesitant to bring up. In addition, regular surveys will allow an appraisal of your policies and strategies.

Create an accessible database of resources that your employees can turn to for seeking help with the help of professionals such as mental health advocates, psychologists, psychiatrists, organizations working in this field, and advocates. These professionals help in structuring the narrative around mental health with sensitivity and any inputs from them can be beneficial.

2. *Sensitize Employees*

As a follow-up to the previous point, it is necessary too because mental health is not an individual challenge rather a collective priority and collective effort. This can be done through sensitization training again with the help of professionals trained to conduct these programs.

3. *Work on Work Culture*

Mental health problems are very much influenced by the social environment individuals are surrounded by, i.e., their identity, especially if they belong to marginalized groups and identities. Hence, promoting diversity and inclusion in your workspace is of key importance because policies and resources around mental health are mitigatory, improving the work culture will keep symptoms and problems at bay.

A healthy work culture for individuals irrespective of their identities should be the primary goal. Tangible changes through policies such as introducing mental health leaves or 4-day weekdays are necessary, but working on developing a sensitive and healthy work culture goes a long way.

4. *Showing Compassion and Empathy*

Trust your employees instead of doubting them. Treating your employees with consideration and compassion itself may ease some of their trouble. Moreover, often, your employees may be facing difficulties outside their workspace which you need to be considerate about in this era of work-life balance rather than chasing productivity at the cost of their mental health.

5. *Respecting Differences between Employees*

Mental health struggles are not experienced in the same way or for the same reasons. People are different so are their experiences. And this also means that they require different approaches to care for their mental health.

6. *Serve as Role Models*

One of the key characteristics of a leader-employee relationship is that the employee learns from their leaders, looks up to them, and mirrors their behaviour. Moreover, if you are advocating for something, you must also practice it.

This emphasizes the importance of your effort in sensitizing and educating yourself such that, you can influence your employees in normalizing mental health in the workplace. If you are a receptive leader, you may be able to influence your employees into being receptive leaders too.

The above changes are not going to be easily achievable because it involves behaviour change, but they are a need of the hour and better late than never. The covid-19 pandemic has been a great teacher in opening our minds to the urgency of paying attention to mental health before it's too late.

While it has threatened us into a mental health epidemic, implementing such changes will surely go a long way in mitigating existing and arising mental health concerns. Workplaces cannot and should not be forsaken from the discourse on mental health. The easiest solution to a problem is acting like it doesn't exist, but the right solution to a problem is facing it head-on.

The concept of Employee wellness is not unheard of. Many organizations across the world offer free gym memberships, mediation classes, smoking cessation programs among many others; what we really need now is a focus and shift towards mental health programs. This is the need of the hour.

Programmes must be culture-relevant and culture-sensitive. While a sharp division often exists between rural and urban settings, the family remains at the core of provision of services and the main link towards involvement in natural community support.

Currently, there are occupational therapy workshops and centres for work activities for people with moderate and severe mental health disorders are carried out all over the country by government, private and non-profit organizations.

The primary aim of therapy workshops is to promote social skills necessary for independent living, including work. There are approximately 300 occupational therapy workshops in the country that ensure temporary employment for people with mental illness who have lost their jobs.

They receive a small stipend for their work. There is one experimental Centre for Work Activities, in which the staffs consist of people with severe mental illness. This centre is supported financially by the State Fund for Rehabilitation of the Disabled.

Political Will and Legislation

There exists a legislation which postulates that disability shall not be a barrier to a meaningful life. With respect to access to work, these laws dictate that reasonable accommodations should be made by an employer and describe what is meant by this concept.

It describes the standards of accessibility for persons with physical or mental disabilities in employment and further defines that "reasonable accommodation standards" will also apply to the private sector. The majority of reasonable accommodation standards pertain to physical disability and include making facilities used by employees readily accessible, the acquisition or modification of equipment or devices, the provision of readers or interpreters, etc.

The provisions that apply most often to persons with mental health problems have to be developed individually and have to do mostly with part-time or modified work schedules, job restructuring to eliminate or exchange auxiliary job functions that increase pressure for the worker, and time off for therapy.

Whereas the accommodations necessitated for physical disability are very often technical or a one-time affair, those required for psychiatric disabilities tend often to be quite simple but will last in time and require an attitudinal change on the part of the employer and, quite often, co-workers.

The law also foresees that the cost of bringing about "reasonable facilities" should not be "unreasonable or unbearable" for the employer.

Reasonable Accommodation for Persons with Mental Health Problems in the United States of America

A Good Practice Initiative #8

LL Mancuso has proposed the following list of accommodations:[25]

1. Changes in Interpersonal Communication.
   - Arranging for all work requests to be put in writing for a library assistant who becomes anxious and confused when given verbal instructions.
   - Training a supervisor to provide positive feedback along with criticisms of performance for an employee re-entering the workforce who needs reassurance of his/her abilities after a long psychiatric hospitalization.
   - Allowing a worker who personalizes negative comments about his/her work performance to provide a self-appraisal before receiving feedback from a supervisor.
   - Scheduling daily planning sessions with a co-worker at the start of each day to develop hourly goals for someone who functions best with added time structure.
2. Modifications to Physical Environment.
   - Purchasing room dividers for a data entry operator who has difficulty maintaining concentration (and thus accuracy) in an open work area.
   - Arranging for an entry-level worker to have an enclosed office to reduce noise and interruptions that provoke disabling anxiety.

3. Job Modifications.
   - Arranging for someone who cannot drive or use public transportation to work at home.
   - Restructuring a receptionist job by eliminating lunchtime switchboard duty normally handled by someone in this position.
   - Exchanging problematic secondary tasks for part of another employee's job description.
4. Schedule Modification.
   - Allowing a worker with poor physical stamina to extend his/her schedule to allow for additional breaks or rest periods during the day.
   - Allowing a worker to shift his/her schedule by 1 hour twice per month to attend psychotherapy appointments.

In the United States, until recently, recipients of social security lost cash and medical benefits if they earned US$ 500 per month. This has now been raised to US$ 700 per month in order to create an incentive for social security recipients to go back to work.

One needs to emphasize once again the necessity of providing continuing support to both the individual and, most often, to the employer, in order to establish a 'working relationship' based on known expectations, cooperation and partnership. Trial periods on the job site have been found to be very successful and predictive of the employer's capacity to 'integrate' the job.

Coordinated Action

To help employers and to facilitate access to work for our clientele, it has been found very useful to regroup potential employers. For instance, the Employers Forum on Disability acts as the authoritative employers' voice on disability as it affects employers and service providers. The Forum is funded in part and managed by over 350 members while the rest is funded by the corporate sector.

The Employers Forum on Disability Employment agenda provides the framework for employers committed to developing best practice in the employment of disabled people.[26] For planning purposes, it has been found very useful to have formal input from representatives of employers and from labour unions that can facilitate the required openness to create jobs for persons with a background of serious mental illness.

While they will benefit immensely from initiatives stemming from the private sector, the most successful programmes will require government support. It is not always easy to decide where the primary responsibility rests among the departments or ministries of a government.

Effective inter-sectoral collaboration will involve the departments of health, labour, employment, education, regional development, social services, etc. A specific formal mechanism which allows for this inter-sectoral collaboration is a highly effective tool.

Potential Predictors of Successful Participation

Given the size of mental health population that can and would like to work, there are very few effective vocational programs available. It would, therefore be, extremely useful to develop criteria that will identify the likelihood of successful outcomes. Such an initiative will have to be based on the three major principles of:

(a) Towards Zero Exclusion
(b) Choose/Get/Keep
(c) Consumer Determination

The variables that can be of relevance in this regard are listed below:

- Work expectation (those who are expecting to be working within a year).
- Attitudes about work as a source of pride and accomplishment (each increment on the scale results in double participation).
- Work history (individuals with fewer than 5 paid jobs since age 15 are unlikely to receive services as those with more extensive work experience).
- Age is negatively related (with each additional 5 years the odds of participation greatly diminish).
- Education is positively related (each increase in educational level yields an almost one-and-half times increase in the odds of participation).

Why is Mental Health at Work so Under-rated

Career therapist and author Vasant Janadhan[27] points out that 10% of the certified absences are due to mental illness, which also accounts for 23% of NIMHANS pharmaceutical costs.

Depression alone is estimated to cost approximately crores of rupees per annum. Besides, absenteeism has an impact on reduced productivity, labour turnover, poor timekeeping and accidents.

The author points out that, even if employers take the view that work does not constitute an etiological factor for mental illness, the fact that there are 30 working days lost to depression and anxiety for every single day lost to industrial disputes makes the issue a paramount one. This viewpoint is now apparently shared by employers, employees and trade unions.

Janardhan is of the opinion that the main issues for research in this field are:

- More accurate prevalence studies of a wide range of different work settings
- Elucidation of risk factors
- Evaluation of techniques for primary prevention
- Evaluation of techniques for secondary prevention
- Evaluation of occupational mental health services, provisions and policies
- More accurate estimation of the impact of minor psychiatric morbidity on sickness absence, work performance, relationships with colleagues, accidents and labour turnover.

Developing Social Firms

Social firms are small to medium-sized firms which have been developed with the primary purpose of providing employment for persons with a disability in a context which is more or less the same as that of a regular firm, while at the same time offering the required support to workers who need it.

In social firms, persons with disabilities work side by side with non-disabled individuals. All are paid regular wages and work on the basis of a regular work contract. They all have the same rights and obligations.

The balance between commerce and care is the single most critical issue which faces social firms, and this balance is achieved differently according to the origins of the firm and orientation of its founders.[28]

Social firms have developed mostly in the last 20 years in order to deal realistically with increasing unemployment ratios and major changes in the nature of work itself, characterized by downsizing, increasing requirement for specialized training, and an ongoing demand for higher productivity. These are all factors that tend to exclude many persons who have experienced severe mental illness.

Using a broad definition of social firms, and including Indian cooperatives, there are said to be in excess of 2800 social firms at this point in the sub-continent offering employment to persons with psychiatric disabilities.

However, there are some key differences between social firms and regular businesses:

- First of all, it is the mission of a social firm to create jobs for people with disabilities and disadvantaged people. Social firms have a social and a commercial mission.
- One of the most important characteristics of a workplace in a social firm is the 'empowering atmosphere' for their employees with disabilities. While in a regular business people with disabilities might be considered as a disturbing factor, social firms do actively recruit from this target group and provide the necessary reasonable accommodations.
- The emphasis is on the potential and abilities of the worker rather than on potential problems and barriers. With this flexible approach work tasks can be arranged and adjusted to accommodate worker needs. This often results in the job being accomplished as quickly and to as high a standard as in any other workplace.

All social firms initially receive support from the state. In the most advanced firms, a full market analysis and business plan must be developed prior to receiving the go-ahead. Several firms, once established, reach 85% self-financing. All firms employ, side-by-side, handicapped and non-handicapped workers.

All are paid the regular rate for the sector of employment in which they work. While the majority of workers are full-time employees, approximately 25% may use the firm as transitional work while 10–15% man power receives internship. A good majority of workers are trained on site and all of them receive ongoing support as necessary.

The firms are involved either in the provision of services (office work, recycling, restaurant, catering, landscaping, etc.) or in manufacturing (textiles, computer hardware, furniture, etc.).

Because of the differing contexts and variations of each individual's disabilities, and because of the lack of evaluative studies with comparative groups, it is difficult to judge the social firm's efficacy solely in terms of economic independence of its members. The performance of an integration company (social firm) may not be judged merely in economic terms, it must also be seen in terms of integration.

Other International Examples

Several examples show the great variety of possibilities which exist in the development of social firms and other types of programmes that promote the employment of persons with serious mental illness. More recently, a number of initiatives have involved the provision of white collar jobs for persons with serious mental health problems, as opposed to jobs which are close to the minimum wage.

In the United States, Project Employ (part of the President's Committee on Employment of People with Disabilities) has identified programmes which offer white collar office occupations.[29] The common features of most of these new programs involve the following:

- Many were initiated by large corporations themselves and corporate contacts were systematically used.
- Individualization of job development is the rule rather than the exception, even though it is more costly.
- Several initiatives came from local governments.

An American Bank

A Good Practice Initiative #9

A large US credit card lender provides a variety of jobs for people with cognitive disabilities. This includes positions in clerical support, mail centre, copy centre, fitness centre, environmental services, fleet services and landscaping.

In 1990, a parent advocate approached the company to discuss jobs for people with cognitive disabilities. The chairman made the initial corporate commitment. An in-house staff member assists the managers and co-workers who are mentors to the individuals with disabilities with techniques to give meaningful instructions, encouragement and needed support.

Of the 36 jobs at the company, 20 are non-traditional. Salaries range between US$ 13,000 and US$ 20,000 annually, plus up to US$ 2,000 in individual and company performance incentives. All personnel are evaluated after six months and are eligible for merit increases.

People receive full company benefits, including health care, life and disability insurance, pension and retirement plans. Thirty five employees with disabilities work 40 hours per week, and one works 20 hours per week.

Source: Supported Employment InfoLines.

There are several effective preventive and promotion programs as well as those for treatment and rehabilitation. Some of the best programs comprise:

1. ***Promotion and Preventive Programs:*** They attempt to create a climate that fosters motivation and commitment, reduce obvious stressful agents and promote harmony among co-workers.

   Good Practices

   - Importance of health education in order to increase awareness of factors affecting mental health and well-being.
   - Screening programs to detect risk factors or early signs of stress-related illness, and
   - Communication, clear work goals and participation of employees in this process.

   In addition, Occupational Health Services and Employee Assistance Programs are instrumental in implementing promotion and prevention activities.

2. ***Treatment Programs:*** They should include the capacity for correct diagnosis, remembering that often mental illness hides behind physical signs and symptoms.

   Good Practices

   - Quick access to and intervention by competent medical and professional staff will be called for.
   - Integral to quick access and early intervention of appropriate medical treatment for individuals is reducing the stigma and shame associated with mental health problems.
   - Often an individual will not seek treatment or will delay seeking it because of the stigma associated with mental illness.

   Furthermore, there is a need for more easily accessible mental health treatment programs.

3. ***Rehabilitation Programs:*** They must emphasize the requirements for a prompt return to work by focusing on necessary accommodations to the work situation, as well as required support to the individual.

   Good Practices

   - Encouraging high levels of client participation in all aspects of the rehabilitation process.

- It also includes the participation of an individual's support system such as family members, a mental health professional, case manager, vocational counsellor and work supervisor.

A successful timely return to work and the identification of necessary accommodations need to involve the client as well as his/her support system.

A Complete Furniture Factory, Spain

A Good Practice Initiative #10

A major Spanish NGO has created 12 service centres employing more than 800 handicapped persons who fill 183 service contracts. In Cabra, Andalusia, they run a commercial furniture factory employing 212 persons, the vast majority having had long stays in psychiatric hospitals.

The factory is very modern and has several separate assembly chains where the needs of individual workers are taken into account. There is also a large showroom and the products are sent throughout Europe and even to America.

Most workers live where the NGO is located and they are very well accepted owing, among other things, to the constant cooperation between the city council and the workshop leaders. Seventy workers live in an Andalusian type of residence with a swimming pool next to the factory.

The NGO also has a research centre affiliated to the University of Cordoba where the emphasis is placed on scientific and technical research in rehabilitation with emphasis on computer technologies. All workshop workers receive salaries equivalent to those of workers in regular industries. The workshop is 90% self-financing.

Like all European programs mentioned here, this NGO receives material help within the framework of the Horizon and Helios 1 and 2 programmes put together by the EU.

Source: Supported Employment InfoLines, 2000, 11(2).

Breaking the cycle of discouragement and eliminating the numerous societal barriers that affect employment are keys to enhancing the economic and social integration of people with mental health problems.[30] We must consider the mental health system and its influence on challenging negative stereotypes as well as encouraging employers to implement good practices.

It is important to recognize that in many parts of the world the mental health delivery system often discourages an individual from entering the workforce or returning to work after a diagnosis of mental ill-health, despite stabilization of symptoms.

A Service Cooperative, Italy

A Good Practice Initiative #11

This cooperative was founded in 1981 as an integrated cooperative because its members both worked together and supported each other. The cooperative has grown from 9 members to more than 500.

It offers:

- *Cleaning Services:* Interior and exterior cleaning in schools, public offices, private homes, industrial buildings and district health offices.
- *Social Services:* Assistance to elderly and handicapped persons, programs for children, and work training programs.
- *Upkeep of Parks and Gardens and Reclamation of Run-down Green Areas Using Specially Trained Staff:* Defence of the environment in cooperation with private individuals, firms and public entities.
- *General Maintenance Activities:* Plumbing, electrical work, house painting etc.

Source: Supported Employment InfoLines, 2000, 11(2).

Although, there is an increasing emphasis on employment and re-employment, there is still a tendency by mental health and rehabilitation professionals to minimize the importance of work for many individuals, particularly for strengthening and maintaining recovery.

Furthermore, the system of financial supports for individuals with mental health disability is a disincentive for employment. Financial concerns are often cited as a major contributing factor to discouraging a person with a mental illness from seeking employment, education and training opportunities. It is important that these issues be fully understood as they impact employment prospects.

Steps can be taken to help reduce barriers to employment and the systematic cycle of discouragement. For example, early and timely intervention, networking and client participation in identifying and setting goals are all elements of effective programmes sponsored by some employers and vocational rehabilitation agencies.

Engaging all individuals in early discussions about work and recognizing that the purpose of early discussions may ultimately help an individual identify realistic goals and strategies for achieving these goals. Early intervention, for example, in recognizing and ameliorating the impact of workplace stress has shown to be effective in reducing stress-related absenteeism.

A Gardening Project in Milan, Italy

A Good Practice Initiative #12

A few years ago, 12 patients were discharged from a psychiatric hospital in Milan, Italy, to be followed up as out-patients. They all found living accommodation either with their families or in apartments with some supervision close to the hospital.

They tended to be somewhat passive until a formal work training program was offered to them in gardening by a cooperative that had been recently created and subsidized by the regional government.

After an apprenticeship of a few months, the cooperative obtained a formal, year-round contract from three suburbs of Milan. This included seeding, planting, looking after flower arrangements and grass and general maintenance of public gardens. Within 4 months of initiating their work, all ex-patients had moved to the areas where they were working.

The project includes two monitors who are professional gardeners. All employees are paid the regular rate corresponding to their job.

Source: Harnois, G.: The Role of Work in Psychosocial Rehabilitation—European Union Symposium on Training and Employment for People with Psychosocial Disabilities, Sweden, October 14-16, 1994.

Accessing resources and referral information to become more knowledgeable in assisting individuals in exploring vocational supports and services are important components of networking. Furthermore, using community resources such as state or local rehabilitation agencies and support groups may aid in the successful return to work of an employee.

For the mental health and rehabilitation professional, in particular, learning about all of the options available within the surrounding community—including details about types of employment programmes, eligibility criteria and key contact personnel—is a good practice in assisting the individual to find employment or re-employment.

An Olympic Task, Montreal, Canada

A Popular Local Initiative #1

The project is an adapted work centre with a yearly budget of $5 million Canadian dollars, of which 25% comes from the Quebec Office of Handicapped Persons (OPHQ). This centre has a staff of 203 persons, of whom 55% have had serious mental health problems.

A small factory at the head location makes carton products for offices. The larger portion of the enterprise has a 5-year contract for cleaning of the Olympic sites and village. There are 11 teams of 12–16 persons deployed around the clock. In order to ensure full availability, 20 persons are on a standby list.

Most of the workers are unionized and are paid union wages. The employees are very proud to wear their company uniforms. There are very few dropouts. In order to lessen the stigma problems associated with mental illness, a special educational program is offered to the non-handicapped employees.

Taking the OPHQ subsidy into account, the company is 75% self-financing. The majority of handicapped employees freely admit that they would be unemployed but for the existence of the program.

The board of directors comprises 10 persons, of which 5 are from the private sector, mostly banking. The board also includes one user.

A Mental Health NGO in Northern Ireland

A Popular Local Initiative #2

A mental health NGO in Northern Ireland—Through Work to Health—is the motto of this NGO which operates in Northern Ireland to promote employment opportunities for people who are recovering from mental ill-health.

It is one of the largest regional voluntary sector organizations in the United Kingdom providing vocational rehabilitation and personal development training programmes with employment placement and support.

Over 1,000 adults participate in a range of programs each year and about a quarter of them move to either full or part-time employment or other training organizations.

A Quality Provision

This success is due to a number of factors. One clearly relates to the encouragement and training provided to the trainees. The organization's efforts have obtained regional and national recognition in the United Kingdom National Training Awards competition in 1997 and 1999.

The other has to do with the strong links which have been established with over 300 of the largest employers in Northern Ireland. Indeed, since its earliest days the work of the organization has been led by businessmen helped by health professionals.

Partnership Working

Great importance is attached to maintaining ongoing links with employers and this is promoted on two levels. One had been secured as the result of the organization being successful in attracting subcontract work—based on quality, price and time delivery—from a range of companies. The other is due to the personal links established with human resources departments by the employment service officers.

This has helped to overcome the stigma which is still attached to mental illness and, more importantly, has ensured that ongoing help is available to both the employer and the trainee once a job placement has been secured. A range of organizations from many parts of Europe has studied the methods employed by this NGO.

Good Mental Health Makes Good Business Sense

The organization has also recently adopted a more proactive approach by encouraging employers to promote positive "mental health in the workplace" policies. This makes good business sense, as there is clear evidence about the loss of production allied to the litigation which can arise if employees seek compensation payments as the result of work-related stress.

To that end, a consultancy and training service to industry has just been launched with the full support of employer organizations, including the Institute of Directors. There is no health without mental health

This NGO is also proactive in promoting a positive understanding about mental health and has launched a 'Design for Life' competition aimed at the student population. Information packs about this innovative competition were circulated to all post-primary schools and youth groups across Northern Ireland. The response was encouraging.

Further information can be obtained from: Cecil Graham, Chief Executive, Action Mental Health, 19, Knockbracken Healthcare Park, Saintfield Road, Belfast, BT8 8BH, Northern Ireland.

Lastly, it is important to recognize the impact of family and/or significant others on an individual's choice to engage in education, training or employment activities. A person recovering from mental illness may be reluctant to pursue work-related goals that may reflect the concerns of the family who fears that stressors may occur that could trigger a relapse.
Within this context, the family and significant others are often relying on the mental health professional for information regarding resources in their communities for rehabilitation and support.

Success Stories

Many business organizations provide employees with resources to improve their mental health and stress management. Some of the exemplary examples are listed below:

1. Prudential Financial
    - Monitors the effect of supervisors on worker well-being, especially when supervisors change.
    - Conducts ongoing, anonymous surveys to learn about attitudes toward managers, senior executives, and the company as a whole.
    - Normalizes discussion of mental health by having senior leadership share personal stories in video messages.
2. TiERI Performance Solutions
    - Focuses on six key health issues—depression, anxiety, obsessive-compulsive disorder, schizophrenia, bipolar disorder and addictions as part of its 'Start the Conversation about Mental Illness Awareness Campaign'.
    - Provides resources to assess risk find information and get help or support using multiple formats to increase visibility and engagement. For example, information is provided as infographics, e-mails, weekly table tents with reflections and challenges and videos (educational and storytelling).
3. Beehive PR
    - Maintains the 'InZone', a dedicated quiet room that is not connected to a wireless internet signal, which gives employees a place to recharge.

- Combines professional and personal growth opportunities through goal-setting, one-on-one coaching, development sessions and biannual retreats.

4. Tripler Army Medical Center
    - Requires resiliency training to reduce burnout and increase skills in empathy and compassion for staff members who are in caregiver roles.
    - Training sessions mix classroom-style lectures, role-playing, yoga and improvisational comedy to touch on multiple learning styles.
5. Certified Angus Beef
    - Provides free wellness consultations by an on-site clinical psychologist. Employees do not have to take leave to access these services.
    - Holds lunch-time learning sessions to reduce stigma about mental health and the services available to employees.
    - Offers quarterly guided imagery relaxation sessions to teach stress management strategies.
6. Houston Texans
    - Provides comprehensive and integrated physical, mental and behavioural health insurance coverage, including round-the-clock access to Employee Assistance Program (EAP) services.
    - Extends EAP access to anyone living in an employee's home, with dedicated programming for those who are caring for children or elderly parents.
7. Aangan, Indian Non-profit Organization
    - Monitor how team members are feeling.
    - Allow them to switch roles, pursue passion projects and even take them out of the field if needed.
    - Experiment with different projects and programs.
8. Point of View, Indian Non-profit Organization
    - Emphasise self-care by taking a day off for their mental health, meeting with a therapist, a yoga class or other practices.
    - Encourage employees to think about themselves and prioritise their mental health.
    - Downtime and rest are imperative to avoid burnout, a phenomenon that is as much emotional and psychological, as it is physical.

9. Buddy System, Indian Non-profit Organization
    - Create a healthy support eco-system.
    - Regularly schedule sessions with counsellors and other similar practices that encourage team members to share, talk about their work, their lives and any challenges they are facing.
    - Confidentiality is the key particularly if the exercise does not include an external counsellor or therapist, and is being conducted internally along with making it clear to staff that talking about their mental health will not affect their job standing.
10. Quest Alliance, Indian Non-profit Organization
    - Create a nurturing work environment.
    - Encourage people to try different things, and even to fail.
11. SNEHA, Indian Non-profit Organization
    - Reach out to professionals and encourage them to openly discuss their workplace mental woes and stressors.
    - Allow people to discuss personal mental problems as well.
    - Train field staff or deal with stress at workshops.
12. Arpan, Indian Non-profit Organization
    - Integrate mental health into employee welfare funds.
    - Have a therapeutic allowance, applicable monthly, for all employees.
    - Also remain open to employees pursuing external avenues of mental wellness.

Summary

Implementing and maintaining mental health and well-being initiatives in the workplace is a shared responsibility. All levels of the organization must contribute to its success. The organization must keep in mind the following while doing so:

- Leadership demonstrating support and care shows the organization's commitment to the importance of employee mental health and well-being.
- Identification of psychosocial hazards in the workplace is an important step to identify opportunities to improve employee mental health and well-being.
- Ongoing review and evaluation of mental health and well-being initiatives at all levels of the organization ensure resources remain relevant and effective.

- Providing and promoting access to high quality behavioural health care, including through remotely delivered evidence-based pathways, ensures that employees have access to their preferred type of care when they need it.
- Integrating these services into a comprehensive wellness program may concurrently promote improved total health outcomes.
- Community partnerships extend the reach and resources of organizations, and provide new opportunities to collaborate and be part of the solution.

These are the recommended practices with real-world implementation examples. While success from these strategies has been inferred from employee experience, it is important to note that real world data to document outcomes from implementation of these strategies across organizations and settings are needed.

Continued efforts by organizations to measure and share successes and failures in implementing workplace mental health and well-being initiatives will strengthen future best practices recommendations.

UNIT–V

Spiritual Intelligence in the Workplace

The phrase 'spirituality in the workplace' conjures up different images for different people. Some might imagine a new age type atmosphere with burning incense and yoga sessions. Others might imagine a religious atmosphere that borders on being repressive and intolerant of diverse viewpoints. These are two extremes neither of which is accurate. A question then arises on what does spirituality in the workplace look like?

Actually, the term of Spiritual Intelligence is mostly credited to Danah Zohar and Dr. Ian Marshall based on their book, SQ: Connecting with Our Spiritual Intelligence.[1] Spirituality comes from within and by large it benefits one's own self. A person who is spiritually conscious is well-aligned with his thoughts and desires and as well as of others. It comes with surety validated by the heart instead of the mind alone and it creates inner meaning and motivation about work, extending inner peace in one's own self with a natural desire to help others grow, learn and develop.

Spiritual Quotient (SQ) helps a person to determine his or her motivations, vision and the overall mission in life. Above all, it gives them a concrete dream, based on which they can design their future action plan to attain these goals. Spiritual intelligence shows how one makes use of their spiritual quotient to live a fulfilling and productive life.

Background

Webster defines spirituality as "of relating to, consisting of or affecting the spirit of, relating to sacred matters, concerned with religious values, of related to, or joined in spirit." The term 'spirituality' is derived from the Latin word 'spiritus' that means vapour, breath, air or wind.

Skelley (1996)[2] discusses three meanings of spirituality:

1. A human capacity for self-transcendence.
2. A religious part of life and the ways the capacity for self-transcendence are actualized by God or the Divine.

3. A specific religious experience that creates self-transcendence that is a Hindu, Buddhist, Jewish, Christian or Muslim faith.

He states that spirituality is not necessarily religious but rather it is a universal capacity for self-transcendence that allows human beings to experience spirituality in daily regular activities including work.

Table 1: Definitions of Workplace Spirituality

Source	*Term Used*	*Definition*
Ashmos and Duchon (2000)	Spirituality at Work	The recognition that employees have an inner life that nourishes and is nourished by meaningful work that takes place in the context of community.
Giacalone and Jurkiewicz (2003)	Workplace Spirituality	A framework of organizational values evidenced in the culture that promote employee' experience of transcendence through the work process, facilitating their sense of being connected to others in a way that provides feeling of completeness and joy.
Kinjerski and Skrypnek (2006)	Spirit at Work	Spirit at work is a distinct state that is characterized by cognitive, interpersonal, spiritual and mystical dimensions. It involves engaging energies characterized by a profound feeling of a well-being, a belief that one is engaged in meaningful work that has a higher purpose, an awareness of alignment between one's values. Beliefs and work. Therefore, having a sense of being authentic.
Kolodinsky *et al.* (2008)	Personal Spirituality	The totality of personal spiritual values that an individual brings to the workplace and how such values influence both ethically related and ethically unrelated worker interactions and outcomes.
	Organizational Spirituality	An individual's perception of the spiritual values within an organizational setting.
	Workplace Spirituality	The interaction between an individual's personal spiritual values and the organization's spiritual values.

(Table contd...)

(Table 1 contd...)

Source	*Term Used*	*Definition*
Lynn *et al.* (2009)	Workplace Religion	(Definition not specifically given). The authors endorse the inclusion of dogma, religious views and belief systems in the workplace spirituality scholarship.
Pandey *et al.* (2009)	Spiritual Climate at Workplace	The collective perception of the employee about the workplace that facilitates harmony with "self" through meaningful work, and transcendence from the limited "self" and operates in harmony with social and natural environment having sense of interconnectedness within it.
Petchsawang and Duchon (2009)	Workplace Spirituality	Feeling connected and having compassion towards others, experiencing a mindful inner consciousness in the pursuit of meaningful work that enables transcendence.
Altaf and Awan (2011)	Workplace Spirituality	The spiritual well-being of an individual in working conditions.
Chen and Sheng (2013)	Spiritual Awakening	Refers to realizing life's value and meaning via experiences through work or workplaces. It is an introspective process, where individuals connect with others, societies, and all beings in the nature in a profound manner, in order to generate a new set of conceptions, awareness and perceptions that go beyond usual sensory experiences.
	Organizational Spirituality	Establishment of an identity and concerns shared within an organization. Employees feel a meaning to life that work creates via conversations, listening and coping with pressures and challenges through spiritual learning and growth.
Adawiyah and Pramuka (2017)	Islamic Workplace Spirituality	Proposed Islamic workplace spirituality as a function of the extent to which an individual's religious world view manifests at work (that is, religiosity) and an individual's alignment with organizational values (that is, workplace spiritual values).

Different Spiritual Perceptions

Part of the sensitivities and disagreements over spirituality in organisations arise from the wide variety of definitions that people have when using the words spirit and spirituality.

One of the foremost authors on spirituality in leadership and organizations is Harrison Owen who admits that people naturally interpret spirituality from a personal frame of reference and belief system, but still need to communicate about it using common language.

In trying to define spirituality it is easier to start by stating what spirituality is not. Spirituality definitely is not the same as religion. Ver Beck (2000: 32)[3] puts it clearly: "Spirituality is a relationship with the supernatural or spiritual realm that provides meaning and a basis for personal and communal reflection, decision and action, while religion is an institutionalised set of beliefs and practices regarding the spiritual realm."

Scholars the world over have defined spirituality in their own different way. However, it is possible to highlight some common themes, which are as follows:

- An animating life force.
- An inner, intangible experience.
- An awareness of connectedness or relationship with something more concerned with the meaning of life.

The main area of difference in defining the spiritual is whether people are simply talking of the inner human spirit or whether they are also talking about a sacred and, to a degree, external Spirit.

Most people appear comfortable with the secular use of the term spirit to refer to an inner human spirit. This inner human spirit includes things like intuition, emotions and love. We use the words such as team spirit, community spirit or say someone is in high or low spirits frequently and we know what is meant.

Rational Intelligence (I/IQ), Emotional Intelligence (EI/EQ) and Spiritual Intelligence (SI/SQ)

It is a long-standing belief that one's Intelligence Quotient (IQ) is the greatest validation of a person's intelligence. However, as days progressed in the 90's, a new concept of Emotional (Intelligence) Quotient (EQ) emerged and changed everyone's perspective of intelligence. And then came the 2000's, where the idea of emotional intelligence evolved and gave rise to the new concept of Spiritual Intelligence.

Human Intelligence is highly complex. Neither IQ alone nor EI of a person would represent the totality of their intelligences. Computers have high (artificial) IQ but not EI. Some animals have little bit of EI along with IQ. But it is not possible for computers or these animals to ask the questions of 'why', to be creative, to change rules, to alter situations, to tamper rigid rules with understanding and compassion, to discriminate between good and bad, to dream, to aspire and to raise oneself out of the mind. EI enables a person to judge what situation he is in and then to behave appropriately within it. That is, if he is working within the boundaries of the situation allowing the situation to guide him, his SI enables him to ask the question "Why should he be there in that particular situation in the first place?" Unlike EI, SI can give him transformative power, power to change the situation by creating a better one, that is, one's SI can help him/her in dealing with the situation by allowing them to guide the situation, to create new values by understanding existing situational values etc.

Thus, according to Robert Feldman[4], IQ is the capacity to understand the world, think rationally and use resources effectively when faced with challenges. It is simply the measure of a person's intelligence in comparison to that of others. EQ is the ability to manage one's emotions rationally and in a positive way. In short it is the ability to recognize, understand and manage our own emotions. In practical terms, this means being aware that emotions can drive our behaviour and impact people (positively and negatively) and learning how to manage those emotions. The Spiritual Quotient concept goes beyond your cognitive and emotional skills. It is living in humility, bearing in mind that you are small part of the vast universe. An understanding of SQ motivates people to balance their work commitments and time with family and inner growth.

Scientific basis on which these Three are related

Neurologically, if one looks at these three intelligences then it can be understood that neo-cortex (at the top surface of brain) is responsible for IQ, sub-cortex (at the lower part of brain) is responsible for EI and the identified spot (called God Spot) responsible for SI is at the temporal lobe of the brain.

Based on the theory of evolution, it is of some special interest to note that sub-cortex got evolved in human brain earlier than neo-cortex. IQ is based on serial neural wiring in the brain whereas EI is based on associative neural wiring (somewhat similar to series and parallel connections in electricity).

SI is based on another type of neural wiring; it is based on synchronous neural oscillations that unify data across the whole brain. It unifies, integrates and has the potential to transform any material based on the other two wiring processes. It enables a dialogue between reason and emotion (between IQ & EI) between mind and body. In fact, it is like a lever of the first order when SI is the fulcrum for growth and transformation.

This fulcrum (SI) is an active, unifying, meaning-giving centre to guide an individual. When we look at the dimensions of EI & SI, one may notice certain overlapping (for example, self awareness) but self awareness in connection with EI is at emotional level dealing with the mind, whereas the same in connection with SI is at the spiritual level, dealing with the very 'spirit' of an individual.

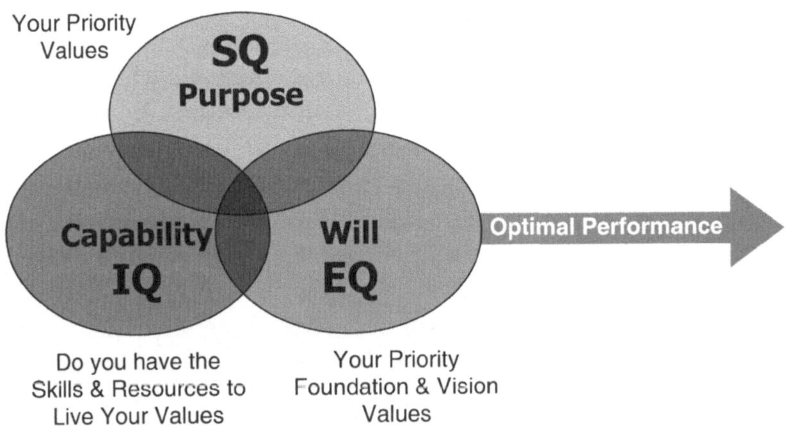

Figure 1: The Three Intelligences
(Adapted from www.souldrama.com)

In an ideal case, these three intelligences should work together by supporting each other. The human brain is designed to coordinate these three—as each one has its own area of strengths, they can function separately too. Human being in general, need not be high or low in IQ, EI & SI simultaneously.

All variations are possible, that is, high IQ & lower EI & SI is possible. One need not have higher IQ to possess higher EI/SI. Ideally, all the three intelligences should be well developed to succeed in life.

Tracing Workplace Spirituality in History

The central value of historical understanding is that it transforms historical givens into historical contingencies. It enables us to see the structures, in which we live, as only one among many other possible experiences.

Through the ages, work has remained a constant feature of human existence, although its nature, content and context have often varied in perspective depending on the prevailing belief system of the day.

For instance, in the classical era (c. 950 bc–550 ad) which was first dominated by ancient Greek and then Roman civilizations, the disciplined pursuit of philosophical knowledge—a withdrawal from an active to a contemplative way of life—was considered a worthwhile endeavour for developing the independent and perfect nature of the gods.

Those who for whatever reasons were compelled to work for others or for a living—such as slaves and wage earners—were held in contempt by the established elites and philosophers of that period who adjudged the time devoted to the philosophical discourse of matters of the state, culture, and governance a far more valuable use of human effort than its application to physical labour.

Though much of the Roman belief system was adopted from Greek civilization, in contrast to the political and intellectual elites', regarded productive labour as a sacred obligation to the gods. Work was tied to honour and societal esteem and considered a path to good or virtuous living.

An important philosophy that further shaped populist perceptions about work in this era was stoicism, which endorsed labour as a virtue to be embraced and emphasized its performance as the fulfilment of both moral and social responsibilities that were required for leading a virtuous life.

Moreover, manual work which contributed to the common good was valued in ancient Roman society, receiving recognition through the agency of the guilds. The guilds were influential associations set up in ancient Roman cities that enabled the development of the handicraft tradition through the practice, supervision, and control of craftwork.

These associations regulated and ensured high standards of quality craftsmanship were attained and maintained, thereby bringing respect to and Roman the practice of manual crafts in general. In this manner, productive labour industry extended from cities to the conquered people living in the diverse territories spread across the vast Roman Empire.

Spiritual Awareness in the Workplace

Homo *Spiritualis* is not characterized by maximizing profit but by an awareness of others and a focus on human flourishing. This understanding is what gives life meaning and purpose, as opposed to materialistic goals alone (Bouckaert 2011).[5] The bottom line is important but not at the expense of the society and the common good.

Spirituality brings another dimension to organizations, a dimension that focuses on human flourishing, that develops character and virtues over culture and values, and that encourages choices that transcend organizational self-interest to ensure the long-term flourishing of all.

Spirituality is often considered as an important driver of the overall well-being of an individual. Given the significance of spirituality in one's life, organizations are increasingly making efforts to ensure that employees use spirituality to engage themselves physically, emotionally, and cognitively in their work.

An effort has been made here to understand the relationship between spirituality and engagement at work and to reflect on its importance to management. Employee engagement is increasingly becoming a top business priority for many organizations because of its positive consequences for employees and employers.

Engaged employees volunteer to engross themselves cognitively, emotionally, and physically in their work. Spirituality within the workplace and employee engagement are constructs that relate to individual emotions & spirituality and there is evidence that the two are related.

On the Right Path to SQ

To begin any process, an in-depth assessment is necessary. One needs to ask themselves where they stand, where they want to go and the gap between the two. The answers to this question will eventually determine the path one will ultimately take.

India Inc has taken significant efforts towards implementing SQ in the workplace. The Future Group—owners of brands like Big Bazaar and Pantaloons—has an in-house chief belief officer.

Individual consultants are set up at the organization as Chief Spiritual Officers. Their role is to understand the zeitgeist of the organization and make sure that everyone (especially the C-Suite) is being driven towards the same goals.

Developing Spiritual Intelligence

Zohar and Marshall have recommended seven practical steps towards developing a better SQ:

1. Become aware of where one is right now. This can be personally, emotionally, or professionally.
2. Develop a goal as to what one wants to see themselves becoming.
3. Start exploring your deepest wants and motivations.
4. Discover and dissolve obstacles.
5. Examine different paths to reach your goal.
6. Commit to a fixed path.
7. Remind yourself that even though the fixed path may fail, there are other paths one can discover.

Models to Foster Spirituality in the Workplace

The research by Mitroff and Denton (1999)[6] titled 'A Spiritual Audit of Corporate America', is highly referenced, not only for its valuable statistical and interview findings but also for its categorization of five different models of spirituality in the workplace.

They are summarized briefly here:

1. *The Religion-based Organization:* This is a workplace spirituality model that is based on Evangelical Christian beliefs such as:

   The word of God is the ultimate business text.

   Satan is the major competitor.

   Prayer is the ultimate communication channel.

   This is an extreme model and has helped to create resistance in other organizations who might want to implement workplace spirituality.
2. *The Evolutionary Organization:* This model is based on organizations, such as youth gatherings, that began as religion-based organizations and has evolved to be more ecumenical. These organizations are still committed to founding spiritual principles while maintaining an openness to change in a pluralistic environment. Religion-based hospitals are another good example of evolutionary organizations.

3. *The Recovering Organization:* Some experts are of the belief that spirituality in the workplace involves a step program. For example, such organizations limiting organizational units to 100–150 members, minimizing status differences, limiting coercive pressures, using self-selection in group decision methods and utilizing mentorship extensively.
4. *The Socially Responsible Organization:* This type of organization is designed to illuminate strong social values and to show that they can be practical in the business world. The organization sees itself as having a binding contract with society, which it realizes through its infrastructure. There is a strong belief that good things happen to companies that support sustainability, social justice, healthy living and other positive social values.
5. *The Values-based Organization:* Some organizations employ the family metaphor for values-based organization, envisioning them as a healthy, extended and caring family. Many of these organizations explicitly operate using the golden rule as a guiding value and are comfortable using words like love and virtue. There is a shared belief that ethical employees working for an ethical company will outperform unethical workers in an unethical company.

The values-based organization is not connected with specific religion or even necessarily with spirituality, but the organization is guided by broad philosophical principles or ideals.

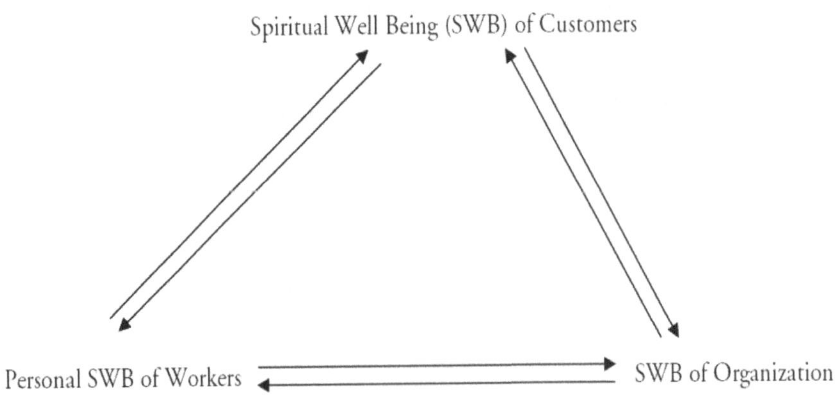

The above diagram visually represents a way of understanding spirituality in a work setting and how everything is interconnected. The spiritual well-being of customers side of the diagram is demonstrated by ways that employees of an organization try to honor customers life experiences and help them create meaning in their lives. The personal spiritual well-being side of the diagram demonstrates the approaches employees use to find meaning, purpose, balance, and completion in their own lives and the manners in which each person's gifts are utilized. The spiritual well-being of the organization side of the diagram demonstrates the how the values and beliefs of an organization support a sense of spiritual well being in individuals and groups of people. It also demonstrates how much feeling of community is present and how clear and meaningful the organizational mission is. It demonstrates how much the organization encourages people to utilize their unique gifts and take risks and how safe employees feel to do that (Craigie. 1999).

Mitroff and Denton also offer a "best practices" model "that guides a leader through deciding which of these models the best fit for his or her organization is. They recommend a hybrid model that is primarily based on the values-based organization and which incorporates the best of the religion-based organization.

Table 2: Models of Spiritual Workplaces

Spiritual Workplace Model	*Key Focus*
Claiming Our Gifts	Understanding one's unique gifts and living them in the workplace.
The Four Aspirations	Supporting the hopes and expectations that employees bring to work: 1. They want to be involved in activity and leadership. 2. People want to find meaning and purpose in what they do. 3. People want to use all of their energies, to use their whole life in their work. 4. They have a need to be seen as individuals, and they want to be involved in the community.
Employee—Employer Dynamics	1. Who or what do I serve? 2. In what ways can I use my gifts as I serve? 3. How can I be of more service? 4. Am I able to be of service without thought of personal gain? (The last model is most accepted in the corporate world).

Spiritual Workplace Model	*Key Focus*
Spiritual Leadership	A causal model that demonstrates the relationship between: 1. Spiritual leadership values, attitudes and behaviours. 2. Follower needs for spiritual survival. 3. Organizational outcomes (most referenced model in academia).
Corporate Spiritual Therapists	The goal is to restore beneficial power that is harmful. Practices include journeying, centering and healthy rituals. Integrity is a core value.
Edge-walking	Five qualities and five skills necessary for integrating spirituality in the workplace: *Qualities:* Self-awareness, passion, vision, integrity and playfulness. *Skills:* Knowing the future, risk taking, manifesting, focusing and connecting.
Universal Spirituality in the Workplace	Expressing truths that go across cultures and traditions.
Self-managing Systems	Systems thinking and chaos theory. Trusting the evolvement of spirituality in the workplace.
Spiritual Intelligence	It builds on models of emotional intelligence. There are four quadrants in it: 1. Self/Self-awareness 2. Universal Awareness 3. Self/Self-mastery 4. Social Mastery/Spirituality in the Workplace

Key Elements

Workplace spirituality has continued to gain acceptance as a topic of study in business schools across the country, presumably with application to practice within organizations. Though initially the topic of spirituality in the workplace may have been viewed as a passing fad, it now seems to have reached trend status.

Management textbooks routinely include sections about "workplace spirituality", and professional organizations such as the Academy of Management offer membership in special interest groups emphasizing spirituality.

Spiritual intelligence is an ability to access higher meanings, values, abiding purposes, unconscious aspects of the self and to embed these meanings, values and purposes in living a richer and more creative life. Signs of high spiritual quotient include ability to think out of the box, humility and an access to energies that come from something beyond the ego, beyond just me and my day-to-day concerns. SQ is the ultimate intelligence of the visionary leader.

According to Danah Zohar, spiritually intelligent leadership can be fostered by applying the following principles:

1. *Self Awareness:* Knowing what I believe in and value, and what deeply motivated me.
2. *Spontaneity:* Living in and being responsive to the moment.
3. *Being Vision-and-Value-Led:* Acting from principles and deep beliefs, and living accordingly.
4. *Holism:* Seeing larger patterns, relationships and connections having a sense of belonging.
5. *Compassion:* Having the quality of 'feeling-with' and deep empathy.
6. *Celebration of Diversity:* Valuing other people for their differences despite them.
7. *Field Independence:* Standing against the crowd and having one's own convictions.
8. *Humility:* Having the sense of being a player in a larger drama, of one's true place in the world.

Table 3: Elements of Workplace Spirituality

Needs	*Author(s)*	*Views*
Self-Discovery	Illes and Zsolnai (2015)	Self-discovery or getting to know their self is a crucial part of the development of business professionals.
Individual Development	Khasawneh (2011)	Individual spiritual development induces a change in behaviour of employees, and thus, results in a change in functions of the organization.
Trust	Rahman, Osmanganj, Daud, Chowdhury and Hassan (2015)	There is an overall knowledge-sharing exchange increase among the members of an organization due to trust.

Needs	*Author(s)*	*Views*
Sense of Purpose	Mitroff and Denton (1999)	Sense of purpose was manifested integrally by the notion of a higher power.
Stress Reduction	Daniel (2015)	Low levels of work stress are felt by employees working in organization with high levels of spirituality in their work environments.
Inner Life	Ashmos and Duchon (2000)	Inner life is about assimilating one's power and using it to live a more satisfying life.
	Rego, Cunha and Souto (2007)	There is nourishment of inner life by meaningful work.
	Albuqueque, Cunha, Martins and Sá (2014)	Inner life means that employees have spiritual needs at work besides cognitive, emotional and physical needs.
Meaningful Work	Ashmos and Duchon (2000)	Meaningful work is about connection between soul and work.
	Rego *et al.* (2007)	Meaningful work dimensions explain self-esteem, job involvement, intrinsic work satisfaction and affective commitment.
	Albuqueque *et al.* (2014)	This dimension assumes work is valued by the employees for reasons beyond their remuneration.
Sense of Community	Ashmos and Duchon	Living in connection to other human beings is part of being alive.
	Albuqueque *et al.* (2014)	Feeling of belongingness to a community is part of what increases the spirituality at work.
Alignment with Organizational Values	Rego *et al.* (2007)	Value alignment dimension explains intention to quit and commitment.
Sense of Contribution to Society	Rego *et al.* (2007)	The sense of endowment to the community is similar to the meaningful work.

9. *Tendency to Ask the Fundamental "Why?" Questions:* Needing to understand things and get to the bottom of them.
10. *Positive Use of Adversity:* Learning and growing from mistakes, setbacks and suffering.
11. *Sense of Vocation:* Feeling called upon to serve, to give something back.

Throughout the 20th century, life in the West became compartmentalized. People started thinking about work, personal and spiritual life as separate "modules" of how they spend their time. We started losing sight of how all those modules penetrate one another.

Workplace spirituality is one manifestation of integrating all aspects of life back into the whole. As we grow as a society, more and more people look for the spiritual dimension of their jobs. Many organizations stop looking at work as something we just get done and forget about. They recognize that what we work on shapes us in more ways than we are aware of.

Humans are spiritual beings and spirituality is a shared human quality that manifests as the yearning we all have to experience life deeply, be present, and feel that we are a part something bigger than ourselves. Work can be a great opportunity to satisfy that yearning.

Spiritual experience is something most people just know. But that knowing often slips away when we try to turn it into a mental understanding. Although definitions differ, one element seems to come up more often than others. This element is the transcendence of self.

Workplace spirituality is a framework or a part of organizational culture that enables exactly that. It creates conditions in which employees and leaders can feel themselves to be a part of something bigger—and, something that matters.

The most straightforward way to this experience of transcendence is through the overall mission of an organization. But, there are also other ways. One of them is through the relationships and interactions that happen in the workplace.

On the other hand, workplace spirituality can also manifest through the responsible behaviours of the employees, such as:

- Active listening.
- Assertively stating one's opinions.
- Drawing healthy boundaries.
- Showing respect for others.
- Responding to conflict and challenges with empathy and compassion.

At the core, workplace spirituality is about a major shift in the organizational culture and values. After decades of shaping organizations around competition, hierarchy, sales targets and profits, many companies are realizing that these are not always the best way forward.

It's often more beneficial for organizations today to embrace values revolving around collaboration, creativity and compassion. This is sometimes described as shaping the workplace from the "inside out". The primary focus of spiritual leadership is on the wellbeing of employees and teams. The management trusts that, with such an approach, the health and efficiency of the organization will naturally follow.

Spirituality in the workplace requires a holistic approach to work and other areas of life. It recognizes that what happens outside of work influences the state of the organization—and vice versa. Such a perspective brings many benefits to the employees and the workplace as a whole.

Although definitions of the 'spiritual' may vary, there is a general consensus amongst writers on what this looks like when applied to organizations and also to leadership. Some of the major elements that are common to most are an emphasis on:

1. Vision and values
2. Service and love for others
3. Empowering others
4. Courage to overcome fears
5. Changing from within
6. The role of a supernatural spirit.

Need for Spiritual Intelligence in the Workplace

Spiritual Quotient makes an individual more responsible and aware of the problems in the society, surroundings, workplace, country and the larger universe too. It makes one humble and to a great extent reduces selfish intentions.

With this intelligence one is thwarted from getting swayed by power, status and money. Instead, it helps build a holistic approach towards the organization where an employee benefits in more ways than one.

Spiritually intelligent employees reduce the burden on the management to intervene and discipline. A spiritually intelligent employee benefits not only by managing his emotions but also by managing work in the most stable approach ensuring self- motivation.

If organizations can help employees tap in their spiritual quotient, then it helps in building a long lasting and a proactive employee-employer relationship, and in turn, enhances the overall employee wellness in the organization.

In a syllabus for a course called 'Spirituality in the Workplace', offered at Woodbury University, Dr. Dhiman (2000)[7] delineates the differences between spirituality and religion. Religion is outward, focused on rites and rituals, while spirituality is focused inward and is non-dogmatic, non-exclusive, gender-neutral and non-patriarchal.

He describes spirituality as "the awareness of the Divine Ground/ Principle of our being as characterized by our effort to live in harmony with the Divine Principle." Spirituality in the workplace attempts to connect to the divine principle through the setting of a workplace and through the process of work, he adds further.

Spirituality in a work setting must be differentiated from an emphasis on job satisfaction. Many qualities and values contribute to both such as open communication, honesty, integrity, and respect.

However, spirituality is distinctive, and it goes further than the above qualities. It is concerned with unity, coherence, and balance in both the individual and organizational life. It acknowledges the sacredness and connectedness to a divine source and to communities of people.

Scholars also echo the importance of differentiating a spiritual workplace from a participative management philosophy. On the surface, the two are similar. Skills and abilities of employees are respected and valued. The manager takes on more of a coaching or mentoring role rather than the authoritative role. Employees are seen as worthy of trust and responsible.

In many corporate settings, work has ceased to be merely a function allowing people to make money, but has evolved, and working people also expect work to fulfil deeper, less tangible needs.

Of course, people have always wanted to 'enjoy' their jobs but enjoyment was considered a bonus rather than a requirement. However, job satisfaction today comprises having feeling in one's work and being connected to a greater purpose.

Organizations have always had a spiritual side simply because they are made up of human beings. In the past, this spiritual side had been kept a secret, denied or suppressed or most likely ignored.

The past thirty years has seen an interest in organizational development that has paralleled an interest in the connection spirituality has to work, and now many organizations are deliberate and reflective in integrating spirituality with work (Skelley, 1996) and (Biberman & Whitty, 1999).[8]

Besides several other factors, organizational structure has changed, which has contributed extensively to the rise in the sprit/work philosophy. Middle management positions have nearly disappeared due to advances in information technology, greater participation of employees and less need for direct supervision to produce quality goods and services.

Spiritual Intelligence Must be Encouraged

Today's workplace is a battle zone with constant fights for market share, visibility, revenues, profitability and talent. As in any war, in the office too, it is the people who invariably get impacted. Pressure to perform amidst workplace and environment challenges affects employee wellness, morale and engagement.

Furthermore, this can potentially lead to stress, dissatisfaction and ill-health. The question remains as to how we can help reduce the drastic effects caused by the modern day work scenario.

We combat these problems by nurturing awareness arising from the spiritual self, promoting flexibility, resilience, hope and power of endurance to break ingrained patterns of behaviour that sap our energy.

Even though external gratification and motivators act as hindrances to a large extent, the inner change of thought process can assure that there is stability ensuring overall employee wellness, propelling them to perform and contribute despite the changing times and expectations.

On an individual level, people are creating workplaces that better serve their spiritual needs. Human beings have a fundamental need for both connection and contribution, and these needs are being met less and less in their personal and family lives. Consequently, people are looking for meaning in their work and professional lives.

In a national survey in 1994, respondents stated that they were searching for practices and values in the work setting that were supportive and open. Their current situation reflected a style of management that was based on financial incentives, fear and punishment.

Respondents sought a work situation where management utilized motivation techniques that were based on the encouragement of creativity, caring, personal satisfaction and personal growth in all areas.

Judi Neal, in her article "Work as a Service to the Divine" interviewed 40 people on a formal basis and over 700 people informally on spirituality in the workplace. The outcome was that work as a spiritual path emphasizes service to others as a path to service to the divine. She found four practices that were common to people who had integrated spirituality into every aspect of their lives being in nature, meditation, journaling and reading spiritual literature.

As a result of 100 in-depth interviews with senior managers and executives on work and its meaning, Mitroff and Denton (1999, page 85)[9] were able to articulate and rank the factors that give people meaning at work:

- The ability to realize my full potential as a person.
- Being associated with a good or ethical organization.
- Interesting work.
- Making money.
- Having good colleagues and serving humankind.
- Service to future generations.
- Service to my immediate community.

Inviting Spirituality into the Workplace

While there are so many benefits of workplace spirituality, the question of how to encourage it is a tough one. Ultimately, this is about a change in culture. How can one person take on such a massive task?

Spiritual life—at work or elsewhere—is not determined by what you manage to accomplish. Rather, it is fostered by your internal attitudes and interpretations of the events that are already happening around you.

This means you can introduce spirituality into your organization, no matter whether you are in a leadership or junior position. You can do so by bringing certain qualities into how you show up when talking to your colleagues at the water cooler, handling meetings, or even replying to emails.

Here are some ideas for how you may implement this in practice:

1. To recognize that everyone has their inner life:

   Practice Self-Awareness: This is the fundamental part to understand others. Being more conscious of your inner life is where you start to appreciate how much is happening in the human mind, body and soul at any given moment.

   Put Yourself in Other People's Shoes: If you don't understand why a team member makes certain decisions or acts the way they do, first assume their innocence. Then ask yourself: What are the possible reasons behind their actions?

Acknowledge Conflict Instead of Running Away from it: Conflict, if approached right, can be an opportunity to deepen bonds within the team. Don't treat it as a threat, but a temporary disturbance. Conflict allows you to get to know others ever more deeply.

2. To create opportunities for meaningful work:

   Share Opportunities for Personal and Professional Growth: If you are a leader, this may mean organizing helpful workshops for your employees. If you are a junior, you can share learning experiences from outside of work with your colleagues to inspire them.

   Do Not be Afraid to do Things Differently: When people get stuck in their work patterns, this kills their creativity and sense of fulfilment. Sometimes, all it takes to revive enthusiasm towards work is to do an old task in a new way.

   Take Breaks and Encourage Others to do the Same: Intentional, well-paced breaks are opportunities to consolidate knowledge and find meaning. They also help you stay more relaxed, even during a hectic day at work.

3. To reinforce the community context in everything you do:

   Ask for Help when You Need It: Your seniors and colleagues will feel that you trust them and value their opinions. Additionally, you will create the experience of solving problems together, which always strengthens the community.

   Give Spontaneous Positive Feedback to Others: All too often, we only give negative feedback and take good work for granted. Acknowledging it out loud will give your team a boost.

   Create a Context for Sharing: This is not necessarily about official meetings, but making space for others to express themselves. You can do that in a coffee break or organize a zoom call just to check how everyone is doing. Do not expect particular outcomes out of this—the point is for everyone to share their experience freely.

Spiritual Intelligence at Work

Spirituality is "the propensity to make meaning through a sense of relatedness to dimensions that transcend the self in such a way that empowers and does not devalue the individual" (Reed 1992).[10] In the context of occupations, it is a sense of wholeness, connectedness at work and deeper values.

According to Karakas (2010),[11] there exist 70 different definitions of workplace spirituality. Yet, there is no single popular definition primarily because of the complexity and the diversity this term has.

Some definitions such as the one that states 'workplace spirituality is our inner consciousness' and 'that it is a specific type of feeling that energizes action at work' are used commonly. However, the concept of workplace spirituality has continued to develop and evolve over the years.

Scholars explicate that the terms spirituality and spiritual intelligence have no connection and have nothing to do with religion or belief systems. With spiritual intelligence happening at the workplace, the environment will be more favourable. A better working atmosphere relates to a higher level of output.

Researchers have been trying to emphasize on the significance of spiritual intelligence, the commitment to righteousness and ultimate wisdom at the workplace.

They are also attempting to show how by developing one's spiritual intelligence, one can develop skills such as intra-personal & inter-personal relations, problem solving, goal attainment, motivation, commitment, responsibility, self-awareness, team spirit, stress management, time management, leadership and transformation necessary for workplace success.

By providing some suggestions on how to develop spiritual intelligence, the author concludes that spiritual intelligence need not be an inborn trait but can be developed, which results in making life and work more meaningful and enjoyable.

This society is undergoing a paradigm shift that affects the manner in which human beings perceive the world, their work and leadership in contrast to the modern paradigm of work (also called the machine era paradigm) with the spiritual paradigm.

The modern paradigm is characterized by rigid attitudes and beliefs about other people and practices in the organization, establishment of specific rules and procedures, a resistance to change, a tendency to rely only on logic and reason and to scorn intuition and any display of emotion, a scarcity belief, the use of win-lose methods in conflict, the use of power and political manoeuvres to maintain a power base, and a difficulty in delegation of power.

Organizations that are based in the modern paradigm utilize more inflexible bureaucratic structures and a top-down chain of command.

Communication is through formal channels & formal policy and via the procedure manuals.

The spiritual paradigm is characterized by openness to change, employees and managers having a sense of purpose and meaning, an appreciation of being connected to the organization as whole, individuals who are able to express spirituality, an abundance mentality, a greater likelihood to trust others, a valuing of intuition and emotion in decision making and the use of win-win methods in conflict.

Organizations based in a spiritual paradigm are generally flatter in structure and there is a greater cooperation and collaboration between individual units of the organization.

Traditional organizations place emphasis on form and function, organizations operating under this new paradigm place emphasis on energy and flow (a state induced by being involved in challenging and intrinsically motivating tasks). They also focus on creating a shared vision that works to inspire employees, and they recognize the part that both positive and negative emotions play in alignment of worker values with organizational values.

In the past, organized religion has provided individuals with community & traditions, myths, rituals and beliefs, and religious bodies have been and are effective vehicles for the spiritual side of human lives.

Of course, organized religion can't directly impact modern organizations due to the diversity of modern workforces. No one religion is appropriate to promote in a work setting instead organization need to uncover nonreligious ways to support and encourage a spiritual dimension of the workplace.

It is important to recognize that developing spirituality in a work setting is more about bringing out a quality that is already present and not about teaching something that is not there. Workers can be allowed and encouraged to talk about spiritual issues—this is the way to bring spirituality to work.

Some scholars describe a work setting that relies on participation and consensus, and many of their suggestions for attaining a true consensus process are derived from work that has been done within the Native American communities. Native American people traditionally have valued a comprehensive view of the world that incorporates the spiritual dimension of life in everyday life.

As the global economy continues to grow, a manager must be sensitive to differences, including differences regarding organizational change. All such activities are entirely voluntary for employees and no one religious doctrine is advocated.

Some specific examples of workplace spirituality are:

- The Container Store motto that states, "Workers are morally obligated to treat customers as they would themselves".
- The Children's Hospital Medical Centre in Cincinnati utilizes team building exercises and meditation in order to improve the level of inclusiveness at work and has held spiritual retreats for staff.
- Avaya (a computer software company) has a designated room set aside for meditation and prayer and has implemented a luncheon series on 'Bringing Forth the Soul in Workplace'.
- Ramunni, Bushka and Sinnamon CPAS pray during consultations with clients.
- KeySpan hired a former priest as the human resources director.

When initiatives focusing on spirituality are brought into the workplace, it is important to question the intent of the programs and whose interests are being served. HRD programs should never exploit workers, spiritual lives or manipulate workers with programs designed to appeal to their need for meaning.

An organization's consistency with espoused deals is one benchmark that determines if promoting spirituality in the workplace is intended to truly benefit the employee as the primary motivation.

Some practices that would indicate such consistency are "flexible hours and job-sharing opportunities", support for employees volunteer work outside the company child and elder care support, compassionate response to worker stress, gender and ethnic inclusivity practices, exercise of social responsibility in the wider community, and clear evidence that the company questions and practices a consistent and thoughtful system of ethics in all areas of its corporate activity, including acceptable boundaries of HRD practice" (Fenwick & Lange).[12]

The spiritual workplace is characterized by various traits such as a revival of the spirit of community in work, shared power and co-management with spirituality as the common foundation, greater value for diversity, global stewardship, service-learning atmosphere, a recognition that human beings have a basic need for "relevance recognition meaning and self transcendence (Biberman J.A. & Whitty M.)."[13]

Spirituality is becoming part of mainstream organisational theory and practice. It's no longer viewed as the preserve of a new age or fundamentalist fringe. In the last five years management journals conferences academic syllabi and popular writers have increasingly focused on the spiritual dimension to organisations and change.

A number of top companies are making explicit attempts to integrate a more spiritual approach in their management practices. Yet in the practice of and writing about NGO capacity building the spiritual dimension is conspicuous by its absence despite the importance of faith-based organizations in development work.

One must remember that the subject of spirituality is a personal, sensitive and flammable. Some attempts to bring spiritual perspectives into organization and management have been reckless, exclusive and even damaging. But the importance of the subject makes it imperative to grow in our understanding and ability to discuss the spiritual more explicitly.

Spirituality, after all, is clearly not the monopoly of any one religion and is informed by a wide variety of faiths. Although the spiritual is very personal, it docs not necessarily follow that it must also remain private.

In any discussion of spirituality and organisation (such as being attempted here), a difference of opinion and interpretation is guaranteed, but these very differences may uncover new understanding about our work and enable us to find ways to make our practice of capacity building more effective.

Table 4: Concept and Meaning of Spirituality in the Workplace

Concept	*Meaning*
Helping personally	To a larger purpose
Helping professionally	Sense of community
Getting to know me	Through breaking bread
Caring what I think and feel	To the organization
Saying "Thank You"	With leaders
Speaking to people	With colleagues/peers Throughout the organization To one's team Through fun
Fair and legal staffing	Formal
Fair professional development	Downward
Fair compensation	Upward
Fair promotion practices	Informal

Concept	*Meaning*
Fair policies and norms	One-on-one
Fair treatment	Transparency
Fair work life balance	Career development Mode of communication Feedback "Safe space" for communication Multilingual
Trust in the organization's strategy	Expecting inclusion
Trust in human resources	Initiating inclusion
Trust in organizational processes	"They told me son"
Being trusted by leaders	Being flexible
Trusting leaders	Self-control
Trust in one's colleagues/peers	Double effort, half the recognition Persistence in proving oneself Checking out (avoiding) Impression management Affinity groups Leaning towards inclusion
Having a mentor or a coach	Recognition/acknowledgement among peers
Needing mentoring	Reinforcing fairness and meritocracy
Actively engaged mentors	Conquering a challenge
Diverse set of mentors	Celebrating performance with others
Formal mentoring programs	Intrinsic enjoyment of reward
Informal mentors	Public recognition and award
Gaining exposure/Getting exposure	Feeling appreciated for hard work
Skill development	Being promoted
Career development	Internal visibility
Being a mentor or coach	External visibility

Source: Bell, E. (2008) Towards a Critical Spirituality of Organization. Cult Organ 14(3): 604–703.

Spiritual Practices in the Corporate Sector

There are many ways in which an organization can consider integrating workplace spirituality. It is most helpful to categorize workplace spirituality practices based on level of analysis, which are known as the "Four Gateways to Spirituality at Work."

These are:

1. Creating personal transformation and individual practices.
2. Developing enlightened leaders and teams.
3. Creating organizational transformation and systemic practices.
4. Joining the global consciousness shift.

Table 5: Seven Levels of Corporate Consciousness

Human Energy System	*Level of Consciousness*
Spiritual	Service
Spiritual	Making a Difference
Spiritual	Internal Cohesion
Mental	Transformation
Emotional	Self-Esteem
Emotional	Relationships
Physical	Survival

Several large organizations including Google have implemented a mindfulness program that is very well-accepted. In 2007, one of Google's original software engineers, Chade-Meng Tan, created a program called 'Search Inside Yourself' that has become a model for other companies such as SAS.

The program incorporates three elements:

Training your attention

Developing self-knowledge & self-mastery, and

Creating useful mental habits.

As a result of this program, Tan was appointed Google's Jolly Good Fellow, and his charter was to "Enlighten Minds, Open Hearts, Create World Peace". The company provides meditation rooms and yoga classes. While the focus is primarily on stress reduction, there is also an emphasis on self-awareness, which Google believes supports greater creativity, and a better working environment.

Table 6: Empirical Research in Workplace Spirituality

Study	*Instrument Used*	*Sample and Method*	*Major Findings*
Milliman *et al.* (2003)	Adapted from Ashmos and Duchon (2000)	Cross-sectional survey. Final sampling consisting of 200 part-time MBA students from a business school in southwest United States (response rate, 88.11%). Structural Equation Modelling (SEM) analysis conducted.	Workplace spirituality has a significant predictive effect on individual experiences of organizational commitment, intention to quit, intrinsic work satisfaction, job involvement and organization-based self-esteem.
Duchon and Plowman (2005)	Ashmos and Duchon (2000)	Sample taken from six work units of a large hospital network in southwest United States. Non-parametric measures (Mann-Whitney Test) used due to small sample size of the work units.	Workplace spirituality predicts work performance at the unit level.
Kolodinsky *et al.* (2008)	Wheat (1991)	Five studies comprising students enrolled for Masters in Business Administration program	Organizational spirituality significantly predicted positive associations with job involvement, organizational identity and reward satisfaction. Similarly predicted a significant and negative relationship with organizational frustration.

Study	*Instrument Used*	*Sample and Method*	*Major Findings*
Rego and Pina e Cunha (2008)	Ashmos and Duchon (2000)/Milliman *et al.* (2003)	Study designed in Portuguese for 361 individuals from 154 organizations. Correlations, regressions and cluster analysis conducted.	The five dimensions of workplace spirituality used in the study predicted higher affective and normative commitment and lower continuance commitment.
Pandey *et al.* (2009)	Designed for the study	Employees in 28 branches of an Indian sector bank responded to questions about the spiritual climate of their workplace. 462 customers drawn from the same 28 branches responded to assessments of their service experience in the bank. Correlation and regression analysis conducted on the average scores obtained for each construct.	Spiritual climate positively related to customers' experience of employees' service.
Pawar (2009)	Adapted from Ashmos and Duchon (2000)	156 out of the 171 working employees attending programs at an educational institute in India provided valid responses (response rate, 91.23%). Hierarchical multiple regression analysis conducted.	Workplace spirituality has significant predictive effect on job satisfaction, job involvement and organizational commitment.

Study	*Instrument Used*	*Sample and Method*	*Major Findings*
Petchsawang and Duchon (2012)	Petchsawang and Duchon (2009)	Two-part study conducted in a large food and baking company in Thailand. Study I involved the random administration of a survey to 250 employees of the company to establish a relationship between meditation practice and a measure of workplace spirituality. Study II was a quasi—experimental study consisting of 60 participants from the same company. Participants in the experimental group completed workplace spirituality questionnaires at three points in time: before, during and after the meditation training. Participants in the control group completed workplace spirituality questionnaires at two points in time only: before and after the meditation training. Work performance measured on the basis of the company's standard evaluation procedures. Correlation and multiple regression analysis also conducted.	Significant positive relationship between workplace spirituality and work performance.

Study	*Instrument Used*	*Sample and Method*	*Major Findings*
Chen and Sheng (2013)	Designed for the study	Two sets of questionnaires administered to financial/accounting personnel and the supervisors at each economic schedule. Questionnaires distributed to a total of 902 companies, 265 companies responded (response rate, 29.38%). Furthermore, 338 valid questionnaires received from supervisors, 650 financial/accounting personnel equally completed the questionnaire. Multi-level analysis conducted.	Workplace spirituality negatively related to motives to unethically adjust/manage earnings.
Gupta *et al.* (2014)	Adapted mainly from Ashmos and Duchon (2000)/Milliman *et al.* (2003)	Cross-sectional study. Sample drawn from 100 payroll employees working in private insurance companies in Punjab. Correlation and regression analysis used.	Workplace spirituality has a significant and positive relationship with job satisfaction.
Daniel (2015)	Adapted from Ashmos and Duchon (2000)	A total sample size of 304 individuals drawn from a variety of industries in the United States and Mexico was used in this study. SEM analysis conducted.	A single dimension of the workplace spiritual measure—meaningful work—was found to be negatively and significantly associated with work stress.

Study	*Instrument Used*	*Sample and Method*	*Major Findings*
Gatling *et al.* (2016)	Adapted from Ashmos and Duchon (2000)/Milliman *et al.* (2003)	190 supervisors working in a large hospitality company responded to the request to participate in the survey (response rate, 89.62%). SEM analysis with maximum likelihood estimation method used.	Workplace spirituality had a significant and negative indirect relationship with supervisors' intention to quit, and this relationship was fully mediated by organizational commitment.
Pawar (2016)	Adapted from Ashmos and Duchong (2000)	The data for the study was collected from 123 participants employed in a variety of organizations and attending a post-graduate program at a management institute in India. Regression analysis conducted to assess the relationship between workplace spirituality and the four well-being types investigated in the study.	Workplace spirituality had a significant and positive relationship with employees' emotional, psychological, social and spiritual well-being.
Zou and Dahling (2017)	Rego and Pina e Cunha (2008)	The data for the two-part study was conducted in southern China and the United States respectively. In China, the data was collected over a span of 1 month comprising 324 frontline service workers. The US sample was recruited online and consisted of 95 participants engaged in various client-facing jobs. Multiple regression analysis was conducted.	Workplace spirituality moderated the negative relationship between surface acting and subjective well-being such that employees reporting high levels of spirituality at work were better protected from the adverse effect of surface acting on subjective well-being relative to employees reporting low levels of spirituality at work.

Genesis and Growth of Workplace Spirituality

Within the last two decades, organizational scholars and practitioners have paid increasing attention to the concept of workplace spirituality, which draws on the notion that people seek to find a sense of meaning and fulfilment in their performance of work.

However, its emergence as a field of interest might also suggest a contemporary approach to an age-old quest of connecting work to a higher purpose, reflecting a trend dating back to antiquity.

We have now reached the stage where people need to know what they should be working for rather than just working. During the last two decades, organizational scholars and practitioners have paid increasing attention to the concept of workplace spirituality, creating opportunities to explore two subjects not typically associated together in contemporary times—the workplace and spirituality.

As an emerging field of interest, workplace spirituality is defined by the search for meaning in the performance of work, crossing over boundaries that hitherto prevented a focus on spirituality in the workplace.

Though the definition of a workplace is fairly straightforward—a setting in which an economic or worthwhile activity takes place—spirituality, on the other hand, is open to diverse views and interpretations.

Spirituality is derived from the Latin root word, *Spiritus* which connotes the vital unseen breath or essence that gives life to all living beings. In its broadest sense, spirituality may be regarded as a process through which the purpose for human existence finds expression in the business of living. It is a thought to encompass a search for meaning, for unity, for connectedness to nature, humanity, and the transcendent.

Current Growth of Workplace Spirituality

Business owners, managers, policy makers, and academic researchers all need to remember, as many surveys indicate, that tens of millions of world citizens are hungry for trans-material, mind-expanding, soul-enriching, and heart-centred (spiritual) values.

The current rise and interest in workplace spirituality also draws its existence from broader social contexts than the deepened understanding of work as a forum for finding and serving God. Ashmos and Duchon (2000)[14] identify five such findings:

1. The massive layoffs and restructurings of the 1990s and the associated demoralizing effect on employees
2. The substitution of the workplace as the primary source of community and connection to other people
3. A growing interest in and acceptance of Eastern philosophies and practices
4. The aging concerns of the baby boomer generation, and
5. The heightened global competitive pressures on organizations.

Setting these trends against an even more complex backdrop of technology-driven change over the years has resulted in organizations and employees struggling to deal with an often hypercompetitive business environment as practically as possible while maintaining an interest in living a meaningful life at work.

Nature of Work as Spiritual Practice

One should work like a master and not like a slave. If working like slaves results in selfishness and attachment, working as masters of our own mind gives rise to the bliss of non-attachment (Swami Vivekananda, 1900).[15]

To work without motive, to work unattached brings the highest bliss and freedom. All thought of obtaining return for the work we do hinders our spiritual progress. In the end it brings misery that comes through attachment and not through work.

Attachment and detachment are key attitudes at work. Attachment to high eternal values and efforts can bring true and long-lasting joy. But attachment to low, transient values, leads to sorrow in the event of failure and pleasure in the event of success.

But the success is short-lived and soon yields to the failure and its trail of sorrow. The secret of success lies in attachment to eternal values, detachment in respect of transient ones. The teaching of detachment has to be understood. Thus, life must be joyful and not be an existence bereft of bliss.

Work by itself is neither high nor low. But the preferences of the ego evaluate all work according to its whims. All work, whether pleasant or unpleasant, should be performed in the sense of duty. The sense of duty teaches us to disregard the false values which ego has attached to life and work.

This negation of ego and its values is also the transcendence of ego itself. It helps to attain freedom from limited vision or universality of attitude and detachment. It is the level headed man, the calm man of good judgment and cool nerves, of great sympathy and love who does good work and so does good to himself (Swami Vivekananda, 1900).[16]

Means are as important as ends in all that we do. Our failures are often due to our ends being beyond our means. If we paid careful attention to means, the results will flow automatically. Means and ends are related to each other as cause and effect.

The central lesson from Swami Vivekananda then is: "Let us perfect the means, and the end will take care of us for the world can be good and pure only if our lives are good and pure. It is an effect and we are the means. Therefore, let us purify ourselves and let us make ourselves perfect."

Spirituality in the Workplace in Recent Times

Work occupies more time than almost any other activity in our lives it allows us to exercise and grow in our major spiritual values found in all spiritual paths just in the course of day to day business decisions and relationships. Therefore, work is one important means to grow towards the experience of union with God.

Spirituality in the workplace can be practiced and fostered in several ways. This will also result in a number of positive outcomes and benefits at both levels—individual and organisational. Today, several organizations in India and abroad incorporate spirituality in the workplace and seek to increase the extent of employee spiritual awareness through the deliberate introduction of spiritual cultural practices.

Within business schools, a number of scholars have incorporated elements of spiritual teaching into the curriculum. They claim to be driven by their own spiritual journey or transformation to deliver highly experiential learning that involves students in meditation, confession, storytelling, dance music and prayer (Delbecq, 2000 and Neal, 1997).[17]

There are several examples of spiritual ethical businesses that enable employees to move beyond the economic imperative for organizing, to see work as a morally superior and worthwhile enterprise.

The examples include Southwest Airlines, whose CEO claims that the company's success is founded on humour, love and soul. Senior managers in so-called socially responsible companies such as Ben and Jerry's and The Body Shop have spoken of the importance of workplace spirituality in a way that suggests it is complementary to their commercially successful ethical business principles. Meditation centres have been set up and religious study groups are held in company time or on company premises.

The Willis Harman Spirit at Work Award honours companies 'for their spiritual policies, programs, or practices that explicitly nurture spirituality in their organisations.' It was inspired by the late visionary futurist Willis Harman. In 2002, two Indian companies—SRFI International Financial Limited, Kolkata and the Times of India, Mumbai—had also figured among the five awardees.

Role of Spirituality in the 21st Century Workplace

The advent of politically charged terms such as diversity, tolerance, and pluralism forces society and its institutions to shed themselves of traditional religious values, systems, and organizations.

Even though religion may still have benefits in the workplace, such as helping to reduce employee burnout, louder voices decry the rigidity and dogma of religion and its ability to influence organizational culture and performance.

Spirituality, on the other hand, although still a somewhat amorphous term, is lauded for its flexibility, intentionality, personality and empathy. While spirituality is centred in the individual's personal belief system and behaviour, and is, therefore more dynamic and experiential rather than static and doctrinal, religion is conceived more in terms of institutionalized sets of rules and dogma.

Benefits to Organizations that Integrate Spirituality

In organizations that foster spirituality, management recognizes that while developing human resources will contribute ultimately to profit, workers are valued and affirmed because that is how the organization operates.

In order to fully understand the idea of spirituality and work, attitude toward employees must be that they are "spiritual beings who are holders of truth, integrity and unique and individual gifts" (Craigie, 1999).[18] Workplaces are reflecting this philosophy more and more.

A Gallup survey conducted in 1998 asked 800 Americans if their spiritual lives had been influenced by their positions. Thirty three percent responded that work was responsible for 'greatly improving' or 'improving' their spirituality.

However, greater profit is a by-product of integrating spirituality into the workplace. Scholars cite a 1994 study of companies that is considered 'visionary', which discovered that organizations that were concerned with core values were ultimately more profitable and enjoyed greater longevity than companies concerned primarily with the bottom line. The companies that were considered successful focused heavily on their contribution to society.

There are claims that other qualities (initiative, responsibility, motivation, commitment and productivity) are also positively affected, and even reduced health insurance costs and a decrease in absenteeism are cited as a by-product.

In addition, more kindness, fairness, democratic principles, and power sharing can be attributed to spirit in the workplace. Employees are empowered, and they thus contribute to the strength of the organization and a renewed competitive energy.

If employees are encouraged to become more conscious of their 'highest' selves and are made aware that the purpose of life and work is both material and spiritual then organizational effectiveness is enhanced (Biberman & Whitty, 1997).[19]

Cultivating spirituality in the workplace benefits everyone involved. It's a win-win situation. The employees, leaders and the organization become enhanced as the values in the workplace shift toward more collaborative and holistic ones.

Although workplace spirituality is a relatively new phenomenon, there are already multiple studies exploring its impact on different aspects of work. Giacalone and Jurkiewicz,[20] the leading experts on the topic, recognize the impact spirituality has on work engagement, satisfaction and productivity:

Employees who view their work as a means to advance spiritually are likely to exert greater effort than those who see it merely as a means to a pay check. Research suggests that employees empowered through policies associated with workplace spirituality are more productive, with the greatest productivity gains seen at the level of unskilled labour.

At the other end of the hierarchy, scholars suggest that leaders who view their work as a means to advance spiritually, at the individual or group level, lead the organization to higher levels of performance.

Apart from those measurable benefits, adding a spiritual dimension to our work has other positive consequences. These are directly felt by individual employees and leaders. Ultimately, they also add to the efficiency and health of whole organizations.

- ***Increased Job Satisfaction:*** A 2016 study found workplace spirituality to be positively correlated with job satisfaction and trust among employees. It's easy to see how this creates a ripple effect and benefits everyone. When any given person finds sense and meaning in their job, all the collective tasks becomes effortless and on-track.

- ***Individual Growth and Fulfilment:*** In spiritual workplaces, there usually is more room for individual expression and diversity of viewpoints. Thanks to that, people know their opinion is valued and become empowered to live and work better. In the long-term, this makes them more committed to their organizations and prevents burnout.
- ***Psychological Safety:*** In a culture where competition is prioritized, people often feel pressured to prove their worth through work-related achievements. This keeps employees on constant edge, never able to relax completely. Conversely, spirituality at work brings out the values of collaboration and understanding, allowing people to feel at ease inside their teams.
- ***Enhanced Creativity:*** Creativity is a natural consequence of psychological safety at work. To be creative means to look for solutions and ideas that were not tested before, and therefore, carry a risk of failure. To explore them, people need to feel that they can afford to make a mistake.

Spirituality in the workplace can bring many benefits that organizations around the world crave. The trick is that these can rarely be imposed from the outside. You cannot force your employees to feel safe or satisfied with their work. These are results of a certain organizational culture—one that's driven by spiritual values of collaboration, trust and understanding.

The question then is: How can one cultivate such a culture in an organization? And the first hint is: The change needs to come from within.

Role of Spirituality in Engaging Employees

Spiritual wellness helps employees find meaning and purpose in life, focus on intrinsic values, experience transcendence and believe in community (Westgate, 1996).[21] Some scholars have argued that employees' spiritual activation is closely related to their physical, cognitive, and emotional functioning.

This attachment leads to greater engagement in the workplace. Workplace spirituality and engagement seem to have a causal relationship, which is primarily based on the spill-over theory. It suggests that satisfaction has a spill-over effect, that is, people with satisfied spiritual life tend to be satisfied in their work life as well (Kolodinsky *et al.*, 2008).[22]

When employees are happy at work, they invest their personal energies fully in their work role. Spirituality at work influences the perceptions of employees about their organization positively. However, it is important that organizations support the cultivation of employees' spiritual well-being to enable them to engage themselves and outperform in the workplace.

This support is majorly in terms of allowing individuals to attain their own spirituality which leads to higher intrinsic motivation, greater organizational commitment and enhanced creativity. All this in turn leads to higher engagement at work.

This means that employees would be more engaged in their work role if organizations allow their employees to express their thoughts and feelings and give room to make use of their full potential. Scholars have extensively reviewed the literature relating to the relationship between workplace spirituality and engagement.

According to Roof's argument, the extent to which employees view their work as interesting is affected by human experience, and spirituality is one of its important components. In other words, spirituality has positive influence on engagement as it makes work engaging in the minds of employees.

It is believed that individuals who score high on spirituality have higher tendency to perceive their work role as significant. Several studies provide empirical evidence of engagement employees displaying positive behaviour at work. Not surprisingly, researchers want to know what drives employees engage themselves in their work.

The need for greater fulfilment in life could be one such motivational factor. It is spirituality that could help employees get the feeling of fulfilment in their life. More studies have provided some evidence that spirituality is positively related to organizational commitment, employee affiliation, growth of values and hope, employee loyalty and emotional psychological contract.

Scholars suggest that like other job attitudes, engagement at work is also beneficial in enhancing strengthening teamwork and emotional loyalty and reducing burnout in presence of spirituality.

Another argument is that spirituality is an inherent dimension of personality, which means that it influences growth and change from within instead of behaviourally influencing outlook, perceptions and coping styles in such a way that they resemble with the mechanisms through which personality traits including locus of control affect work.

Some scholars have argued that spirituality at work may be understood as a basic constituent of motivation required to fulfil higher-order needs as described under Maslow's needs hierarchy theory, Herzberg's two-factor theory and Vroom's ERG theory (Saks 2011).[23]

These needs, if fulfilled, prove to be much more effective compared to fulfilling certain practical requirements. Since engagement at work is characterized by absorption that occurs at the cognitive level, scholars have argued that the spirituality attaches meaning to work that helps employees engage themselves in their work.

A 360 Degree Well-being Approach for Employees

Corona virus is yet another hurdle disrupting the lives of employee wellness and happiness. This disruption, coupled with the threat of contracting this potentially deadly virus is causing people to experience anxiety, stress and uncertainty.

This pandemic is one of the biggest menaces the world has had to face, which has given rise to employee grievance all over the world. Similarly, changing work patterns have put pressure on organizations to pay attention to employee wellness like never before.

Studies have shown that COVID-19 has resulted in a spurt in employee misery. Even though organizations are making all-out efforts to keep the employees motivated remotely, a void that is not being filled to the brim is evident.

An employee benefits from Spiritual Quotient by enabling themselves to be motivated and stay strong despite the changing times. A strong spiritually minded person will not only be able to stay grounded and work but also incorporate stability and will power in their lives.

If organizations today develop mechanisms to instil spiritual intelligence in their workforce, then it is certain that the employees will not only be strengthened to beat the current pandemic but also meet any adversity in the days to come.

Importance of a Spiritually Intelligent Manager

Management is an integral part of both current and future organizations. A managers' intelligence is a pivotal competency that contributes to organizational success. Spiritual quotient is a type of intelligence that enables managers to make strategic decisions in the current complicated business world.

The concept of the spiritual quotient of managers presents a new aspect contributing to organizational and employee benefits, inspiring the two to work seamlessly and achieve success and dignity.

A spiritually intelligent manager derives performance by understanding, supporting and helping the employee tap into their inner strengths. They motivate and inspire employees to be the best version of themselves, keeping them ever aligned to the goals of the organization while focussing on employee wellness.

It is important now more than ever, in the current scenario of changing paradigms in expectations and competition, as there is undue pressure among the employees in a workplace.

A manager with the perfect amount of SQ will be able to guide the employees, though all the ups and downs will help sail through the most difficult of times, as we are currently in. They bring the best out of people, leading to a better workplace, in turn reducing micro-management and creating an environment where humanistic values are uplifted and given importance.

The fact cannot be denied that a manager must have the right blend of emotional and spiritual intelligence to garner to the changing needs and also adhere to the norms of the organization by aligning the employees' personal mission and vision to that of the organization.

Managers do not see themselves as bosses as much as they see themselves as 'team leaders'. They are attuned to seeing themselves as servant leaders, and desire to perform meaningful work while facilitating meaningful work for employees (Lee & Zemke, 1993).[24]

Leadership and its Spiritual Aspect in Organizations

Leadership is often the key to the success or failure of organizations in all contexts whether business, religious groups, the military, academic institutions, etc. Leadership is referred to as 'the critical difference' in a literature review cited by Bhindi and Duignan (1997).[25]

Leaders have the ability to foster spirituality in a work setting. Some of the ways that they can accomplish this are by:

- Defining the organizational purpose and making it come alive—Helping employees participate in the purpose.
- Developing consensus around a vision for the organization.
- Inspiring, rather than compelling employees to work for the vision.
- Bringing out the gifts of employees.

- Providing employees with the support that they need (tangible, emotional or spiritual) so that they may make creative contributions.
- Acting as a servant leader in the manner of the historical religious figures (Christ, the prophets, the saints, the Buddha, Gandhi, Mother Teresa, and the Dalai Lama).
- Being willing to pursue their own spiritual journey and tending to their own spiritual well-being.

The "new" leaders are able to merge their skills with an approach that is gentle and compassionate. They have performed self-examination and are aware of themselves on every level—emotionally, physically and intellectually. They are the 'renaissance' leaders.

Outstanding leaders have several unique qualities such as a personal foundation of spirituality, a commitment to serving people that they delight in, compassion and a recognition of the sacred, right livelihood (an alignment of work with spiritual values), selfless service etc.

Boozer and Maddox make a distinction between the transformational leader and transactional leader. Transformational leader is concerned with leading people toward their own self-actualization, and they inspire people to a greater sense of purpose.

Transactional leaders, on the other hand, rely upon techniques such as identification of roles, negotiation & compromise, and there is an implicit agreement that people will help the leader achieve his or her goals in exchange for some kind of payment. A transactional leader relies upon the imagery of economic exchange. (Boozer & Maddox, 1992).[26]

Much of the language that is in regard to leadership originates from spiritually-based words. For example, 'inspired' comes from spirit, 'enthusiastic' evolved from the Greek word 'entheos' that means possessed by a god and 'devoted' comes from a Latin word meaning to bow to a deity.

Employers and Employees with a High SQ

- Employers with a high Spiritual Quotient encourage and motivate employees better.
- Employee engagement becomes a crucial parameter in organizations where SQ is high.
- Employees work for satisfaction and to the best of their ability and not just for salaries.
- Routines are not mundane but are nurturing and fulfilling.

- There is a better alignment of employer-employee-organizational needs.
- Performance levels are higher and traditional methods to measure performance are replaced by goal-driven outcomes.
- Work life balance improves drastically.
- Issues like stress, emotional disturbances, mental pressures etc are eliminated from the core.
- Holistic well-being is assured and visible.

Spirituality as the Basis for Business Leadership

Over the last 100 years, four distinct leadership contexts have emerged. These are:

1. *Paternal—Mechanistic:* It operates on the philosophy of survival of the fittest (win-lose). Since the goal of the leader is to maximize wealth through command and control mechanism, employees were considered as dispensable and interchangeable entities.
2. *Humanistic:* Where people were allowed to actualize their objectives and simultaneously maximize wealth by meeting organizational objectives (win-win). Employees, who are treated as a resource, have to be managed sensitively.
3. *Holistic:* The goal gets slightly broader and wealth maximization of all stakeholders occurs. Employees are assets and the leadership objective is to invoke a common purpose and build a value system.
4. *Spirituality-based:* A paradigm shift in the way business is managed. Wealth maximization is no longer the end goal of a leader and the business. It is a means to achieve the bigger goal, spiritual fulfilment and selfless service to all the stakeholders.

On the issues of discipline and reprimand, spiritually inclined corporate leaders need to distinguish between the actions and the actor. Condemn the actions but not the actor.

If it is essential to reprimand or retrench, assess the contributory factors of failure (organizational and the individual) initiate gentle disciplinary action to amend, view the likely consequences for his dependents. Even after that, if it is essential to retrench, do it for the sake of the ultimate good.

Spiritual leaders aiming for transformation should constantly engage in dialog that helps to transcend the inner shared meaning. Studies have shown that spiritual leaders must lead by example to be successful.

The literal meaning of spirituality has changed a lot. It now means elite work framework. In order to crack the modern-day human resource challenges like inspiration, engagement, corruption, motivation, stress etc both of the academicians and corporate experts depend upon deep sense of being able to break down in order to get better industrial results.

Spiritual Leadership and the Bottom-line

An organization achieves its highest level of performance if the spiritual mindset is established and maintained among its workers. One of the six executives in the 2003 study, Dr Richard King of the King International Group in Pasadena, stated this train of thought: "When you employ spirituality and leave room for discussing it, you can far exceed the normal business profit and return parameters that are occurring under the current way of doing business. I think that by using the process of spirituality & beginning to enhance creativity and innovativeness and taking people to different levels, the end result of that can be far better returns than what we have today This is because we are multiplying productivity so much."

King's statement is in perfect coherence with Dr Stephen Byrum from the Spiritual Leadership Institute who claims that, "When you create an environment where people's beliefs are respected and they are encouraged to be the best human beings they can be then it can have a positive impact on your bottom line."

Scholars assert this perspective by asserting that organizations high in workplace spirituality outperform those without it by 86 percent. Such organizations also reportedly grow faster, increase efficiencies and produce higher returns on investments" Garcia-Zamor (2003).[27]

There has been ample empirical evidence that spirituality in the workplace creates a new organizational culture in which employees feel happier and perform better bringing together the motivation for work and the meaning in work increases retention.

Employees also may feel that belonging to a work community, which is an important aspect of spirituality, will help them when things get rough in the future. In such a humanistic work environment, employees are more creative and have higher morale, the two factors that are closely linked to good organisational performance.

Practical Implications

Since spirituality plays a key role in affecting work engagement, it is of prime importance for managers and organizations to appreciate and encourage the concept of spiritual wellness. Steps in this direction are expected to benefit the individuals, teams, and organizations.

The know-how of this relationship may have the following implications at different levels. Krishnakumar and Neck (2002)[28] explained how spirituality can be enhanced in the workplace at the individual level. They suggested "the spiritual freedom model."

According to this model, if managers can implement spirituality at work, it would lead to increased sense of meaning and purpose in the employees' life, which would help the employees experience satisfaction and fulfilment.

The authors suggest that care needs to be taken while implementing spiritual principles in the companies as it may lead to the inability of employees to pronounce and practice their own set of spirituality principles. The underlying reason is the differences in beliefs that individuals have.

It may eventually lead to dissatisfaction, and employees would fail to derive meaning from the day-to-day operations. Therefore, managers need to appreciate and acknowledge these differences and for clusters of employees holding similar spiritual beliefs. Even if employees know that the ultimate results will be the common good, there could be a possibility that employees with different belief feel constrained in the way they would like to express their spirituality.

Therefore, being an individual-specific factor, spirituality at work should be viewed and implemented from employees' perspective instead of the organization's perspective. This kind of approach would result not only in greater organizational performance but also better personal development. This approach is particularly important in today's diverse workforce.

Managers need to encourage employees to speak freely about their spiritual values and help them to find a fit between their own values and the company's values. Here, the spiritual freedom model may help as it is based on the "spiritual freedom" concept in the workplace. So, organizations do not establish a common code for spiritual principles.

The authors argued that allowing and rather encouraging employees to express their spiritual beliefs freely would result in positive consequences at work. Some of such positive consequences include higher engagement, creativity, honesty, trust, personal fulfilment and organizational commitment. It is suggested that spirituality can be used to do change management.

Change through spirituality would mean changing things inside out instead of the conventional top-down or bottom-up approaches. It is because spirituality works on changing the attitudes of employees toward changes which increase the effectiveness of the change.

However, precautions should be taken while making changes. It is because the conflicts, clashes, and sense of purpose at work may be harmed if the spirituality is impacted negatively by the changes. On the contrary, a workplace rich in spirituality is likely to energize employees and encourage them to perceive their organization in a positive manner.

To enhance spirituality at team level, a mood chart is highly recommended. It is an emerging technique that helps in adapting to the requirements of a new project. A mood chart, for example, gauges the extent to which an innovation team is feeling demoralized. It can be defined as a graph which shows the fluctuations in the mood levels in terms of rise and fall over a period of time.

It enables the manager to predict the mood episodes, and thereby, record the responses to medications. It has the following details: medications, hours of sleep, and one's mood.

The authors argued that since mood has a direct relationship with productivity, negative emotions are also to be recorded and to be understood in light of the impact these would have on productivity.

Similarly, it is important to capture "group mood" using mood charts. Thus, if the management finds a link between group moods and their productivity, it can do human resource intervention in the form of introducing solutions for enhancing one's mood.

For organizations to strengthen the spirituality perspectives to improve employee performance, five factors are of paramount importance. These factors include:

(a) Social Participation
(b) Team Correlation
(c) Opportunity for Inner Life
(d) Job Satisfaction, and
(e) Alignment between Personal and Organizational Values.

Organizational Asset

Workplace spirituality is tough to measure because it is tough to define. Amin Mohamed *et al.* (2004)[29] have proposed three domains of spirituality definitions:

1. Spirituality Predispositions or Catalysts
2. Spirituality Actions, Behaviours or Experiences, and
3. Spirituality Outcomes or Consequences

Other scholars believe that spirituality in the workplace has been under-researched because it is non-material in nature and it is thought not to exist. Intellectual bias by management scholars is another reason that workplace spirituality is studied so infrequently assert that integrating a sense of spirituality into the workplace helps to improve employees' intuitive abilities, levels of innovation, teamwork experience, level of employee commitment, and ability to create powerful visions—all of which are positive outcomes.

Workplace Spirituality and Fulfilment

At the end of the 20th century, people have begun to face spiritual emptiness, moral abnormalities, twisted social values, greed, and all kinds of crimes, against the backdrop of the formation of knowledge economy and the acceleration of material satisfactions due to technological advancements. This has caused an imbalance between material and spiritual life. (Bhunia and Das, 2012).[30]

Since the industrial revolution, many theorists have tried to capture the correct essence of managerial productivity blended with harmony in the workplace, which includes the new era of a post-modern 'flat world'.

Spiritual discussions are surfacing, and spiritual management is being suggested for leaders who want to thrive in an era of the knowledge economy. Scholars believe that the discovery of a spiritual dimension of work started a movement that can be traced back to the late 1980s.

There are good reasons to believe that workplace spirituality is more than an impermanent trend. On the contrary, the concept carries a much more substantial meaning and its potential contribution to a more rounded understanding of human work, of the workplace and of the organizational reality in general is worthy of examination.

Harrington *et al.* (2001)[31] describe a shift occurring at the turn of the century, where employees experienced a fundamental change of work values. This ushered in spiritual exploration as a profound culture shift and introduced the notion of "workplace spirituality."

Most current spirituality research focuses on individual feelings of spiritual fulfilment. But more work is needed on organizations themselves and hard data to further develop workplace spirituality. Some progressive organizations seem to accept a variety of dimensions for inner life, meaning, connectedness, and transcendence.

It is being more evident that modern organizations are obligated to create a corporate culture that addresses the whole person (spiritual, mental, emotional, and physical). If organizations wish to thrive and survive as globalization continues to shrink our world, a plan is needed to consider the whole-person when developing the workforce.

The pros and cons issues, as scholars clearly see, are:

1. Workplace spirituality is becoming a prerequisite for meaning and fulfilment in the workplace.
2. There is a void in research that focuses on how to measure purpose and workplace spirituality and fulfilment from an organizational perspective.

Workplace Spirituality and Creativity

Research suggests that there is a connection between workplace spirituality and creativity. Experts have identified seven dimensions of workplace spirituality of which creativity is one of them. These are:

- *Creativity:* Directly related with additional elements like the use of colours, laughter or humour, and freedom to utilize any available method to increase productivity.
- *Communication:* Basically acts as the tool that connects humans to work cooperatively.
- *Respect:* The respect shown to each other.
- *Vision:* Basically the ability to be farsighted.
- *Partnership:* It is the responsibility of task-based work commitments for a group or partners.
- *Positive Energy Force:* Prevents negative activities like violence in workplace, sexual harassment, discrimination, confrontations, lack of respect, loss of productivity, and non-conducive work conditions.
- *Flexibility:* It is the ability of an individual to adapt in dynamic situations and allowing individual trust to change according to current demands.

Organizational Spirituality and Interpersonal Interactions

Organizations necessarily evolve as a result of the interactions they comprise. Interactions imposed by external, formal structures pave the way to the evolution of other forms of interactions. Both externally defined and emergent interactions ultimately define the quality of an organisation (Feldman & Rafaeli, 2001).[32]

Organizational Spirituality and Values & Ethics

Spirituality in the workplace would be incomplete if one fails to delve on values and ethics. Values elevate an individual to higher and purer level of consciousness. Organizations focus more on building skills through training but seldom concentrate on educating employees on values.

Comparing value systems of Japan and China vs. America brings out certain interesting management ethos of these countries. In American culture, values such as humility and gratitude are considered timid and unprofessional though they have steered Japanese firms to unlimited success.

While commenting on India, scholars chide on how dependent it is in emulating either American or Japanese management styles rather than developing its own based on the Indian psyche.

Rooted in the deep structure of Indian culture and society, values such as respecting people as embodiments of the divine, cooperation and trust (oneness in all), 'Chitta Shuddhi' (purification of mind) through noble thoughts like compassion, friendliness, humility, gratitude, containment of greed, inspiration to give (sense of sacrifice), renunciation and detachment can enrich the Indian management ethos tremendously.

Workplace Spirituality and Workplace Bullying

Workplace spirituality is a pervasive force that affects both individuals and organization at a variety of levels. Studies have shown that both work and personnel-related factors could trigger workplace bullying (Van den Brande *et al.*, 2016).[33]

Moreover, the impact of workplace bullying on individuals can be serious and most of the negative impacts happen on the individual level. So, how a phenomenon as workplace spirituality could be implemented to benefit individuals who face systematic workplace bullying?

Interestingly, keywords search of "workplace spirituality and workplace bullying" yields no results in Google's Scholar, Thomson Reuters' Social Science Citation index, Elsevier Scopus, and EBSCO's business and management databases. However, when the keywords are refined some related researchers are identified.

Perhaps, workplace bullying and workplace spirituality could be discussed both at individual and organizational levels. At organizational level, workplace spirituality and spiritual traditions can be implemented to create a better and more positive environment.

One of the ways of achieving that could be through institutionalizing underlying values and norms. In fact, the aforementioned values and norms, which stem from spirituality, would certainly be useful to reduce tension among the victims and perpetrators of workplace bullying.

The component of "sense of community" can be embedded into associated values. If the member of organization shares these values, then they would find acceptance. However, consensus is required for their establishment. Nonetheless, this could be valid at mostly organizational level but it would influence individuals. It creates barriers and limits individual behaviour.

Spiritual organizations can also be more successful to reduce work-related bullying factors such as role stressors. From an individual level, the impact of workplace bullying on individuals can be seen from various aspects. However, the important question is how workplace spirituality and spiritual traditions can be used to cope with workplace bullying.

There are different coping methods that could help individuals with workplace bullying. These are reappraisal coping, active coping, confrontive coping, direct coping, social support (problem-focused coping), and self-care (emotion-focused coping. Coping styles also mediate the relationship between stressful life events and mental health.

One of the main issues perhaps is to prevent workplace bullying occurring in the first place. There are three main sides in case of workplace bullying:

- Victims
- Perpetrators, and
- Witnesses.

If values and norms are embedded into the organizational consciousness—informal institutional framework—then individuals would require checking if actions they were taking would be appropriate. This cannot be said for formal rules and regulations as already it is by law workplace bullying is forbidden and there are serious consequences if it is committed in many different countries.

This may provide a mechanism where individuals could know what is expected of them. Workplace spirituality and so-called spiritual organizations could be natural places where such framework could be appropriately implemented. It should also be noted that spiritual organizations could be places that traditional norms and established strong organizational values could be changed.

However, the opinion is that this is most helpful for the prevention phase. So, how can workplace spirituality and spiritual traditions be helpful for victims? Research from around the world has shown that workplace bullying is one of the strongest reasons for workplace stress and causes long-term physical and psychological health issues (Hoobler *et al.*, 2010).[34] At the same time, engaging in workplace spirituality and spiritual traditions are found to lower stress factors at work.

If victims opt to use emotion coping strategies, victims are more likely to opt for emotion coping strategies such as denial or avoid problem avoiding strategies. Then, perhaps, prevention becomes more important as the denial of the problem would not be easily solved by the establishment of values, norms, and attitudes.

Spirituality and Organizational Performance

At the heart of every organization, whether public or private, is the requirement to succeed. Organizations must carry out their mission, fulfil their goals, and ultimately produce. In other words, organizations that do not perform do not last.

Organizational performance is not the result of a single entity or person. To produce a greater number of widgets or graduate an even larger number of college students, each year requires the combined forces of many people within the organization.

Protocols, rules and regulations, automation, and processes are certainly important, but in the end unless the human element works in tandem with the organizational components, success is limited. Working in tandem is working in community.

Organizations do not perform well when there is a gap between the individual's spirituality and his or her position in the workplace. Workplace spirituality provides the opportunity for the individual to express himself or herself more fully and completely, especially when (s)he knows who (s)he is has significance for what he (s)knows.

Several top CEOs of Fortune 500 companies to small construction businesses have contended that spiritual practices, such as meditation or lunch room discussion of spiritual values, contributed to a more positive organizational environment.

Researchers opine that there are three perspectives or typologies of spirituality that 'enables or leads to organizational performance':

1. The first is the human element, where spirituality promotes holistic employee well-being and quality of life, and in turn the spiritually content employee is a more productive employee. Experts say that spiritually content and motivated employees demonstrate less signs of 'stress, burnout and work holism' thereby contributing to a better work environment and a more productive workforce.
2. A second perspective is the philosophical approach, where spiritually motivated and spiritually practicing employees demonstrate greater self-contentment at work and find more intrinsic purpose in their work and workplace. Providing employees with the opportunity to express themselves and their spirituality in the workplace leads to more satisfied employees, and more satisfied employees often are more productive employees.
3. The third perspective is directly linked to Follett's integrative process thesis, where spirituality leads or contributes to a greater sense of interconnectedness and community.

Over and over, today's workers identify their top concern: being disconnected from who they are as a person and the work they perform. Low morale, lack of support for the mission of the organization, and distrust of management and leadership reflect low levels of participation in and connectivity to the greater workplace community.

Spiritual Intelligence (SI) is that intelligence which is required when one begins to open up to his/her spirit's (soul's) journey and to quest for a greater understanding of life. Spiritualism is one of the philosophical doctrines in which it is believed that the 'spirit' exists as distinct from matter and that, 'spirit' is the only reality. Indian scriptures refer to this term as 'Atma' or soul.

SI is the intelligence with which we balance meaning and value for life and place our lives in a wider context. It is the soul's intelligence connected to wisdom from beyond the ego, or unconscious mind; it is our conscience, compass, the hidden inner truth also.

SI makes spirituality possible, but this need not always depend on any sectarian religion. It is used to deal with existential problems and to get guided—to live a life at a deeper level of meaning; to have an understanding about who we are and what things mean to us and our place in the world.

Based on the theoretical and experimental considerations of Zohar and Marshall (2000), academicians and professionals have started discussing about a quotient to represent an individual's Spiritual Intelligence—i.e. Spiritual Intelligence Quotient—SIQ or properly known as SQ.

The following are some of the major concepts of SI/SQ as reflected in the work of Zohar and Marshall:

- SQ (SI) is used to grow our human brains. Spiritual intelligence helps an individual to become transformed for a better life.
- Spiritual intelligence is used when one need to be flexible, visionary or creatively spontaneous.
- It helps in dealing with existential problems. It gives an insight of what life's struggles are about. SQ is our conscience.
- SQ helps in understanding the meaning and essential motive behind all great religions.
- Spiritual intelligence helps in the integration of intrapersonal and interpersonal intelligences. So spiritually intelligent individuals will be good in management of their things as well as that of others.
- Spiritual intelligence helps an individual to go beyond his immediate ego/ self to live a life at a deeper level of meaning.
- It is through spiritual intelligence that one can fight with the problems of good & bad, and life & death.

Changing from Within

Spiritually-based organizations and leaders believe that we are part of an inter-connected whole. If we want to change that whole, we must change ourselves. Margaret Wheatley (1996)[35] points out: "The source of change and growth for an organization or an individual is to develop increased awareness of which it is now if we take time to reflect together on who we are and who we could choose to become, we will be led into the territory where change originates."

For an individual or an organization to be open to such change, they need to be self aware without being self-centred. Various scholars emphasize that effective leaders are highly self-aware and more likely to move quickly and confidently and in different directions without needing to be consistently right and in control. Leaders and organizations need to look at their glasses rather than just through them.

NGO Capacity Building

Although the corporate has been stirred by this focus on spirituality in management, the field of NGO capacity building has remained largely untouched as yet. This is quite surprising given that the core elements of a spiritual approach to organisations are the very elements that are claimed to define NGOs and set them apart from other types of organisations.

NGOs are seen to be value-led and their visions are to make the world a better place. The new corporate 'gospel' of empowerment and participation has been central to NGO development theory and practice for many years. But as yet, few capacity building programs really focus on such issues of values and empowering servant leadership.

Instead they continue to emphasise learning the management techniques to fit in with the planning and reporting systems of donors. In addition, despite the prevalence of many faith-based organisations in the aid sector, even less have risked integrating the concept of a higher power into change programmes. Capacity building has remained a professional and secular activity.

The reasons for this dichotomy are many and complex. To some degree the NGO sector has been inoculated and built up a healthy resistance to repeating past mistakes whereby religion was a source of conflict and oppression. Significantly, an increasing proportion of NGO funding is coming from official sources.

Many of these donors are also still languishing in dated management thinking from the 1970s (such as logical framework planning) and have not caught up yet with recent developments in post-modem management theory. They still optimistically believe that they can control another country's devel opment.

In addition, such sources also regularly emphasise the danger of misusing public funds for proselytising. This encourages faith-based organisations to separate the spiritual from the physical aspect. As a result the spiritual dimension to development and change is downplayed, even ignored.

This picture, however, appears to be changing and from a somewhat surprising direction. Experts identify 'a resurgence of interest in the developmental role of faiths, even in such non-spiritual organisations as the World Bank.' In 2001, the World Bank invited representatives of nine of the world's religions for dialogue about development in consultations for the World Development Report.

There are obvious dangers in emphasising the spiritual dimension to capacity building, it could easily be manipulated into unhealthy and exclusive regulations or into intolerance of others with differing beliefs. But if we approach the subject in humility, knowing that no-one has a monopoly on truth, there is potential for mutual growth and learning.

If indeed a spiritual dimension does exist and has potential to help us transform organisations, then we should find out more so that we can try and harness that energy more consciously. The overwhelming developmental challenges of today require that we look beyond the security of our past practice.

Most of the conventional Western discourses ignore or dismiss the spiritual, moral and cultural dimensions of human well-being as irrelevant to development practice. And yet for most parts of the world, innermost attitudes and behaviour towards change are not motivated by economic or political interests.

Rather are many people moved by deep underlying moral and spiritual assumptions that reflect and explain reality and that support the values that guide their decisions about whether to change or not to change?

Until very recently, most organizations used asset-based management. The real value was in tangible often immovable commodities. In agricultural times, assets were land jewels and precious metals. From the industrial revolution until the very-late 20th century, money became the asset that was often invested in factories and means of production.

Under the above conditions, employees were incidental to the wealth of a company or a person Certainly they were needed, but it was more for brute force work or domestic servant chores neither requiring high levels of education or complicated training.

Therefore, workers were more-or-less replaceable and not seen as having any real value to the enterprise. In those times, managers had some real control over the firm's assets.

During the information age, capital for investing in ventures is no longer a scarce commodity. When internet giants Yahoo and Amazon can be started with almost no capital financing and become some of the largest US corporations, one realizes that capital has lost its edge as the major force for creating successful enterprises.

Today, we have a growing segment of employees called knowledge workers. More and more organizations are dependent on their skills, intelligence and wisdom. Robots and assembly lines have replaced the need for manual labour, but what are needed are smart, hardworking employees.

They are the real assets of modern companies. And unlike in past ages, those assets can walk out the door if they don't like how they are being treated. There seems today to be a spiritual reawakening of organizations around the world.

We are experiencing marketplace adjustments and awareness of what Karman and Hormann (1990)[36] discuss as the fundamental fact about us—that we are spiritual beings inhabiting a spiritual universe, and that denying this is an error condemning any social structure to failure. If so, we are operating in a world based on spiritual principles and laws, as well as the more familiar physical principles and laws.

Outcomes of Spiritually Intelligent Workplaces

In the early days of the emerging field of workplace spirituality, scholars and practitioners hypothesized that companies that were more spiritual were more likely to experience positive outcomes such as greater employee commitment and job satisfaction, reduced turnover, higher productivity, high levels of customer service and improved reputation in the marketplace.

The major critique of the field at that stage was that claims were being made that had not been substantiated by quality research studies. Since that time, significant progress has been made in outcomes research. On the basis of research in the field of workplace spirituality, it can be summarized that spirituality supports organizational performance.

These findings can be sorted into three different perspectives:

1. The human resource perspective focusing on developing employees' well-being, leading to positive outcomes of increased morale and commitment, increased employee well-being and increased employee productivity.
2. The philosophical perspective focusing on developing employees' sense of purpose and meaning, resulting in increased fulfilment, job satisfaction, hope, creativity and reflection.
3. The inter-personal perspective focusing on developing employees' sense of community and connectedness, leading to increased attachment to the organization, increased loyalty, belongingness and high-quality connections.

Mainstreaming of Spirituality in Management

The academic world of management has witnessed an explosion of interest in spirituality as a new dimension of management. The present spiritual trend is probably the most significant trend in management since the 1950s. There are numerous conferences, articles, books, influential websites and courses springing up on the subject.

The American Academy of Management formed a special interest group on Management, Spirituality and Religion. Harvard Business School now hosts an annual conference on Leadership, Values and Spirituality while there are at least 12 other conferences each year in the United States alone on spirituality in the organisations.

In the United Kingdom, the Cranfield School of Management has an MBA elective on Spirituality and Organisational Transformation. Major academic journals such as the Journal of Organisational Change Management had two special issues on spirituality in 1999 and another in 2003.

The Journal of Management Psychology also had a focus issue on spirituality in 2002. This led to the launch of a new journal—Management, Spirituality and Religion in January 2004.

There has been a convergence of thinking and practice in the three fields of organizational change, organizational behaviour and leadership. According to Lee Robbins of the Academy of Management (2003),[37] "Leadership—particularly transformational leadership—depends heavily on spiritual perspectives, values and assumptions of leaders and on how these perspectives connect them to potential followers."

Mahatma Gandhi had once said that, "Such power as I possess for working in the political field is derived entirely from my experiments in the spiritual field". The interest in spirituality is not confined to the rarefied atmospheres of academia. Organizational consultants and popular writers such as John Adair, Peter Senge, Tom Peters, Peter Vaill, Steven Charles Handy and Harrison Owen are increasingly explicit about the spiritual dimension to organizational life.

John Adair, arguably the most famous author on leadership, concludes: "The vital difference, the X factor, which enables you to transcend limits, is called inspiration. There is guidance and help available in strategic leadership from God, or as if from a god if you would prefer it."

Steven Covey says, "I believe that there are parts to human nature that cannot be reached either by legislation or education, but require the power of God to deal with." Or as Owen points out, "Real or lasting change is rarely, if ever, affected by memo and command. Such change occurs when the spirit changes."

These spiritual perspectives in organizations have also permeated the 'real world' of actual management practice. Wagner-Marsh and Conley (1999)[38] observe that "a great number of highly diverse firms are moving ahead with attempts to instil a spiritual approach to their corporate cultures."

They highlight Fortune 100 firms such as TD Industries, Xerox, Exxon and the Bank of Montreal which "all have a spiritual dimension to leadership and management development programs." Hewlett Packard, Semco, Ben and Jerry's and Toyota are also identified as implementing a spiritual approach to management.

Other large firms such as Boeing have Christian, Jewish and Muslim prayer groups while others have what they call Higher Power Lunches. Research in the United States by Biberman and Whitty (1997)[39] revealed that an increasing number of managers are turning to various types of meditation and spiritual disciplines to cope with their turbulent work environments."

This finding is echoed by Howard's UK research which found that "in the midst of high-flying business careers, participants talk explicitly about prayer and reflection upon wisdom literature as the foundation of their ability to have discernment."

Paul Wong (2003)[40] concludes, "The movement to bring spirit and soul to business is no passing fad. It continues to grow and shows no signs of abating. Clearly something significant is stirring the corporate world."

It is increasingly recognised that as much as 75% of planned humanistic change fail. This has led people to look for more innovative and deeper solutions to organizational change issues. Change efforts led by logic and brute sanity do not seem to have worked well.

Rogers Harrison (1995)[41] points out, "I have never in all my years as a consultant seen anyone change an organization in any fundamental way through rational planning." He encapsulates the dilemma when he says, "the tools and approaches that have got us where we are today are not the ones we can use to advance to another level. The real answers to our dilemmas lie in the dark beyond the circle of illumination given by our current concepts and methods.

Andrew Kakabadse, one of the leading management thinkers today, believes that one of the reasons for this lies in ignoring the invisible world, the spiritual, the collective unconscious, the underlying order of things. Another thinker Dorothy Marcic asserts "the bewildering organizational problems are rooted at least partially in a lack of awareness of spiritual laws and its relevance to the workforce."

She believes that most organizational change programs fail because they do not go far enough. They do not deal with core issues of spirit and love and ultimately do not deliver. There is a realization that most change programs—while attempting to catalyse 'life' and energy have inadvertently been focusing on inert matter, such as systems and structures.

The recent progression in natural sciences thinking has also had a profound impact in moving spirituality into the mainstream. Insights from the natural sciences have shown the world to be an individual whole, a web of relationships in which any action has complex, non-linear and unpredictable effects.

According to Ackerman and Banner and Gagne, spirituality and consciousness is the core of dynamic evolutionary systems, and thus, must be included in analysis and practice of organizational change and management.

Recent socio-economic trends have also pushed spirituality into the forefront of organizational thinking and practice. The increasing insecurities from downsizing, mergers and globalisation have made people look for their security beyond their job. Such trends have also increased the stress levels on those left behind.

The rapid technological change has been dehumanising to a degree by making people feel both eminently and imminently expendable. As Peter Vaill (1989)[42] describes: "More than ever, individuals find themselves in a world of permanent white water, experiencing a lack of meaning in their lives and an attendant sense of spiritual desolation."

In addition, as the West has been enjoying unparalleled prosperity over the last two decades, some people have found emptiness in affluence and consequently have started looking beyond the material in search for meaning. This search has been further encouraged by the disillusionment and alienation arising from corporate scandals (termed by some as the Enron Effect).

Coupled with a concurrent breakdown of many traditional institutions such as the family, the workplace is now seen as one of the most important sources of community, and therefore, an important place for exploring and finding spiritual meaning in life.

World class organizations are discovering that this continued success depends on creating workplaces based on unity, justice, integrity, respect and service. These are spiritual virtues and they form the basis of moral teaching of the main religions.

For decades, we have denied the importance of these lines our organisational lives and have developed a more material view of man, one that ignores the deeper issues of seeking meaning in life and work.

Little recognition has yet been given to the moral and spiritual foundations. Without this foundation, however, it would be impossible to create the new management paradigm. For example, managers could never think about creating a shared vision if they did not assume the spiritual virtue as a worthy goal.

Similarly, worker commitment requires a sense of purpose and teamwork. Nor could profit sharing exist in the absence of a sense of justice, which also underpins the concept of equality in employment opportunities.

As a result of new management approaches, we have moved from business focusing on tasks to ones focusing on processes and customer needs. Competitive firms focus their attention on serving the real needs of customers. They have customer-friendly systems operated by employee who are attentive, responsive and willing to help. This is the mark of what we care calling the new management virtue of service.

Integrated Model of Workplace Spirituality and HR's Role

Spirituality means various things to various people. Some believe it to be informal and personal while some view it as universal, non-denominational, broadly inclusive and tolerant and still others see it as a basic feeling of being connected with one's complete self, others and the entire universe. Spirituality is often expressed in the broadest sense as organizational and personal aspirations vis-a-vis goals, values and ethics. There are people who have a somewhat broader perspective of what spirituality in the workplace means. These perspectives see spirituality at work as akin to values and ethics, and thus, an important component of organisational success. As a result of the findings to a phenomenological study in 2003, spirituality in the workplace can be simply defined as, "an experience of inter-connectedness among those involved in a work process, engendered by individual goodwill, reading to the collective creation of a motivational organisational culture, itemized by reciprocity and solidarity, and resulting in enhanced overall performance, which is ultimately translated in lasting organisational excellence."

The model clarifies how an encouraging organisational culture can be created through the application of these themes, and what the results of this culture will be. Figure 1 below demonstrates the incorporation of the themes and the effects they have on the organisation's performance and ultimately, its bottom line.

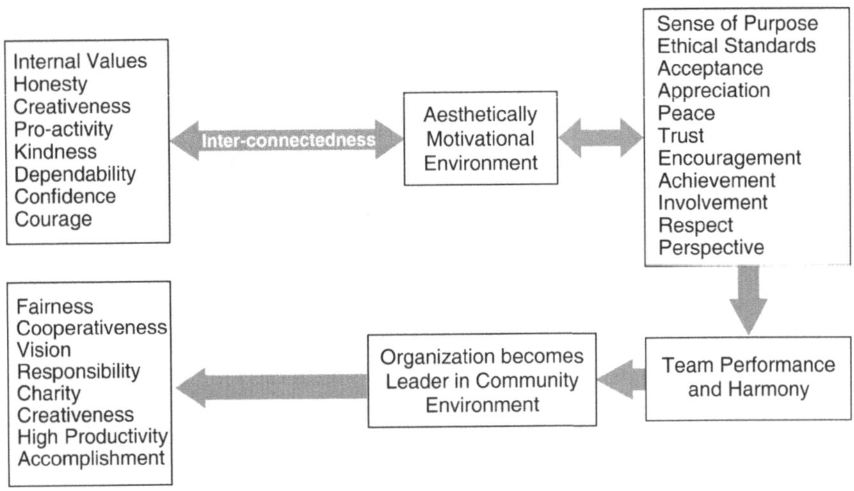

Figure 1

Figure 1 is a schematic presentation of what this researcher established as her final definition of spirituality in the workplace. The figure depicts the following:

- The figure incorporates internal integrated and external factors that were distinguished in the course of this study
- The individual in the figure harbors a set of internal values, which are honesty, creativeness, proactively, kindness, dependability, confidence and courage This set of values typifies the worker that performs at his or her highest level of spiritual awareness.
- Due to this spiritual awareness and the internal set of values this worker realizes his or her interconnectedness with the work environment.
- Together with other spiritual workers the workplace should be enhanced to an aesthetically motivational environment consisting of and exuding all or most of the listed items between sense of purpose

and perspective. This list represents the elements of a workplace that nurtures the spiritual mindset.

- In a workplace that nurtures the spiritual mindset and where workers realize the value of interconnectedness and an aesthetically motivational environment, team performance and harmony should be practiced.
- Due to these strong elements the organisation should perform well, and may become a leader in its industry and community Because of the values encouraged and maintained by the workforce of this leading organisation the organisation should distinct itself in its industry and community and maintain is leadership through performances of fairness cooperativeness, vision responsibility charity, creativeness, high productivity, and accomplishment The prospering organisation should, in turn, recognize the value and input of its workforce and do everything to maintain this workforce by increasing job satisfaction and self-esteem within the workers Finally, a workplace that provides job satisfaction and a good feeling about the self (self esteem), should encourage the spiritual mindset within its workers, consisting of values such as honesty, creativeness, proactively, kindness, dependability, confidence, and courage.

Role of HR in Organizational Spirituality

In the field of human resource management, the involvement of spirituality is increasing day-by-day. Academicians to corporate practitioners are all vying to incorporate it for its potential of redressing workplace woes.

By successfully adding one more dimension (karma capital) of Indian spiritual values to workplace, the essential HR principles of employee engagement, motivation and managerial effectiveness can be judiciously tackled.

The industrial scenario has expanded tremendously. Defining HR policies in an organization and its growth prospects is key function that needs deep understanding of its employees' needs.

Work environment and the appropriate strategies for successful HR management is rapidly changing. Dr Ross McDonald, a senior lecturer in the management and employment relations department at the University of Auckland, identifies two main factors as significant in this change.

He says, "The declining influence of traditional religions (particularly in the West) provides a constant reminder of greed laws and ways of acting. A public concern over issues such as modern competitive business practices and globalization is resulting in a cheapening of deeper spiritual values and their conversion into fleeting management tools or fads."

The October 2003 issue of HR Focus claims that "keeping workers happy is difficult in these times of layoffs, greater workloads, longer hours, and smaller raises, but it is not impossible." This source clarifies that the secret to achieving workers' happiness is, "finding out what matters most to your organisations workers, and then providing it."

The article suggests the following attention for man to focus in order to maintain a satisfied workforce:

1. Avoiding layoffs
2. Offering desirable benefits
3. Good communication, and
4. Giving employees the flexibility to balance work life issues.

Kulesa (2003)[43] reveals two other issues for HR departments and managers to keep in mind: "Top performers pay special attention to high-level issues of corporate leadership. In addition, high performers seek an environment in which their efforts will be rewarded, not with higher pay necessarily, but with enhanced development and career-path opportunities."

He stresses that senior leaders providing a clear sense of direction, communicating decisions to employees, and in turn being respected by employees is equally important. Kulesa says that "High performers' concerns are much more strategic than those of other staff, reaching to the very heart of the organization's purpose, strategy, and positioning in the marketplace."

There is a heightening expectation that HR will shift its role from simply providing the delivery mechanism to become a new business driver of change, says Dr Lawrence Lyons (2001).[44]

Dr Lyons continues, "HR is the only function with the relevant people focus to create the soft strategies businesses now need to deliver profits. However, unless HR gets its house in order there is a real danger that other business functions will win the race for the strategic high ground."

Eminent scholars and corporate experts point out the truly great places to work—such as the Fortune 100 companies—are not great because of their perks and benefits, but because of their organizational cultures and policies that promote meaningful work and a nurturing, supportive workplace.

Tom Chappell, CEO of Tom's of Maine, offers creative and easy-to-initiate ideas for HR managers to make any company a more spiritually satisfying place at little or no cost. Some of Chappell's ideas on how HR can help establish a spiritually satisfying workplace are:

- Help employees connect with nature by bringing in natural features, (such as plants).
- Holding outdoor meetings when possible.
- Allowing staff to take exercise breaks to promote physical and spiritual wellness.
- Stage frequent company celebrations to acknowledge milestones and achievements.
- Honour creative expression by decorating the workplace with employee made art.
- Create an evolving mission statement employees are proud to live by.
- Rotating those attending outside events.
- Start holding meetings in the round, thereby creating feelings of egalitarianism.
- Encouraging employees to get to know each other better (hobbies, likes and dislikes).
- Encourage employees to take turn at answering customer correspondence.

Rosner (2001) cites consultant Martin Rutte, who offers a simple four steps action plan for HR directors to better address spirituality at work:

- **Step 1:** Make it safe, permissible, and comfortable to have the conversation about spirituality in the workplace, if people choose Begin talking, writing, and communicating in a gentle, non threatening, non-dogmatic manner Respect others' points of view and the degree to which they wish to participate (Rosner 2001, p. 83).
- **Step 2:** Seek help from the many resources available. There are myriad sources filled with ideas, conferences, books, speakers. [and] discussion groups. (Rosner, 2001, p. 83)
- **Step 3:** Allow a form to evolve to help expand spirituality in your workplace. This can be anything from a regular discussion group to a shared project or activity to a speaker series Agree on a method and time. (Rosner, 2001. p. 83)
- **Step 4:** Evaluate what is working and what is not working. Then correct what is not and nurture what is. And don't forget to celebrate (Rosner, 2001, p. 83).

A 2003 doctoral study on spirituality in the workplace comprising a combination of extensive reading on the topic and in-depth interviewing of business executives in Los Angeles, has led the author of this article to believe that spirituality in the workplace has all characteristics of good management behaviour, in which workers at all levels are respected and valued, and where reciprocal understanding and cooperation are nurtured, while backstabbing and internal competition are discouraged.

According to this study, spirituality in the workplace, thus, involves an environment where inter-connectedness among workers is optimal, because all workers participate in the work-process with their best mindset, and perform to their best capacities.

They get encouraged by the overall atmosphere of helpfulness and accessibility at all levels, the friendliness, understanding, atmosphere of trust, and the general feeling of 'wellness' that prevails. This whole set of good and encouraging behaviour expresses itself through optimal performance from all workers, resulting in optimal performance of the organization.

Optimal performance of the organization leads to longevity for the company, translated in enhanced job security, which in turn, increases the devotion, dedication and self-esteem of the workers. This results an upward spiral that simply cannot go wrong in any way.

Workplace Spirituality and Effective HRM

The notoriety of idea of spirituality at workplace is expanding exponentially in the field of human assets administration. With growing number of organizations in the industry, it has become very important to improve the working environment for employees.

It has been reported by many researchers that workplace spirituality is accounted for the out worldly existence that should be related with larger amount of hierarchical effectiveness with equal amount of rate of return.

Spirituality at workplace helps in ploy to have a sense of being able to create their performance level according to their potential. Several research scholars have also started to explore the motivational aspects which play an important role.

Workplace spirituality has advanced as a compelling answer to manage deficiency of employee engagement. Various organizations have come up together to find a solution to create a spiritual place, where an employee can work with their complete potential.

The level of engagement of employees at work is clearly related to their spirit at work. Their level of engagement at workplace is directly related to their feeling of completeness and job satisfaction. The literal meaning of spirituality is the sense of completeness.

Employee engagement incorporates the synchronous set-up of all parts of one performance, that is, cognitive, physical and emotional. This means an ideal spiritual workplace should have complete employee involvement. Workplace spirituality gives freedom to employees to express various facets about themselves—not just physical but intellectual as well.

According to Indian spiritual values, it promotes employees to have complete dedication and responsibility for the organization. A company cannot grow without their employees' dedication so devotion for the organization brings confidence and faith for each other.

The Bhagwad Geeta also states that an employee must work towards benefit of the company and abandon any kind of personal differences. This kind of theory brings a common linkage between the employees and their workplace spirituality.

Indian Philosophy in the Workplace

A post-modern management paradigm is emerging emphasizing on spiritual principles and practices as opposed to the current prevailing modern management paradigm. Academicians as well as business practitioners the world over are now showing keen interest in the topic of spirituality it the workplace. Nevertheless, some have a sceptic view to the issue.

They consider it to only be yet another passing management fad, where we look to others to know what's "in or how it can be the next salvation" at work. These notions can be easily and effectively dispelled if we become aware of the strong theoretical foundations of spiritual and its applications that are deep-seated in ancient and contemporary Indian philosophical thought.

The concepts in our 'Sanatan Dharm', 'Vedant' and 'Bhagwad Gita' being eternal have practical relevance and applicability even in our modern world today. These thoughts are also echoed amongst thinkers like Swami Vivekananda, Sri Aurobindo, Mother Teresa and others.

Work exists for two spiritual reasons:

1. For developing spiritual awareness in everyone, including shareholders, managers, employees, customers, suppliers and society.
2. For serving others as an expression of our spiritual growth.

Given the nature of modern society—an exploding information base, global markets, fast-changing product demands, a diverse and demanding population and a labour pool increasingly composed of knowledge workers—traditional management alone will no longer work. The 21st century worker looks for meaning in his work, not just efficiency and effectiveness (Mitroff and Denton, 1999).[45]

A shift in the consciousness of workers and managers at all levels of organizations is beginning to occur as they seek to find more meaning, purpose and fulfilment in their work. Academicians as well as business practitioners' the world over are now showing keen interest in spirituality in the workplace. Though some doubts exist, they can be effectively dispelled when we become aware of the strong theoretical foundations of spirituality and its practical applications.

Every nation and culture has its own approach to the subject of management, forms of group life and workplace activity. America and Japan are highly specialized in the field of management and have their own philosophies relating to it. Richard Tanner Pacsale and Anthony G Athos discuss the successful management philosophy and practice of the Matushita Electric Company in 'The Art of Japanese Management'.

An entire chapter dedicated to spiritual values surmises that national service through industry, fairness, harmony & cooperation, struggle for betterment, courtesy & humility, adjustment & assimilation and gratitude can work wonders for a spiritually invested workplace (Swami Jitatmananda, 1995).[46]

Japan and India as eastern countries have a common spiritual background. Yet, it is only recently that Indians have recognised the value of their own traditions and heritage and its relevance to management in the Indian context. If people have no knowledge of their own philosophy of life and work, they imitate western philosophy and methods cosmetically.

Therefore, their actions are ad hoc and limited understanding makes them bereft of self-respect and apologetic at best. This also weakens their national resolve and capacity to seek and assimilate the real philosophical and spiritual elements of their own culture.

Indian Management Thought

Modern management tries to rouse people to action in order to get work done. India ethos seeks to rouse the 'whole man', the essential divinity and infinite strength within. The awakening of essential internal man assures all success both external and internal.

India has always taught people to put spirit above matter to make internal excellence lead the quest for external excellence. The Advaitha Vedanta inspires us with a positive outlook, exhorts us to live and work with zest, and to transform our crass self interest into enlightened self-interest.

Unlike many religious ideologies, whether Indian or foreign, Vedanta does not look down upon man seeking of material or sensory values in the concept of 'Purusharthas'. Vedanta finds an honoured place for all desires and urges of man, from material and sensory to moral, ethical and super sensory of transcendental.

Putting spirituality to work is not an intellectual exercise. Instead, it focuses on the source of our essential nature as human beings. It leads us to bring forth the most meaningful, uplifting, and practical course to take in life.

Swami Vivekanand (1900) exhorts us to "Put yourself to work, and you will find such tremendous power coming to you that you will feel it hard to bear even the least work done for others awakens the power within."

Future Directions in the Field

Although some conceptual and measurement progress have been made since the early days of scholarship, underlying the concept of workplace spirituality are multiple dimensions and meanings that require acknowledgment and proper scrutiny, suggestive of new ways of scholarship in the field.

To this end, there is a need to support the ongoing development in the field by properly theorizing and delineating what workplace spirituality is while addressing current concerns about the current reductionism that tones down the essence of the concept.

However, this does not suggest that workplace spirituality scholars are to jettison the current quantitative approach which at the moment seems to be fairly developed, rather, scholars are encouraged to theorize and incorporate mechanisms and processes that will advance the field beyond direct relationships that simply focus on just the predictor and criterion domains.

For instance, this could include work that enhances the understanding of the moderating and mediating influences of workplace spirituality on the relationships between already widely studied constructs—such as organizational culture, workplace health, leadership, human quality of treatment and organizational citizenship behaviour—and their antecedents and their outcomes.

Future Research

Further research should continue to initiate the relationship between organizational performance and workplace spirituality while also probing possible moderators and mediators of this relationship. Next, research in future should strive to pinpoint reasons for the evident disconnection between workplace outcomes and individual-level spirituality.

Finally, future research should work toward the establishment of basic relationships between workplace spirituality and workplace outcomes through empirical analysis.

Conclusion

Eventually, the complexities of the modern society and the modern workplace converged to re-emphasize the need for people to do meaningful work in order to live a fulfilling life. Due to this development, within the last two decades, organizational scholars and practitioners have paid increasing attention to the concept of workplace spirituality.

An attempt has been made here to take a broad look at the dynamics facilitating the recent emergence of workplace spirituality as a field of interest from its historical foundation to the more current literature that has evolved. Though the concept in itself is not new, the ways and means by which it is evolving do call for new research approaches and methods that encourage conversations from multiple perspectives to further develop the field.

Spirituality at work is increasingly gaining popularity among scholars and practitioners primarily because it helps employees experience a strong bond with their work emotionally, physically, and cognitively. These experiences lead to greater engagement in the workplace that in turn leads to higher individual and organizational productivity.

Operationally, workplace spirituality has been measured using several scales, but the commonality across all those are mindfulness and connectedness.

UNIT–VI

Future Trends

Future Trends—Quality of Work Life

The concept and nature of work have undergone numerous changes over the years. During the 19th century, workers wrestled to safeguard their right to determine how and when they would work. This was the great age of cooperatives, strikes and political movements led by small artisans defending individual methods of working against the factory system.

As the 20th century progressed, workers were gradually trapped within the formal economy of jobs and factories, and tussled to control the amount of labour they would have to give to the system in order to live. This was the age of the eight-hour day struggle, for weekends off, holiday and sickness pay, of a decent wage and guaranteed employment.

The defeat of these struggles has reduced the ability of the working class to oppose the intensification and casualisation of work, while increasing their dependence on the bosses to obtain the means to live. For some, working time has increased beyond the eight-hour shift into overtime and additional part-time work.

An employee cannot say no to do overtime work. In low wage industries, workers get overtime work as a favour from managements and union leaders. Companies avoid laws requiring premium pay for overtime by calling it 'overstay' or offering 'hardship allowances' instead of overtime pay. Additionally, there has been a huge change from long-term employment with its often-better pay and conditions to sub-contracting and self-employment.

In this manner in the "new economy" there are several changes in the nature of economic activity, such as strong growth in the services sector, increased levels of productivity growth and globalized markets. Work in the new economy is deemed to be different to work in the old economy because the spreading of information and communications technologies (ICT)[1] has changed the way in which firms do business and create value.

ICT has augmented the flexibility of capital goods, making capital investment more productive and encouraging firms to substitute capital for labour. This trend contributes to the globalization of markets, has changed the nature of work and its ramification for quality of work life of people.

The pressure of competitiveness due to globalization and privatization has resulted in many far reaching changes in the work place. Companies are designing their work systems around the following four props:

- Virtual Organizations
- Flexible and Adaptive Workforce
- Contingent Pay, and
- Democratic Governance at Workplace.

Shifting Focus

Keeping people engaged in organizational work and making them realize that they contribute to the mission of the organisation is a key challenge. The following Table 1 provides insights into the shifts depending on whether a company is engaged in traditional agriculture or manufacturing or information technology leveraged manufacturing and service sector.

Table 1: Shifting Focus in the Realm of Work[2]

Aspect	*Traditional Agriculture*	*Early/ Traditional Industry*	*Post-Industrial Service/Hi-tech*
Wealth	Land	Money	Mind/Information
Skill/Effort	Brawn-Muscle	Machine Tending	Brain/Mind Attitude and ability matter, not just skill
Management Philosophy	Unilateral	Pluralistic	Egalitarian
Management Style	Autocratic	Paternalistic	Collegial
Employment Context	Master – Servant	Employer – Employee	Partners
Relationship	One-sided Dependence	Interdependence	Mutuality and Independence
Communication	Top – Down	Two – Way	Transparent
Motivation	Fear	Favour	Fairness
Performance Appraisal	Information Confidentia, Boss	Formal, One – Way	Formal, Open, Participative Appraisals
Control	Direction and Control	Inducement	Consensus/Commitment

Upcoming Trends

The details of some changes are mentioned below:

I. *Job Insecurity and Work Intensification*[3]

1. In 1974 at the Eicher factory in Faridabad, 450 workers produced 80 tractors per month. Supervisors then drove workers to make 150 tractors in a month. An incentive scheme was introduced in 1978 and workers started producing 500 tractors a month, then 1,000 in 1982 and 1,500 per month in 1988.

In 1989, a re-engineering plan was implemented. The number of workers was halved, though they still had to produce the same number of tractors, and the incentive scheme was discarded. Eicher then used the latest "human resource development" scheme to reduce the number of workers further and goaded them to produce 2,000 tractors monthly.

At some time, incentives were given when a tractor was assembled in 15 minutes. Now it is done in 10 minutes without incentives, and the management wants it done in seven. The unions in the factory have fought the worker's cause and fought it well—their members are allowed to take all of nine minutes, not seven, to assemble a tractor.

Among industrial wage-workers, incentives for increased production are often used to make workers supervise intensification of their own bodies. Incentives are meant to lure workers to give more than normal production. The increased levels of production become the new norm—to be met without incentives. The management then begins a new cycle of increasing work-load and intensity.

A major study conducted in 1999 reported that "the root cause of job insecurity and work intensification lies with the reduced staffing levels pursued by senior managers in response to market pressures from competitors and dominant stakeholders".

That same study revealed that 60% of employees in the United Kingdom claimed the pace of work and the effort required to do it had greatly increased, resulting in poor general health in the workforce and tense family relationships. Stress and ill-health are made worse by job insecurity.

Of course the two are used together to exploit workers more intensively: "if you want to keep your job, work harder" and "unless you work harder, you will lose your job". Thirty per cent of the workforce works longer than 48 hours a week, with 39% reporting an increase in working hours.

Between 2000 and 2002 alone, the number of men working more than 60 hours per week rose from one in eight to one in six. The number of women working long hours has doubled. Fifty per cent of workers report inadequate or very inadequate staffing levels and as production and quality suffer, performance appraisal systems are introduced, causing more stress and worry.

A major source of job insecurity is the distrust employees have of their bosses. Few employees consider their managers have any faithfulness towards them. The longer one remains in a state of insecurity the more his physical and mental well-being deteriorates.

II. *Flexibilization and Casualization*

Flexibilization is often presented as the creation of flexible working patterns. Many employees have no objection to flexible hours and working but it is the imposition of flexibility that provokes so much opposition. Interestingly (and not surprisingly), those with interesting jobs are greatly in favour of flexible working. For them it means more time with their family members, more leisure and quality time. They claim to be able to work smarter and harder.

Study after study show, however, that this choice is not open to working class people in cul-de-sac type jobs. The working class response to flexibilization—a high labour turnover, absenteeism, low commitment and poor performance—is matched by the reduction in benefits, performance management techniques and rigorous monitoring of work and working.

The report SMEs and Flexible Working Arrangements, by Shirley Dex and Fiona Scheibl, of the Judge Institute of Management, Cambridge, is published by The Joseph Rowntree Foundation that found that flexible working arrangements, practiced informally, are far more common in small organizations.

The researchers divide types of employer into three groups in terms of their adoption of flexible work: holistic, selective, and resistant—in other words, those who go for it, those who do a bit and those that don't. The Britain government introduced the Work-Life Balance Campaign in 2000.

The campaign was to help employers to recognize the benefits adopting policies and procedures to enable employees to adopt flexible working patterns. This would help staff to become better motivated and more productive because they were better able them to balance their work and other aspects of their lives.

Conversely, casualization is the process by which the power of employers to give or refuse to give employment is greater than before. Many bosses are introducing 'zero hour' contracts, where there is no assurance of work and one is permanently on standby.

This has the benefit to the bosses as workers are not having any rights or protection under the law. The risk associated with the uncertainties of unplanned economies, of having to pay idle workers for instance, is transferred to the workers themselves. Many millions of jobs have always been or are rapidly becoming casualized.

III. *Macdonaldization*

Donaldisation (the modern form of Taylorism) is a system of producing goods and services in which the work process is broken into its smallest part, systematically analyzed, re-engineered to maximise profit and replicated in each and every working environment that produces those goods.

Making things becomes a series of entirely independent, discrete, controllable actions, eliminating independent thought and creativity. Employees become estranged from the process, required to perform a series of meaningless tasks. Such alienation from the work produces depression, anger, an unthinking and uncaring remoteness from other people.

Everywhere this process is used the bosses are happy with the amount produced but appalled by its low quality. The labour turnover in these factories is evidence of the determination of people to resist their exploitation. The bosses get rid of any worker who shows signs of resistance or who are too demoralised to produce efficiently.

This system is also often known as Toyotism, after the Toyota, Japan factory system introduced in the 1960s and 1970s. The level of control over workers has been deepened by the introduction of individual work contracts and other processes that impose obligations to produce on the individual while weakening collective agreements and relationships—creating what is known in Europe as the 'diffuse factory'.

What is new about Toyotism is "just-in-time" production and prompt reaction to market requirements; the imposition of multi-jobbing on workers employed on several machines, either simultaneously or sequentially; quality control throughout the entire flow of production and real-time information on the progress of production in the factory.

Production is often come to a standstill and work-teams, departments or even the whole factory called to account. Anybody who shows a waged-worker's indifference to the company's productivity requirements and decides not to join "quality control" groups etc., is stigmatised and encouraged to leave.

How the useful is divided from the not-so useful is a science in itself. Increasingly, consumption and leisure are being 'McDonaldised'. Now we expect to be able to find the same brand names throughout the world. Culture is increasingly global but it also increasingly mass-manufactured and distributed, designed for mass appeal.

IV. *Commodification*

Work used to be a purposeful and meaningful activity. There was spiritual contentment in working and co-operating to meet the needs of oneself, one's family and people. People chose the work they did if they could and invested much of their personality and abilities in the making and production of useful, better or beautiful things.

Today, the supremacy of consumption as a social good and conferrer of social status on people as individuals has made the product far more important than the producer. Work has died away to have a personal value for those who sweat. In many cases it does not have a social value to society.

Large amounts of work are simply about the reproduction of capitalism. It matters only because this is the means by which capitalism rationalises itself and produces the means—money—for its own continuation. The activity produces nothing, except money, whose social value is zero.

Work only matters in terms of what is produced—the commodity—and the social and personal value of what is produced to the person consuming it. Of course, many people realise this but are themselves trapped by the artificial need and desire to consume.

We become our own gaoler! It is through consumption that the majority channel their aspirations—to pleasure, to a sense of meaning and personal identity. Our aspirations to freedom have been transferred from the workplace to the rest of our lives but the commodification of personal life and leisure has simply built more cares around our life.

The refusal to work must be accompanied by the refusal to consume (and vice versa), to participate in the reproduction of everyday life through the production and consumption of useless commodities via a co-modified process: work.

V. *Rescheduling Working Arrangements*

Alternative ways of scheduling the days and hours of work are increasingly common. These arrangements reshape the traditional schedules, such as the 40-hour week and 8 to 5 day, in ways that better accommodate individual needs. These arrangements help employees balance work with their non-work responsibilities and activities, and are among the innovations commonly found at "family friendly" employers.

Compressed Workweek

A compressed workweek is any work schedule that allows a full-time job to be completed in fewer than the standard five days. The most common compressed workweek is the 4–40, where 40 hours of work are accomplished in four 10-hour days.

Someone working a 4–40 often benefits from increased leisure time, more three-day weekends, free weekdays to pursue personal business, and lower commuting costs. The organization can benefit, too, in terms of reduced energy consumption during three-day shutdown, lower employee absenteeism, improved recruiting of new employees, and the extra time available for building and equipment maintenance.

However, some workers complain about increased fatigue from the extended workday and family adjustment problems. Customer complaints occur due to service interruptions and breaks in work coverage.

Part-Time Work

Part-time work has become increasingly common in modern society. It has also proven controversial in some important respects. There are two kinds of part-time work:

1. Temporary part-time work is where an employee is classified as "temporary" and works less than the standard (for example, 40-hour workweek), and
2. Permanent part-time work is where a worker is considered "permanent" but works fewer hours that the standard workweek.

Organizations sometimes employ part-time workers in order to hold down labour costs and more easily adjust staffing to peaks and valleys in the business cycle. Both temporary and permanent part-time work can benefit people who hold full-time jobs elsewhere, or who only want to work part-time for personal reasons.

Job Sharing

Job sharing is dividing one full time work between two or more people according to a schedule agreed to among themselves and the employer. The two typically work different parts of the week with some overlapping work time in the weekly schedule to coordinated activities. This works for some people, but the major challenge is finding a partner with a compatible work style and pace.

Telecommuting

Telecommuting describes work done in the home or in a remote location via use of a computer and/or facsimile machine linked to a central office or other employment locations. Sometimes this arrangement is called flexi place. Teleworkers may be described as those who spend a substantial proportion of their time at home and who use telephone and computers in the course of this work.

Studies of teleworking identify the main advantages as:

- Reduction in office costs
- Increased motivation and productivity
- Improved recruitment and retention
- More opportunities for those with family responsibilities and the disabled
- Increased flexibility
- Improvement in equal opportunities
- Meeting employee demands
- Reducing the time, cost and stress of commuting to and from work, and
- Less absenteeism.

The main disadvantages to the employee are social segregation and difficulty of self-motivation. So far as an employer is concerned, they are those of ensuring effective communication & management and the difficulty of ensuring that the worker complies with health and safety requirements.

For teleworking to succeed there needs to be significant mutual trust between the employer and employee along with clear goals and procedures for the workers involved.

Shift Work

It has traditionally been used in manufacturing environments to maximize productivity from fixed resources and costs. More recently, shift work has become a feature of the 24/7 service economy and a by-product of globalization. For example, supermarkets and computer help desks are now typically open 24 hours a day, seven days a week.

Nowadays, a computer user calling for technical support during regular business hours is likely to end up speaking with a technician working the "graveyard shift" in India. Despite its extensive use in certain environments, shift work poses some practical challenges for some employers.

Call Centres

One of the recent developments in organizations has been the growth of call centres. These are functions within organizations designed to respond to a large volume of calls from customers, or to generate sales, and comprise a large number of operators, usually at least 10, whose role is to provide a first line of service to callers. They are sometimes described as the battery farms of the information age.

Call centres bring with them a whole thrust of different issues for organizations to confront. These include:

- How to maintain motivation and morale in such an environment.
- How to measure and reward performance.
- How to avoid high levels of stress arising from the intensive nature of work, and
- Ensuring that the call centre staff has the required levels of skills and training.

Hybrid Work Arrangements

A fall-out of the post-covid work culture, it allows employees the flexibility to work from home while still maintaining some in-person collaboration. More than 700 employers' worldwide reported that 87 per cent of employers will embrace greater flexibility post-pandemic, with most planning a hybrid onsite/remote-work model. This was reported in the March 2021 Mercer Survey.[4]

Some employers are implementing technology to manage occupancy such as online platforms or cell phone apps that allow workers to book workspace when they want to be in the office. The term "hoteling" refers to having telecommuters reserve an office or workstation for their in-office days in lieu of assigning them a permanent workspace. Hoteling can cut an organization's office space requirements and reduce costs.

Snowbird Programs

Such a program allows employees to transfer to an organization's location in a warmer region during winter months. A telemarketing operation or help-desk call centre can be physically located anywhere. Such an example is not practiced in India.

In a snowbird program, an organization might be able to attract a better and larger labour force (including older persons) if, for example, it had a program allowing employees to spend winter months working in Florida or Arizona. Pharmacy Company CVS Caremark, with 2 lakh American employees, offers a snowbird program that allows pharmacists to migrate south to places such as Florida for the winter.

VI. *Growing Relevance of Knowledge Work*

Over the years, relevance of knowledge work has been increasing. The nature of knowledge work is significantly different from traditional industrial work. Charles Despres and Jean-Marie Hiltrop of the International Institute of Management Development, Switzerland has defined these differences of knowledge and traditional forms of work. These differences are illustrated in Table 2.

Table 2: Difference between Traditional Work and Knowledge Work[5]

HRM Dimension	*Knowledge Work*	*Traditional Work*
Employee's Career Formation	External to the organization through years of education and socialization	Internal to the organization through training, development, rules and prescriptive career schemes
Employee's Loyalty	To Professions, Networks and Peers	To the organization and its career systems
Skills/Knowledge Sets	Specialized and deep, but often with diffuse peripheral focuses	Narrow and often functional
Locus of Work	In Groups and Projects	Around Individuals
Focus of Work	Customers, Problems and Issues	Tasks, Objectives, Performance

HRM Dimension	*Knowledge Work*	*Traditional Work*
Skill Obsolescence	Rapid	Gradual
Activity/Feedback Cycles	Lengthy from a business perspective	Primary and of an immediate nature
Performance Measures	Process effectiveness potentially great, but often erratic	Task Deliverables Little (as planned), but regular and dependable
Impact on Company Success	A few major contributions of strategic and long-term importance	Many small contributions that support the master plan
Organizational Structure	Hierarchic, Mechanistic, Atomic	Holographic, Organic, Overlapping
Control of Work	Vested in the supervisory process	Vested in the Individuals
Managerial Functions	Functions	Process
Authority Power	Hierarchical Position, Command and Control	Professional Influence, Communication
Control of Work Outcomes	Remains with Central Management	Negotiated between Supervisors and Groups of Knowledge Workers

Prophesying the Future

A report published by the government of the United Kingdom—'Work in the Knowledge-Driven Economy'—takes a look at what work might be like in organizations of the future.

It concludes that for many in this generation, the world of work will be very different to that of their parents. It warns we must all prepare for change and will need new skills in the work-place of the future. The report envisages that:

- The move from manufacturing to service sector jobs and from blue collar to white collar jobs will continue.
- White collar clerical work will decline whilst highly skilled knowledge-based jobs will grow.
- Service sector employment will become increasingly important as the 'human touch' will be difficult to replicate with machines.
- Teleworking could grow substantially.

The report develops two possible scenarios of the world to help understand how the future of work might change. These are:

'Wired World'

Depicting an economy composed of a network of individuals, working on projects through the Internet. In it, individuals will no longer be able to rely on the 'comfort zones' created by larger companies (personnel advice, legal, marketing, technical and financial expertise). It is a world where individuals develop sets of skills and a knowledge base and sell these to other individuals or companies.

'Built to Last'

Describing a world in which large companies use incentive packages and other powerful mechanisms to keep the knowledge of their employees in-house.

The future will contain elements of both scenarios and whatever the mix, if as predicted the speed of change increases, people will have to become more adaptable. This has implications for the skills that we need and the way we learn.

Organization, in the past, gave more importance on innovative technology for higher productivity surpassing the needs and mental state of its employees. This created a negative impact on the working environment among the employees. Thus, it was realised that societal support goes hand in hand with technical innovations.

This integration can only be made through quality of work life programmes. Quality of work life refers to all the organizational inputs which aim at the employee's satisfaction and enhancing organizational effectiveness. Having concern with the life on the job is not new.

The increased upheaval of union activities in the 30s and 40s, through. Even before that, labour was vigorously collective bargaining and legislations, led to improved working conditions protesting management attempts to change the work environment.

A study by Professor Robert F Hoxie, Chicago University in 1915[6], reported how the unions, particularly the machinists, were fighting scientific management techniques.

In the late 1950s, the term QWL was used to stress the prevailing poor quality of life at workplace and it was first defined then in terms of people's reacting to work, particularly an individual's job satisfaction and mental health. In the new economy, emphasis is placed upon the latest technology, most ground-breaking management practices, and state-of-the-art office buildings.

However, these are of no worth without the talent, commitment and contribution of a quality workforce. Every organization must do its best to provide a working environment that is inclusive, enriching and encouraging to all employees. This spirit must be visible in all work processes and benefits.

Modern Workplaces

In today's world, the structure, content and process of work have changed. Work is now:

- More cognitively complex
- More team-based and collaborative
- More dependent on social skills
- More dependent on technological competence
- More time pressured
- More mobile and less dependent on geography.

Today, people will also work for an organization that is likely to be very different due to competitive pressures and technological breakthroughs. Organizations today are:

- Leaner and more agile.
- More focused on identifying value from the customer perspective.
- More tuned to dynamic competitive requirements and strategy.
- Less hierarchical in structure and decision authority.
- Less likely to provide life-long careers and job security.
- Continually reorganizing to maintain or gain competitive advantage.

Although many factors ultimately contribute to the changing patterns of work, organizational theorists point to two key drivers:

1. Increasing pressures on organizations to be more competitive, agile, and customer focused—to be a "lean enterprise".
2. Communication and information technology breakthroughs, especially mobile technologies and the Internet that enable work to be separated from time and space.

How Work is Changing

Over the past two decades, a new pattern of work is emerging as knowledge economy realizes the full potential of both new technologies and new organizational models. The changes fall into the following domains:

- Cognitive Competence
- Social and interactive competence
- The new "psychological contract" between employees and employers
- Changes in process and place.

Cognitive Overload

Vastly increased access to information has made work both easier and more difficult. The ease comes from ability to rapidly locate and download information from diverse websites. The difficulty comes with the need to consume and make sense of new information in a timely fashion.

Information overload, coupled with time pressures and increased work complexity, lead to what psychologists call "cognitive overload syndrome (COS)." Symptoms of COS include stress, inability to concentrate, multitasking, task switching, and a tendency to focus on what is easy to do quickly rather than what is important.

Social and Interactive Competence

In a 2011 report on the changing nature of work,[7] the National Research Council called attention to the importance of relational and interactive aspects of work. As collaboration and collective activity become more prevalent, workers need well-developed social skills—what the report calls "emotional labour."

Good Social Skills are Necessary for:

- *Team Work and Collaboration*—Conflict resolution and negotiation skills are essential to collaborative work. Conflicts often occur about group goals, work methods, assignments, workloads, and recognition. Team members with good conflict and negotiation skills are better equipped to deal openly with problems, to listen and understand different perspectives, and to resolve issues in mutually beneficial ways.
- *Relationship Development and Networking*—Sharing important information, fulfilling promises, willingness to be influenced, and listening are building blocks of reciprocity and the development of trust. When workers trust one another, they are more committed to attaining mutual goals, more likely to help one another through difficulties, and more willing to share and develop new ideas.

- *Learning and Growth*—Many organizations strive to be learning centres—to create conditions in which employees learn not only through formal training but through relationships with co-workers. Learning relationships build on joint problem solving, insight sharing, learning from mistakes, and working closely together to aid transmission of tacit knowledge. Learning also develops from mentoring relationships between newcomers and those with experience and organizational know-how.

How Workplace is Changing

The changing workplace is driven by the organizational issues and enabled by technologies that support mobility and easy access to information. These pressures and opportunities, however, have not resulted in a specific new workplace model.

Many models and ideas exist concurrently, with designs depending upon the organization, its work practices, culture and customers. Table 3 highlights key drivers, solutions and potential issues raised by the solution.

Table 3: Drivers, Solutions, and Issues of Changing Workplace

Drivers	*Workplace and Technology Solutions*	*Issues and Concerns*
Increased use of teams and cross unit work, more pressure for communication and information flow	• More meeting space • Greater variety of meeting spaces (open & enclosed, large & small) • Smaller individual workspaces • Greater interior visibility to support awareness • Mobile supports (phones, laptops, PDAs, wireless) • Personal video, instant messaging, desktop team software • More use of project rooms • Displayed	• Increased noise • Increased distractions & interruptions • Potential for "over communicating" • Cultural barriers to behavioural change • Individuals working longer hours to compensate for lack of time to do individual tasks • Expectations that workers are always available

Drivers	*Workplace and Technology Solutions*	*Issues and Concerns*
	information and work progress • Small rooms for individual focus • Lockers for personal belongings	
Greater use of dispersed work groups - often global	• Increased use of video conferencing, computer-based team tools • More reliance on conference calls • Greater need for mobile technological supports for meeting rooms • Use of facilities beyond normal working hours	• Expansion of the workday to accommodate geographically dispersed team meetings • Loss of opportunity to develop trust through face to face interaction • More difficulty managing and coordinating • Very high dependence on technological reliability
Continual reorganization and restructuring	• Flexible infrastructure to support rapid reconfiguration • Mobile furnishings	• Acoustical problems with loss of good enclosure • Potential for reduced ergonomic effectiveness
Reduced costs/more efficient space use	• Shares or unassigned workspaces • Centralized filing system • Reduced work-station size and increased overall densities • Greater overall spatial variety to enable different kinds of work to be accommodated at	• Increased distractions and interruptions • Increased noise • May meet with employee resistance • More difficult for paper intensive work

Drivers	*Workplace and Technology Solutions*	*Issues and Concerns*
	same time	
Improved quality of work life and attraction of new workers	• More equitable access to daylight, views and other amenities • More equitable spatial allocation and workspace features • Amenities for stress reduction and quite relaxation	• Resistance from those who support hierarchical space allocation

The Age of New-Normal

The COVID-19 pandemic has given a jump-start to flexible work arrangements, especially remote work. With many states issuing stay-at-home orders and allowing only essential businesses to keep their physical locations open, unprepared employers were forced to implement flexible work options on the fly.

As social distancing orders are lifted, and businesses reopen, employee requests for flexible hours and remote-work arrangements will be part of the new normal. Now that many employers have experienced how successful telecommuting can be for their organization or how work hours that differ from the normal 9-to-5 can be adopted without injury to productivity, offering flexible work arrangements have become more commonplace.

Even in the absence of a pandemic, flexible work arrangements can improve recruitment and retention efforts, augment organizational diversity efforts, encourage ethical behaviour and help the organization's efforts to be socially responsible. Employers can experience cost savings, improved attendance and productivity, and an increase in employee engagement.

Weighing Opportunities and Challenges

Many Indians now consider work/life balance and flexibility to be the most important factors in considering job offers. In fact, 81 percent of employees said they would be more loyal to their employers if they had flexible work options, according to a 2020 survey by FlexJobs.

However, offering flexible work arrangements can involve a paradigm shift for organizations, especially smaller ones that may not have the critical mass of technology, budget, management and competitive flexibility necessary to make extensive use of flexible work arrangements.

Opportunities

Flexible work arrangements offer numerous benefits to both employers and employees. Such benefits include:

- Assisting in recruiting efforts.
- Enhancing worker morale.
- Managing employee attendance and reducing absenteeism.
- Improving retention of good workers.
- Boosting productivity.
- Creating a better work life balance for workers.
- Minimizing harmful impact on global ecology. Certain flexible work arrangements can contribute to sustainability efforts by reducing carbon emissions and workplace "footprints" in terms of creation of new office buildings.
- Allowing for business continuity during emergency circumstances such as a weather disaster or pandemic.

A company-wide Unilever policy permits more than 1 lakh employees—everyone except factory production workers—to work anytime, anywhere, as long as they meet business needs. Leadership identified the following benefits when making a business case for the policy:

1. *Travel:* Conferencing technology like Skype would reduce travel expenses.
2. *Technology:* Upgrading technology would help the company stay competitive and build Unilever's brand as a best place to work. Costs would be offset by other savings.
3. *Real Estate:* Cubicles and offices would be converted to communal facilities, thereby reducing space requirements by 30 percent. Sites would be converted gradually as leases expired.
4. *Health:* Onsite fitness facilities would increase employee satisfaction, help reduce illness and cut insurance costs.
5. *Work Life Balance:* Empowering workers would enhance work life balance. Satisfaction ratings would rise and recruitment would become easier.

6. *Sustainability:* Reduces travel, office energy costs and paperwork would decrease the environmental footprint.
7. *Retention and Engagement:* Flexibility would enhance the employer value proposition, improving retention and supporting diversity.

Challenges

Managers tasked with implementing strategic goals-related to flexible work arrangements need to keep many things in mind:

- Keeping programs relevant to workers' real needs/wants.
- Focusing on the unique needs of specific groups of workers without creating a second class of workers and without engaging in unlawful disparate treatment or disparate impact discrimination.
- Communicating broadly to achieve the benefits of flexible work arrangements.
- Exercising caution when eliminating a program that is not working or is no longer relevant to enough workers. Any loss of a benefit can impair morale, even if only a few workers had used it. Employers should consider phasing out unproductive programs over time.

In addition, managing the change from a traditional work environment to one with more flexible work arrangements can create or throw a spotlight on various managerial trouble spots, such as:

- Upper management's resistance to change.
- Control issues, especially in terms of supervision of work.
- Working as a team with far-flung members and highly variant schedules.
- Maintaining safety and security of personnel and data.

Emerging Technologies

As we already know, emerging technologies are affecting today's world, from the way people make phone calls to the way companies operate. With this in mind, it's vital to say that the chance the working environment will change in the next decade is high.

The tech industry is a fast-growing sector. As a result, the nature of work, working dynamics, and the notion of the workplace are also evolving. Under those circumstances, it's not a surprise that employees should learn new skills to stay relevant.

Nowadays, employment requirements are higher and competition is just as harsh. In that case, the workforce needs to understand how new technologies are affecting today's market, workers have to get familiar with new inventions to meet new demands.

The future of work can be uncertain. However, in order to have a clear image of how the future could be, we have to pay attention to what companies need. Given that, here are some aspects of how new technologies will affect the future of work.

Less Manual Tasks (Automation)

Undoubtedly, emerging technologies are changing the nature of work. As a result, these techs are reducing the need to perform several repetitive tasks manually. A few years ago, having automated machines that could help during a product's development process was unbelievable. But thanks to technologies like machine learning, today it's possible.

- Automation has side effects: Job roles that include only manual tasks are disappearing, fewer candidates will be hired for their manual skills, and more employees will be retained for their creative and strategic thinking skills.
- Repetitive tasks are time-consuming: Automation allows workers to focus on more important tasks like solving problems, designing products, and interpreting data. In the future, employers will seek out candidates that can continuously learn new skills. It's because while the tech industry changes fast, the ability to learn new things will become more valuable.

Generally speaking, specific knowledge will need to be continuously updated, and workers will need to adapt. If you're versatile and like learning new things, you'll be able to be part of the world's next workforce.

Different Working Methods

Automation is not only changing the nature of work but also how work is done. The implementation of artificial intelligence (AI) technology in the manufacturing processes is helping companies to increase productivity. As a result, more companies are using robots to build their products.

On the other hand, AI is not only affecting manufacturing. In fact, it's also changing the way administrative processes are carried out. For example, when we talk about postal services, years ago it was the postman who delivered the mail. After some time, thanks to the tech market evolution, we are able to use emails.

But, nowadays, it is totally different, AI systems can send and receive emails automatically. Also, mobile developers have built mail applications so customers can use their smart phones to manage their emails.

Given these points, it's realistic to expect that in the future, more companies are likely to implement the use of robots and automated systems in their processes. As a result, job roles will be redefined, and organizations will need to train their employees to maximize the human-machine effect.

More Remote Employees (Work from Home)

Since new communication platforms allow companies to communicate overseas, remote working has transcended all boundaries. In the same way, it's important to realize that tech talents have become popular because of their capability to work remotely. For example, tech professionals like database administrators, cyber security and data scientists, are able to work from home. For that reason, they don't need to waste time moving from their home to their workplace.

Remote work has allowed companies not only to reduce costs but also make their employees happier. While working from home, tech talents can spend more valuable time with their family members. Given that, more and more tech professionals demand remote working benefits.

Additionally, remote work allows companies to hire candidates from any country. They can hire qualified tech professionals that demand lower compensation and benefits. In other words, remote working enables organizations to achieve their goals in a cost-efficient way.

While the tech market continues to grow, and new technologies are being created, remote working will be essential for companies to run. With this in mind, it's important to realize that if you can work remotely, you have one step into the future. Otherwise, if you are not able to work remotely, your job role will probably be displaced, and you'll need to change careers.

Given these points, enrolling in coding boot camps is an excellent choice to be ready for future challenges. Springboard is a company that offers courses in fields like UX design, data analytics, and software engineering. Their part-time programs allow you to learn enterprise-level skills in only six months.

Also, the company allows students to learn from the comfort of their homes as classes are taught online. When joining Springboard's team, students can receive support from experienced mentors that will help them launch their new tech careers.

Springboard offers several financing options for those who the money can be a barrier. Its financing options are designed to fit students' needs, from deferred tuition to upfront payment discounts.

Less Physical Infrastructure

With the implementation of cloud computing and remote working, companies have been able to reduce their dependence on physical infrastructure. Decades ago, companies needed large rooms to place their database centre. However, thanks to cloud storage, companies have been able to remove their physical database infrastructure.

Nowadays, data is one of the most valuable resources for companies. For that reason, organizations need to keep their information safe. The use of cloud computing services allows companies not only to store their data but also to keep their information safe. As a result, more organizations are using cloud computing services to store their data.

Additionally, while organizations continue hiring more remote workers, the need for physical office infrastructure will be reduced. In fact, in the future, physical office spaces may no longer be needed as everybody will work from home.

Thus, emerging technologies are reshaping the future of work. They are changing from the way the job is done to where the job is actually done. Given that, it is crucial to say that learning new tech skills or starting a new tech career will be necessary to be ready for future challenges.

Creativity and Innovation

As technology absorbs many jobs once done by people, creativity and innovative thinking are increasingly thought of as an important source of not only competitive advantage but also future jobs. Along with automation, the off-shoring of routine work is leading many business forecasters to predict that the majority of jobs remaining in developed countries like the United States will emphasize a new set of skills.

Though the ability to think logically and analytically will remain important, they predict that organizations will also place greater importance on "right-brained" capabilities such as big-picture thinking and the ability to bring together disparate ideas to create new synergies, products and services.

While the management practices that support creative and innovative thinking may be less straightforward than managing task-oriented, routine jobs, their use may ultimately turn out to be more rewarding for managers and human resource professionals not only because these practices highlight the importance of effective human capital management as a driver of value, but also because constructing an environment where creative skills and abilities thrive may lead to greater employee engagement, motivation and success.

HR and Drivers of Creativity and Innovation

With non-monetary factors so important to current levels of "return on innovation" and creativity and innovation considered such critical skills for future success by corporate leaders, HR clearly must consider strategies to improve the creative environment of the workforce both now and in the future.

In doing so, HR professionals will need to take into account a number of factors, including the best ways to measure creativity and innovation, team versus individual creativity, motivation, training for creativity, and the influence of broader demographic and societal trends on access to creative workers.

The following table categorically shows the knowledge and skills to look forward to in the near future:

Table 4: Top 10 Skills Expected to Increase in Importance Over 25 Years[8]

Rank	*Basic Knowledge and Applied Skill*	*Percentage*
1.	Critical Thinking/Problem Solving	77.8
2.	Information Technology Application	77.4
3.	Teamwork/Collaboration	74.2
4.	Creativity/Innovation	73.6
5.	Diversity	67.1
6.	Leadership	66.9
7.	Oral Communications	65.9
8.	Professionalism/Work Ethics	64.4
9.	Ethics/Social Responsibility	64.3
10.	Written Communications	64

Balance

The work life balance is the state of equilibrium where a person equally prioritizes the demands of one's career and the demands of one's personal life. Some of the common reasons that lead to a poor work life balance include:

- Increased responsibilities at work
- Working longer hours
- Increased responsibilities at home
- Having children

Often, work takes precedence over everything else in our lives. Our desire to succeed professionally can push us to set aside our own well-being. Creating harmonious work life balance or work life integration is critical, though, to improve not only our physical, emotional and mental well-being, but it is also important for our career.

According to Chris Chancey, career expert and CEO of Amplio Recruiting, good work life balance has numerous positive effects including less stress, a lower risk of burnout and a greater sense of well-being. This not only benefits employees but employers, too.

When creating a schedule that works for you, think about the best way to achieve balance at work and in your personal life. Chancey said that work life balance is less about dividing the hours in your day evenly between work and personal life and, instead, is more about having the flexibility to get things done in your professional life while still having time and energy to enjoy your personal life. There may be some days where you work longer hours so you have time later in the week to enjoy other activities.

Here are eight ways to create a better work life balance, as well as how to be a supportive manager:

1. *Accept that there is No 'Perfect' Work Life Balance*

When you hear "work life balance," you probably imagine having an extremely productive day at work, and leaving early to spend the other half of the day with friends and family. While this may seem ideal, it is not always possible.

Heather Mohanan, founder of the career mentoring group #Bossin Heels, says that so far as work life balance is concerned, one should keep the following in mind:

- Don't strive for the perfect schedule, strive for a realistic one.
- Some days, one might focus more on work, while other day's one might have more time and energy to pursue your hobbies or spend time with your loved ones.
- Balance is achieved over time, not each day.
- It is important to remain fluid and constantly assess where you are versus your goals and priorities.
- At times, your children may need you, and other times, you may need to travel for work, but allowing yourself to remain open to redirecting and assessing your needs on any day is key in finding balance.

2. *Find a Job that You Love*

Although work is an expected societal norm, your career should not be restraining. If you hate what you do, you are not going to be happy, plain and simple. You do not need to love every aspect of your job, but it needs to be exciting enough that you don't dread getting out of bed every morning.

Career therapists recommend finding a job that you are so passionate about you would do it for free. They believe that if your job is draining you, and you are finding it difficult to do the things you love outside of work. You may be working in a toxic environment, for a toxic person, or doing a job that you truly don't love. If this is the case, it is time to find a new job.

3. *Prioritize Your Health*

Your overall physical, emotional and mental health should be your main concern. If you struggle with anxiety or depression and think therapy would benefit you, fit those sessions into your schedule, even if you have to leave work early or ditch your evening spin class. If you are battling a chronic illness, don't be afraid to call in sick on rough days. Overworking yourself prevents you from getting better, possibly causing you to take more days off in the future.

"Prioritizing your health first and foremost will make you a better employee and person," said Monahan, adding "You will miss less work, and when you are there, you will be happier and more productive." Prioritizing one's health does not have to consist of radical or extreme activities. It can be as simple as daily meditation or exercise.

4. *Don't be Afraid to Unplug*

Cutting ties with the outside world from time to time allows us to recover from weekly stress and gives us space for other thoughts and ideas to emerge. Unplugging can mean something simple like practicing transit meditation on your daily commute, instead of checking work emails.

Anuradha Kishore, a leading career counsellor of India, says, "Taking the time to unwind is critical to success and will help you feel more energized when you are on the clock."

5. *Take a Vacation*

Sometimes, truly unplugging means taking vacation time and shutting work completely off for a while. Whether your vacation consists of a one-day staycation or a two-week trip abroad, it's important to take time off to physically and mentally recharge.

According to the States of America Vacation Studies-2018[9] conducted by the United States Travel Association, 52% of employees reported having unused vacation days left over at the end of the year. Employees are often worried that taking time off will disrupt the workflow, and they will be met with a backlog of work when they return. This fear should not restrict you from taking a much-needed break.

"The truth is there is no nobility in not taking well-deserved time away from work. The benefits of taking a day off far outweigh the downsides," said Chancey. "With proper planning, you can take time away without worrying about burdening your colleagues or contending with a huge workload when you return," says Amrita Singh, who is an expert and well-known counsellor who helps students and employees realize their dreams.

6. *Make Time for Yourself and Your Loved Ones*

While your job is important, it should not be your entire life. You were an individual before taking this position, and you should prioritize the activities or hobbies that make you happy. Experts say that achieving work life balance requires deliberate action.

"When planning time with your loved ones, create a calendar for romantic and family dates. It may seem weird to plan one-on-one time with someone you live with, but it will ensure that you spend quality time with them without work life conflict. Just because work keeps you busy does not mean you should neglect personal relationships," says ICF certified career therapist Jagadish Kund.

7. *Set Boundaries and Work Hours*

When you leave the office, avoid thinking about upcoming projects or answering company emails. Consider having a separate computer or phone for work, so you can shut it off when you clock out. If that is not possible then use separate browsers, e-mails or filters for your work and personal platforms.

Additionally, Chancey recommended setting specific work hours. "Whether you work away from home or at home, it is important to determine when you will work and when you will stop working. Otherwise, you might find yourself answering work-related emails late at night, during vacations or on weekends off," he adds further.

One can also advise notifying team members and your manager about boundaries beyond which you cannot be accessible because you are engaged in personal activities. This will help to ensure that they understand and respect your workplace limits and expectations.

8. *Set Goals and Priorities (and stick to them)*

Set achievable goals by implementing time-management strategies, analyzing your to-do list, and cutting out tasks that have little to no value. Pay attention to when you are most productive at work and block that time off for your most important work-related activities.

Avoid checking your emails and phone every few minutes, as those are major time-wasting tasks that derail your attention and productivity. Structuring your day can increase productivity at work, which can result in more free time to relax outside of work.

Flexibility can pay off for employers in the long run. "As we look ahead, it is clear that in order to remain competitive, employers must find ways to offer flexible work options if they want to attract and retain top talent," said Hank Jackson, president and CEO of the Society for Human Resource Management.

Enhancing Quality

Jeff Davidson, who is a highly successful work life expert, believes that there are six elements of enhancing quality in work life balance:

1. ***Self-Management:*** Taking care of personal needs, such as eating, sleeping, exercising, plays a significant role in your work life balance. For instance, when you don't sleep well, you are tired and that impacts your work, too. And, more importantly, how you manage your own needs is only up to you.
2. ***Time-Management:*** Deciding on priorities and how you will finish all tasks on time can be challenging. At the same time, you need to deal with personal assignments, as well. Davidson suggests setting goals and selecting important & urgent tasks and working on them first. This is the essence of the Eisenhower Matrix Technique, which can improve your time management skills.
3. ***Stress Management:*** Hearing various noises at the workplace and dealing with distractions, either from other colleagues or from outside, can lead to stress. So to decrease stress levels, one needs to find a way to adapt to this kind of environment. Besides, Davidson points out that one should avoid multi-tasking because switching between projects and tasks can be stressful, too.
4. ***Managing Change:*** No matter where your work and what you do, it's likely that your job requires you to get used to frequent changes. To manage these changes better, you need to ensure that the volume of the change does not overwhelm you. This applies to any modifications in your private life, too.
5. ***Managing Technology:*** The technology you use should make your life easier, not more complicated. Remember that you rule technology, not the other way around.
6. ***Managing Leisure Time:*** Taking time off is a vital element of achieving a work-life balance. Besides, be sure to spend your leisure time doing various activities, in order to avoid monotony.

Skills Integration

A set of discrete skills can help you find ways to integrate the work life domains. You can learn these skills and with practice you can master them. You can achieve a kind of integration that will, in turn, help you have the impact you want to have and lead a life in which you stay true to yourself, serve others, and grow as a person. This integration is the key to leading a meaningful life.

To replace conflict with a sense of completeness, or integrity, does not require turning your whole world upside down. Instead it requires figuring out how to take incremental steps that are under your control and that move you in the direction you want to go, while bringing others along with you.

In pursuing one's passions, whether vocational or non-vocational, you can extract the special something that is unique about you and convert it into something that helps make others' lives a little better. It is not only thrilling to discover a way to do what you love and to love what you do, but it usually results in your having better market value, too.

For example, when you start, or maybe even a long time after you start, your band fails to gel. The parts don't sync, the instruments clash, and individuals fail to meld into a whole. But you work with what you have, combining disciplined structure, practice, increasing competence, concentrated effort, dedicated commitment, and trial and error.

You refine your skill so that you can produce the sound you hear inside your head, the melodies that stir your soul. Each instrument has its limits. Each has a specific contribution to make to the whole. For a jazz quartet to produce great music, discipline is as important as improvisation and serendipity. It's not magic, even if the result is often magical.

People Stories

To help one learn skills and see them in action, one must study the exemplary skills work life integration of the following six extraordinary people: Tom Tierney, Sheryl Sandberg, Eric Greitens, Michelle Obama, Julie Foudy and Bruce Springsteen.

These individuals have found ways to integrate work and the rest of life to achieve greater harmony in different areas of their lives. Taken together, these six exemplars illustrate what each skill looks like in action.

These profiles are based on extensive research into public information available—biographies, articles, books and recorded interviews available on the Internet. My goal is not to tell their entire life stories or provide complete pictures of them but rather to highlight key episodes in their lives that personify QWL skills integration. We can learn from their example on how to apply skills in our own lives.

Six Models

Each of these six models is a complicated mix of drives and desires, wants and weaknesses, confidence and self-scrutiny—just like you and me. And all of them are evolving. These models are:

1. *Tom Tierney*

Envision Your Legacy	Weave Disparate Strands	See New Ways of Doing Things

Outcomes: Tom Tierney is the chairman and co-founder of The Bridgespan Group, former CEO of the powerhouse global consulting firm Bain & Company and co-author of the philanthropy guide Give Smart. Throughout his accomplished career, Tierney has sought creative ways of fitting together the domains of his life, including learning from his children about what really matters.

He has built organizations that encourage personal growth by, for example, rewarding results and not face time and by motivating people with an inspiring vision of contribution to a greater good.

Discussion Question: What is Tom Tierney's method for focusing on his legacy?

2. *Sheryl Sandberg*

Convey Values with Stories	Build Supportive Networks	Resolve Conflicts Among Domains

Outcomes: As COO of Facebook, Sheryl Sandberg has redefined what it means to be a leader. Especially now, following the launch of her book-cum-social movement, Lean In, she is a powerful advocate for new models for women's advancement in society, ideas she conveys with the confidence of a seasoned storyteller.

Her candour about the challenges she faces in resolving conflicts among different parts of her life—as an executive, a catalyst for social change, a friend, a wife, a sister, and a mother—and about the non-traditional means she employs for doing so, make her a persuasive role model.

Discussion Question: How does Sheryl Sandberg's commitment to creating connections in the service of women's advancement help her company?

3. *Eric Greitens*

Hold Yourself Accountable	Apply All Your Resources	Focus on Results

Outcomes: Former Navy SEAL Eric Greitens, humanitarian, author and founder of a non-profit organization, has experienced many lifetimes' worth of adventure. He graduated from Duke, was both a Rhodes Scholar and a Truman Scholar, and attended Oxford. After completing PhD, Greitens forsook high-paying career opportunities for a chance to become a Navy SEAL, enduring a stint of military training often referred to as the hardest in the world.

For his service in Iraq, he was awarded a Purple Heart, and—after a difficult search for a meaningful next step to take—he went on to found The Mission Continues, an organization that helps heal wounded war veterans by guiding them to be of service in their communities.

Discussion Question: When does Eric Greitens hold himself accountable for achieving meaningful results?

4. *Michelle Obama*

Align Actions With Values	Manage Boundaries Intelligently	Embrace Change Courageously

Outcomes: Michelle Obama, the former First Lady of the United States and the first Afro-American woman in this position, stepped carefully into the role. The self-described Mom-in-Chief explains that she considers her daughters to be her first priority, even if this stance rankles' those who would have her do more in seeking broader political and cultural change.

In making sure her own children were receiving the most nutritious food possible, she began to advocate for better nutrition through the national initiative Let's Move! Her policies have won national acclaim.

Discussion Question: Why does Michelle Obama manage the boundaries among her different roles?

5. *Julie Foudy*

Know What Matters	Help Others	Challenge the Status Quo

Outcomes: Julie Foudy is a soccer champion who, in 1991, as a member of the US national team, won the first Women's World Cup. She was part of the iconic US soccer team that garnered Olympic gold in 1996, silver in 2000 and gold again in 2004. But she has done much more beyond the soccer field. She has led an array of organizations that promote athletics for young people, empower young women, and advocate for social causes.

Foudy's success is an outgrowth of her passion for soccer, her insistence on pursuing the most fruitful expression of her talents, and her ability to fuse all the important parts of her life—her soccer teams, her family and her advocacy for worthy causes.

Discussion Question: How did Julie Foudy figure out what was important to her?

6. *Bruce Springsteen*

Embody Values	Consistently Clarify Expectations	Create Cultures of Innovation

Outcomes: Although it may seem counter-intuitive to think of a rock-and-roll hero as an exemplary leader, Bruce Springsteen is the real deal. Springsteen has said that he creates music "to make people happy, feel less lonely, but also to be a conduit for a dialogue about the events of the day, the issues that impact people's lives, personal and social and political and religious.

With his hard-won clarity of purpose, derived from years of painful self-scrutiny, it follows naturally that he makes clear what he expects from the people around him, whether members of his band or members of his family. He's called "The Boss" for a reason.

Discussion Question: What does Bruce Springsteen do to encourage innovation?

The lives of these sterling men and women in business (Tom Tierney and Sheryl Sandberg), in public service (Eric Greitens and Michelle Obama) and in sports and entertainment (Julie Foudy and Bruce Springsteen) defy the myth of the zero-sum game, in which success in your career means failure in the rest of your life, and vice versa.

All of them, like the rest of us, have struggled, and their examples will help you see how you can cultivate a life in which values, actions, social contributions, and personal growth exist in harmony, like a great piece of jazz music. This is a life in which disparate pieces fall into place, not every day—that's the impossible myth of "work life integration"—but over the course of time.

Table 5: Work Life Skills Integration as Illustrated by Six People Models[10]

Skills Integration	*Tom Tierney*	*Sheryl Sandberg*	*Eric Greitens*	*Michelle Obama*	*Julie Foudy*	*Bruce Springsteen*
Be Real *Act with Authenticity*	Envision Your Legacy	Convey Values with Stories	Hold Yourself Accountable	Align Actions with Values	Know What Matters	Embody Values Consistently
Be Whole *Act with Integrity*	Weave Disparate Strands	Build Supportive Networks	Apply all Your Resources	Manage Boundaries Intelligently	Help Others	Clarify Expectations
Be Innovative Act with Creativity	See New Ways of Doing Things	Resolve Conflicts Among Domains	Focus on Results	Embrace Change Courageously	Challenge the Status Quo	Create Cultures of Innovation

Social Protection Goes Digital

When COVID-19 hit Paraguay, the crisis and its associated lockdown measures quickly reshaped the way social policy is implemented in the country. Many programs that depended on face-to-face contact to reach participants suddenly found themselves unable to conduct their usual outreach.

In response, many have turned to digital channels—a shift that has caused not only challenges, but also some promising successes. For example, the Tekopora Program, Paraguay's flagship conditional cash transfer initiative run by the Ministry of Social Development (MDS).

The program targets people facing poverty and extreme poverty in a country where around 23.5% of the population lived in poverty in 2019—a percentage that certainly increased in 2020 due to the pandemic.

It currently covers approximately 45.8% of this population (around 165,000 families). From a territorial perspective, Tekopora reaches the country's 17 departments and at least 254 districts. Its main objective is to improve the quality of life of vulnerable families and communities, facilitating their access to food, health and education, in order to cut the intergenerational transmission of poverty.

Prior to the pandemic, participants of the Tekopora cash transfer program received regular visits and training from a coach, known as a family guide, who followed up on the progress of families within the program. But with quarantine measures in place, visits and face-to-face training were temporarily suspended. Many other activities, from targeting to training to monitoring, also had to be suspended or adapted starting in March 2020.

This situation presented families in the Tekopora Program with a double dilemma. On the one hand, they were already dealing with the negative socioeconomic impacts of COVID-19 prevention measures dictated by the government. And on the other hand, they now faced the possibility of feeling "abandoned" by this essential public program right when they needed it most.

WhatsApp-Driven Outreach Campaign

The pandemic has made this challenge increasingly common all over the world. Families living in poverty and extreme poverty have been forced to rethink their livelihood strategies after the major economic shock and drastic income declines the crisis has provoked.

Moreover, the long period of confinement the world has endured has also had significant non-economic impacts, such as increased conflicts and gender-based violence within the home, which take a particularly heavy toll on disadvantaged populations. Making matters worse, people have had to navigate an ocean of (often bad) information, riddled with fake news, about COVID-19.

The support provided by family guides is essential for Paraguayan families living in poverty and vulnerability, who constantly face economic, social and psychological tensions and challenges.

In this context, MDS and Fundacion Capital have been working since 2019 in a five-year alliance funded by Co-Impact to promote the social and economic inclusion of families in poverty through systems change.

In response to the challenges the Tekopora Program has faced, we joined forces to find a timely and scalable alternative to face-to-face training and coaching, in order to reach the thousands of participants who were suddenly deprived of any contact with their family guides.

This led to the "Tekopora Te Acompaña" (Tekopora Accompanies You), a digital campaign that sought to provide information & tools to prevent and mitigate the impacts of corona virus and to ensure that families, despite the physical distance, maintained contact with the program through direct channels. Our intention was to increase these families' capacities to face the crisis and decrease their vulnerabilities.

The campaign was built on six thematic areas: food and nutrition, income and work, health and self-care, education and learning, housing and environment, and participation and coexistence. It was implemented between May and October of 2020.

In terms of outreach mechanisms, the campaign used communication channels that were popular among the target population. The main dissemination channel for "Tekopora te Acompaña" was WhatsApp.[11] To increase trust and engagement, the messages were sent by the family guides themselves.

Human Component of QWL Flexibility

The campaign employed different formats (for example, text, audio clips, images and short videos) to overcome literacy barriers and maximize flexibility. The "human component" of the strategy was secured by using storytelling as a communication resource and leveraging peer-to-peer learning delivered by a fictional character based on the target population.

The whole campaign centred on Ña Carmen, a character who faces struggles similar to those of participants of the program. She shared tips, experiences and actions to help people overcome these challenges.

Input from field coordinators and family guides were instrumental in informing the messaging strategy throughout the campaign's implementation. For instance, their voices and experience gave more depth to certain content, and the Guarani language (the most commonly spoken language in the country's rural areas) was used in video and audio content, strengthening their effectiveness.

"Tekopora te Acompaña" represented an important innovation within MDS programming. It was implemented through WhatsApp—the first time a massive digital training campaign (one targeting hundreds of thousands of people) was conducted by the Paraguayan government.

This main communication channel also enabled a multiplying effect, in which program participants helped disseminate this content to more people external to the program by forwarding the messages they received.

In fact, in a survey conducted with a sample of participants, 80% of recipients affirmed that they had shared the content with friends, neighbours and families, especially through WhatsApp groups.

Learning from Campaign's Success

Opinions of the campaign were positive among field coordinators and family guides. From over 400 field coordinators and family guides surveyed by Fundación Capital, 96% considered the campaign necessary.

This represented impressive acceptance among the field team of a tool that enabled them to carry out their functions. Likewise, 77% of the field coordinators and family guides considered the campaign to be useful and timely in supporting them in carrying out their roles.

Furthermore, they believed the campaign had served the participating families as well: "Participants put what they learn into practice and proudly show us what they do. The campaign made it possible to strengthen the formation of families," said Marisol, a family guide from the program.

Feedback from the families confirmed that Tekopora Te Acompaña's outreach was significant and empowering. Of the participating families consulted, 74% stated that they knew about the campaign and had received its messages through WhatsApp.

This represents a high percentage of diffusion, and acceptance of the campaign was similarly high: 92% considered it both necessary and useful in helping them cope with the situation.

Importantly, all the participants surveyed affirmed that they had learned something new from the campaign and put the advice into practice, and that they would recommend that others receive this advice. This confirms both the program's usefulness and its replicability.

Finally, based on this small evaluation, participants expressed the most interest in three main topics: tools and means of growing food in family gardens for self-consumption; care of the home, involving both the management of children and intra-household relationships; and prevention and care of COVID-19 and dengue (which is also an alarming epidemic in the country).

Tekopora te Acompaña was created to respond to pressing needs during the pandemic, but its positive results and overall acceptance suggest that there is a promising space for similar interventions after the crisis has ended.

Digital channels cannot entirely replace human interactions, but they can be an important complement to them, strengthening communication and providing timely support to participants of social protection programs, while helping field staff in their work.

Combined strategies that leverage both face-to-face and digital channels can further strengthen these programs—for instance, by reinforcing in-person training via personalized counselling delivered digitally. It is gratifying to see these efforts bear fruit in the current crisis, enabling participants like Ña Cata and Marta to stay connected—even during a global pandemic.

Workplace Wellness Revolution

Remote work is nothing new in India. Before corona virus, India had several employees working from home. However, the pandemic forced thousands more into isolated work environments almost overnight.

According to a November 2020 survey, more than 375 executives, less than 5% said their companies are currently working in person from an office or plan to do so in the next 12 months. Over 94% of respondents confirmed that they are working 100% remotely or in a mixed scheme.

This drastic shift to remote work, coupled with all of the other stresses related to the COVID-19 pandemic, has increased anxiety and burnout for workers and left many companies without enough time to plan how to address the impact on their employees' mental and physical health.

According to a global study of more than 12,000 executives released by Oracle and Workplace Intelligence in October 2021, 70% of people reported feeling more stress and anxiety at work this year than any other year before.

These increased levels of stress and anxiety are having a negative impact on the mental health of 78% of the world's workforce, causing additional stress (38%), lack of work life balance (35%), burnout (25%), depression due to lack of social activity (25%) and loneliness (14%).

The report also indicates that the pandemic is adding new pressures to everyday workplace stressors, impacting people's ability to meet performance standards (42%), to handle routine and tedious tasks (41%), and to manage workloads (41%).

The upside of these alarming statistics is that companies have become more aware of the need to provide their employees with support for their mental wellbeing, and many are adopting digital solutions to support workers' mental health.

Leveraging Technology to Improve Employee Wellness

There are many ways technology is finding its way into employee wellbeing programs, and workers are embracing it. In fact, 68% of respondents to the Oracle and Workplace Intelligence survey said they would rather talk to an artificial intelligence (AI) bot than their boss about stress and anxiety at work, and 80% are open to a bot therapist or counsellor.

A substantial number of people (29%) believe bots can help provide quick answers to health-related questions, an unbiased environment to share their problems (30%) and a judgment-free zone (34%). AI tools also help workers automate tedious and repetitive tasks, freeing up time to be more productive, decreasing their workloads and reducing stress.

In light of this increasing acceptance, more companies in both India and globally are offering digital wellness programs to employees as part of benefits packages—a meaningful advancement.

In response to the pandemic, more than 51% of companies surveyed by Runa offer wellness benefits to employees in popular areas such as stress management (63%), physical activity (39%), and financial wellness (35%).

Many employers are turning to start-ups to help them rapidly introduce or improve employee wellness programs. One such global company is the health-tech enterprise Vittude, which provides online therapy programs. The company has seen a 300% hike in its corporate clients since the advent of corona virus).

Lack of Digital Wellness Solutions[12]

Despite numerous such signs of progress the world-over, a significant portion of the population in the country still lacks easy access to digital health and wellness solutions. According to the Oracle and Workplace Intelligence study, only about 7.6% of the Indian population has downloaded a health application compared with 22% in North America and 15.1% in OECD countries.

When it comes to mental health, the results are all the more pathetic. This clearly shows that the workplace wellness market is still under-served. Although 51% of employees in the said their companies have added mental health services or support as a result of COVID-19, 76% believe that the management could do more to protect the mental health of its workforce.

Nevertheless, it is clear that the pandemic has pushed mental and emotional health issues firmly into the spotlight. Not only are more workers looking to their employers for mental health support, but more companies are also realizing that employee wellbeing impacts nearly every aspect of their businesses, and that they must do more.

With studies showing employees with higher rates of wellbeing are more likely to be engaged, enjoy their work and recommend their organization, it is in companies' best interests to continue to boost their focus on wellness. And as remote work becomes the standard for many organizations, blurring the lines between our personal and professional lives, it will be important for these efforts to offer digital options.

With remote work becoming ever more widespread in India, the market potential for tech-fuelled employee health and wellness solutions—from on-demand counselling and monitoring services to apps and chatbots—will likely continue to grow, even after the pandemic ends.

From Efficiency Designing to Resilience Designing

Since the start of the pandemic, traditional business hours have gone out the window. Instead, professionals are working around their family schedules. Now more than ever, the phrase "business hours" is devoid of meaning.

During the pandemic, "business hours" has morphed into "any hours", or more precisely, "all hours" so it should be no surprise that burnout has become a serious and growing problem.

Pre-pandemic, the priority was generally to have been to hire staff that would create efficient organizations. Mid and post-pandemic, the emphasis has shifted firmly in the direction of resilience. Whereas built-in redundancy or overlaps in skills might previously have been seen as inefficient, today, it is seen as a sensible precaution.

This certainly encompasses another sub-trend, which is that employers are coming to understand the critical importance of building employee healthcare and wellbeing (including mental health) strategies into their game plan. Many are now trying to take more responsibility for helping their workforce maintain physical, mental, and financial wellbeing.

A challenge here that companies will come up against in 2022 is finding ways to do this that hit objectives without being overly intrusive or invasive of employees' privacy and personal lives.

Ensuring a workforce is healthy enough to keep a business running is clearly a critical element of resilience, but it also covers the implementation of processes that are more flexible, with built-in redundancies to provide cover when disaster strikes, resulting in operational efficiency becoming compromised. These processes are sure to play an increasingly big part in the day-to-day lives of workers as we move through 2022.

A 2019 Gartner organization design survey found that 55% of organizational redesigns were focused on streamlining roles, supply chains and workflows to increase efficiency. While this approach captured efficiencies, it also created fragilities, as systems have no flexibility to respond to disruptions. Resilient organizations were better able to respond and correct course quickly with change.

To build a more responsive organization, design roles and structures around outcomes to increase agility & flexibility and formalize how processes can flex. Also, provide employees with varied, adaptive and flexible roles so they acquire cross-functional knowledge and training.

"Diversity leaders will need to be involved in role design and creation of flexible work systems to ensure that employees of all backgrounds and needs are considered when the organization designs new workflows," said Ingrid Laman, Vice President (Advisory), Gartner.

Explicit Employee Encouragement

Citigroup CEO Jane Fraser made news this week when she banned internal Zoom calls on Fridays simply to give employees a brain break and help them refresh. Acknowledging how the pandemic has blurred the line between work and home, Fraser also encouraged employees not to communicate after their "business hours" so that they could have time to reset and recharge.

Leaders like Jane Fraser should focus on developing a company culture that encourages resilience building and work life balance. This is good for individuals and for the bottom line—happy employees are more productive, and burnout is a primary obstacle to happiness at work.

With that in mind, here are some suggestions for what leaders can do to help their teams thrive:

- Be a good role model of resilience building and employee empathy. This will have a big impact on your team members' work life balance as well.
- Encourage all employees to use vacation time (and not work while they are gone) and take vacation yourself. Research strongly supports the idea that truly disconnected vacation time is critical for staving off burn-out and increasing employee productivity.

- Help employees feel that they can connect—by designating someone else they can put on their out-of-office messages, and maybe even allowing them to have e-mails deleted while they are gone.
- Decide on your company's 'communication hours', and strongly discourage team members from sending work-related messages to one another outside of these hours. Designate a specific channel, like text messages, to use for emergencies outside of these communication hours.

A leader plays a critical role in the company culture. Building resilience and making employee empathy the company's cultural heritage cannot be evaluated in a vacuum, and the company culture will shape employees' attitudes and behaviours.

Less Focus on Roles, More Focus on Skills

"To build the workforce one will need post-pandemic, focus less on roles—which group unrelated skills—than on the skills needed to drive the organization's competitive advantage and the workflows that fuel this advantage," as per the 2019 Gartner organization design survey[13].

Skills are critical because they address core business challenges, with the competencies needed in a workforce to overcome those challenges. Roles, on the other hand, describe the way individual members of a workforce relate to an overall organizational structure or hierarchy.

We have certainly seen this trend gestating for some time, with the move towards more "flat" organizational structures as opposed to strictly hierarchical teams with a direct reporting, chain-of-command approach to communication and problem-solving.

By focussing on skills, businesses address the fact that solving problems and answering their core business questions is the key to driving innovation and success within information-age enterprises.

From the worker's point of view, focusing on developing their skills, rather than further developing their abilities to carry out their role, leaves them better positioned to capitalize on new career opportunities. This shift in focus from roles to skills is likely to be a key trend for both organizations and workers during 2022.

Future Trends—Mental Health

Mental health is gaining visibility and services are becoming more accessible, creating a growing need for psychiatrists—medical doctors who specialize in treating mental illness and a range of disorders that affect people of all ages. Also in high demand are the services of non-physician providers who offer counseling and support services in areas such as behavioral disorders, substance abuse, and other types of mental health issues.

Mental Health and Technology

The future of psychiatry will likely be increasingly personalized—and patients may not even need to leave their homes to access care. Already, virtual therapy websites set patients up with online sessions, allowing them to access therapeutic support they otherwise might not receive. This brings easily accessible therapy to rural communities and to people who may not feel comfortable going to a therapist's office. Many insurance policies now cover these virtual treatments, and increased availability in internet bandwidth and camera technology means those sessions can be just as effective as seeing a therapist in person. Additionally, shifting public perceptions around mental health issues have lessened the stigma of seeking treatment. As the number of public figures willing to speak openly about their battles with mental illness continues to grow, so does the acceptance that mental health problems are common and treatable.

Trends in Psychiatry

It's possible that the future of psychiatry will involve advanced technology and techniques such as deep brain stimulation—implanting activated electrical nodes inside the brain—which has already proven effective in the treatment of Parkinson's and other movement disorders. Deep brain stimulation, however, isn't yet fully understood to the point where it's ready for psychiatric use.

Career Opportunities and Mental Health

A social science degree is an excellent place to consider starting if you're eager to pursue a career in psychiatry or a related area and make an impact in the future of mental health. While you need to earn a medical degree to become a psychiatrist, many start off on this path through an undergraduate degree in social science. This degree not only lays the groundwork for a future career in psychiatry upon completion of additional schooling and training, but it also opens doors to a wide array of job opportunities.

Implementing and maintaining mental health and well-being initiatives in the workplace is a shared responsibility. All levels of the organization must contribute to its success. The organization must keep in mind the following while doing so:

- Leadership demonstrating support and care shows the organization's commitment to the importance of employee mental health and well-being.
- Identification of psychosocial hazards in the workplace is an important step to identify opportunities to improve employee mental health and well-being.
- Ongoing review and evaluation of mental health and well-being initiatives at all levels of the organization ensure resources remain relevant and effective.
- Providing and promoting access to high quality behavioural health care, including through remotely delivered evidence-based pathways, ensures that employees have access to their preferred type of care when they need it.
- Integrating these services into a comprehensive wellness program may concurrently promote improved total health outcomes.
- Community partnerships extend the reach and resources of organizations, and provide new opportunities to collaborate and be part of the solution.

These are the recommended practices with real-world implementation examples. While success from these strategies has been inferred from employee experience, it is important to note that real world data to document outcomes from implementation of these strategies across organizations and settings are needed.

Continued efforts by organizations to measure and share successes and failures in implementing workplace mental health and well-being initiatives will strengthen future best practices recommendations.

Future Trends—Workplace Spirituality

The complexities of the modern society and the modern workplace converged to re-emphasize the need for people to do meaningful work in order to live a fulfilling life. Due to this development, within the last two decades, organizational scholars and practitioners have paid increasing attention to the concept of workplace spirituality. An attempt has been made here to take a broad look at the dynamics facilitating the recent emergence of workplace spirituality as a field of interest from its historical foundation to the more current literature that has evolved. Though the concept in itself is not new, the ways and means by which it is evolving do call for new research approaches and methods that encourage conversations from multiple perspectives to further develop the field.

Spirituality at work is increasingly gaining popularity among scholars and practitioners primarily because it helps employees experience a strong bond with their work emotionally, physically, and cognitively. These experiences lead to greater engagement in the workplace that in turn leads to higher individual and organizational productivity. Operationally, workplace spirituality has been measured using several scales, but the commonality across all those are mindfulness and connectedness.

1. *Workplace Hyper-spirituality:* The post-industrial 'workplace' of today is still deeply moored in the traditional, century-old forms of Weberian top-down bureaucratic organizational frameworks and driven by Tayloristic principles of efficiency and worker productivity.

From this perspective, anything outside the status quo has been viewed with suspicion since it may upset the normalized ideal 'workplace' and could have impact on the bottom line for domestic and global companies, as well as public and private universities.

In Europe and especially the United States, the evolving movement of the last three to four decades of workplace spirituality has been presented by human relations gurus as something to be experimented with as an "add-on" to the toolkit for employee motivation, which might even lead to greater job satisfaction, retention, and productivity.

If employees must leave their faith and spirituality at the doorstep to their work, we return to the old antiseptic, bland world of faceless bureaucracies. The authentic form of practicing spiritual inclusiveness at work takes on at least three various classifications: spirituality, faith, and religion. Scholars now advance a fourth dimension: hyper-spirituality.

In trying to navigate the scholarly debate between religion versus faith within the Academy of Management, Miller (2007)[47] suggests there is a more nuanced, blended reality, and they do not stand in diametric opposition, especially when applied to the work setting. Miller suggests 'faith' be considered an overarching rubric that includes both broadly constructed and narrowly practiced expressions of religious belief.

Hyper-spirituality is a business construct that was not an add-on to the formational ethos of certain prominent faith-based institutions. Service learning, social justice, and collaborative transformational leadership are major dimensions that complete intellectual and practical structuralism in a hyper-spiritual workplace.

In recognizing such characteristics of spiritual human development and cognizance, these institutions also have a larger sense of meaning and purpose within their institutional symbolic workplace domains.

Striving toward a commitment to people-hood, the Pepperdine University is attempting to apply experiential learning to their strategic objectives, and ensures ethical and multidisciplinary approaches to faculty and administrative service outcomes.

Fulfilling its commitment to the larger off-campus community, the Whizin Center for Continuing Education enrols about 12,000 participants in non-credit mostly religious-themed programs.

The Boston College Center for Ignatian Spirituality fulfils a mission that is used by other similar religious universities in assisting members of their university community to reflect on the deep origins and spiritual knowledge that transforms, inspires, and impacts its prospective and existing personnel.

To better assist its members to reflect on and understand more deeply on the meaning of their spiritual and religious mission, all faculty and staff participate in semester retreats, one-on-one conversations, and spiritual direction with other institutions who offer dialogs that open a forum encouraging and instilling learning from each other's unique spiritual experiences to better advance their professional responsibilities and obligations.

Through a national association that is specifically designed for administrators and faculty, they are informed about the principles and standards of working in a higher education institute, and further grow their basis and understanding of spiritual wellbeing and workplace behaviour. Further, the Center offers its faculty and staff a Pilgrimage Seminar to explore the context in which they live out their vocation as educators.[17]

Therefore, in a hyper-spiritual environment, individual development is tied to collective spiritual growth. There is also a correlation between faith-based derivatives that encourage ethical inclusive risk-taking.

2. *Organizational Spiritual Intelligence:* Workplace spirituality supports the underlying assumption that organizations should encourage

spiritual experiences in working environments. As a line of enquiry, it is necessarily broad, in order to encompass some disparate and overlapping interests and perspectives within the community of its scholars.

The study of workplace spirituality may also include enquiry about spiritual, practice tools, such as meditation, prayer, using crystals, and healing practices, such as reiki or indeed, Feng Shui, widely adopted in all manner of businesses in Asia. By definition, workplace spirituality is concerned with spiritual experience and specifically how it manifests in the context of the workplace.

Workplace spirituality brings to the attention of organizations that every human being has both an inner and an outer life and that the two are related. This interrelationship focuses inquiry on exactly how employees bring their whole selves with their respective and often variant spiritual values, to the workplace, in ways that fulfil personal and organizational goals.

In terms of fulfilling organizational roles, workplace spirituality has contributed to the intensification of research into the antecedents, correlates, and outcomes of spirituality in these settings. The principles of workplace spirituality have attracted the attention of international executives, managers, consultants, and academics alike.

Companies that have staged promising interventions of a spiritual nature, such as Ouimet-Cordon Bleu Inc., Cordon Bleu-Tomasso Corporation, The Body Shop, IBM, Microsoft, Reliance, Amway, Southwest Airlines, and Timberland, have reported tangible outcomes in the form of increased profits and efficiency (Chawla and Guda 2013).[48]

Despite some reluctance to accept that adopting a spiritually salient component of an organizational identity will necessarily give rise to performance and 'bottom-line' improvements, arguments to the contrary, suggesting the benefits of organizations adopting workplace spirituality principles, are becoming compelling.

3. *Personal and Organizational Spiritual Identity:* Scholars suggest that Organizational Spiritual Identity (OSI) is an appropriate focus for workplace spirituality. Organizational spiritual identity is conceptually and logically rooted in notions of the organization, spirituality, and identity. Experts believe that a discussion on them will result in the nature of personal or individual identity and spiritual beliefs, as they relate to organizational identity and organizational spiritual identity.

The notion that organizations can claim to have an identity or that some organizations strategically engage in and foster practices that are spiritual in nature is not new. However, work linking spirituality and identity in organizational contexts are, curiously, less well explored.

The acceptance that personal and organizational identity, spiritual or otherwise, is fluid, and has the ability to change, is crucial to developing an argument that the process of conducting a spiritual audit in an organization with the intention of influencing it.

Organizational spiritual identity exists, or is only supportable, when considered in relation to the personal spiritual identities of employees as its members. The spiritual relationship between individual and organization is therefore, reciprocal and draws up the premise that an individual is viewed as the catalyst for setting spiritual workplaces in motion.

4. *Employee Well-being Services:* Classes in yoga, meditation, prayer, breathing and silence before meetings for reflection and chanting are all spiritual activities that are often encouraged in organizations as part of initiatives to enhance not only the well-being of employees but also the entire work environment.

Many mega-companies such as IBM, Microsoft, and Reliance, have adopted training programs along these lines. Although many of these spiritually orientated practices are associated with Asian beliefs, they are not, as a matter of course, embedded into organizational practices in that region.

One Thai study, however, reported on an intervention in a large baking company. Initiated by the CEO, the organization introduced paid time, spent on meditation training and learning about Buddhism, with positive results on a number of levels.

5. *Self-reflexivity:* As an approach to workplace spirituality, self-reflexivity summons one to consider the reciprocal relationship between the inner self and the socio-cultural container of experience. Contextual stories of being and becoming are often intimately interwoven and unfold through the multiplicity of lived experiences.

In other words, we are not separate from our previous history or knowledge. We are detached from the spiritual traditions that we may firmly hold and their ability to sway the changing landscapes of societal life, including the workplace.

Self-exploration of one's inner identity can help assess one's position on the experiential continuum of spirituality. This moving force of lived experiences can also serve as a catalyst of spiritual realization within one's intrapersonal self.

Knowing who you are and what constitutes your beliefs and value system is a critical component to self-reflexive contemplation. Spirituality from a self-reflexive approach transcends the natural scope of human thought or reasoning, emanating from an experiential knowing in the heart.

This experiential knowing may not be fully understood through intellectual reasoning alone, for it is only the individuals who can declare their spiritual level. People's life experiences, beliefs, and values constitute their foundational perceptions and worldviews.

UNIT–VII

Case Studies on QWL, Mental Health and Spiritual Intelligence

Introduction

Changing demographics in the labour force in India and other countries, together with a recruiting crunch in some organizations, have encouraged an increasing number of employers to consider the work-life balance of their employees.

At the same time, recognition of work-family disconnects, especially for working mothers, is growing. Organizations are responding by introducing flexible work arrangements.

Each of these case studies highlights the conditions and requirement necessary to make work-life programs and practices successful. Developed for an undergraduate/post-graduate audience, these case studies explore five different flexible work arrangements in five different organizations in India and abroad.

These are real-life case studies that demonstrate a range of work-life initiatives. The case method is qualitative & relative and each study is a snapshot in time to reflect the reality of their organizational life.

CASE STUDY #1

Organizational Culture and Work Hours at WL Gore & Associates Inc.

Background

It is a global privately held company headquartered in Newark, Delaware. It employs approximately 8,000 employees (called associates) in more than 45 locations worldwide. Founded by a husband-and-wife team in 1958, its manufacturing operations are clustered in the U.S., Germany, Japan, China and Scotland.

The company produces proprietary technologies with versatile polymer polytetrafluoroethylene (PTFE) used in products in the health care and leisure industries. It is known not just for its innovative products, but also for its innovative business style (WL Gore's written business objective is "To make money and have fun").

Corporate Culture and Working Hours[1]

The organizational culture is founded on a team-based environment where teams are organized around opportunities and leaders emerge. Teams are fluid and comprise followers and leaders. Associates have no defined job titles, only general task/responsibility areas. Leaders emerge naturally by demonstrating special knowledge, a skill and/or experience that will move the business objective forward.

The roles of leaders and followers are interchangeable by work projects. All associates have a sponsor or mentor assigned to guide them to "chart a course in the organization that will offer personal fulfilment while maximizing their contribution to the enterprise." In this way, associates can alternately, and simultaneously, be a leader, follower and sponsor.

Enabling this corporate culture of teamwork is a commitment to four basic principles that drives organizational activities:

- Fairness to each other and everyone with whom they come into contact.
- Freedom to encourage, help and allow other associates grow in knowledge, skill and scope of responsibility.
- Ability to make one's own commitments and keep them.

- Consultation with other associates before undertaking actions that could affect the company's reputation by hitting it 'below the waterline.'

The associates are not managed but instead manage themselves by being fair, meeting commitments and consulting others as appropriate. Consequently, there are very few company policies, procedures or rules. Practices develop naturally and do not need to be framed in policies. There are no policies and procedures, therefore, that explicitly relate to quality of work life.

However, the company's approach to QWL can be seen in its approach to working hours. There are no set working hours as people make commitments and keep their commitments.

Outcomes

It is widely believed that the corporate culture of WL Gore & Associates Inc encourages a qualitative work life that directly contributes to the award-winning success the company has long enjoyed. John Kennedy, a Gore leader and senior associate says, "Our culture and principles drive very high performance from individuals and teams, who are empowered and results-oriented with a strong 'can-do' attitude."

WL Gore's approach to quality of work life contributes to its repeatedly being included in Fortune magazine's best companies list.

Way Forward

Continuing to develop associates is seen as central to sustaining the corporate culture and principles that foster quality of work life at WL Gore.

Learning Points

- When they are part of a clearly understood management style, quality of work life can work without being supported by formal policies and procedures.
- QWL can be an integral part of a holistic management approach.
- Organizations should focus on life issues for employees/associates and actively work on these as well as carry out development to ensure improvement strategies.

- Good leadership and mentorship are important to encourage employees to balance work and their personal life.

Discussion Questions

1. What are the key elements in the corporate culture at WL Gore that may prevent employees from taking advantage of there being no set work hours?
2. How would you describe the management style and management responsibilities in this company?
3. What are some challenges employers may face when trying to implement WL Gore's distinctive approach to quality of work life in different countries of its operations?
4. What elements of this company's QWL approach could be adopted by other organizations?

CASE STUDY #2

Job Sharing at Motorola

Background

Motorola was founded in 1928 in the United States of America, and currently employs more than one lakh people worldwide. Today, it is harnessing the power of wireless, broadband and the Internet to deliver embedded chip system-level and end-to-end network communications solutions for the individual, work team, vehicle and home. A variety of long established QWL arrangements are the company's mainstay.

They include part-time work, dependency leave, an employee assistance program (EAP)[2], job sharing, health care, special shift arrangements (non-standard shifts), study leave (time off work to complete sections for formal qualifications) and emergency holidays (when annual leave needs to be taken for non-holiday time).

In 2000, there was a major change in work hours that was intended to standardize shifts throughout the whole organization. Today, full-time Motorola operators work seven 12-hour shifts over a two-week period, on the basis of four days one week, and three days the next. When the work hours were changed, employees were offered job sharing, either on the day or night shifts.

Job sharing means that two people share a full-time job between them, splitting equally the number of hours worked. Though not commonplace, it has been an occasional practice at Motorola-UK for some time now.

Results have shown that the transition to new shift patterns, including job share, allowed Motorola to retain key skills and avoid external recruitment. It also led to the company meeting its performance metrics in the face of stiff global competition and remaining competitive.

Most job sharers work very closely together to meet their combined job requirements without manager involvement. This can easily change during their holiday leave periods because temporary holiday employee is unlikely to be very familiar with the regular sharing system between the two main job sharers. Managers may then need to standardize and open discussion when developing policies on how people are treated at work with respect to QWL arrangements.

Way Forward

Motorola plans to have ongoing reviews of job-sharing practices, together with evaluation of business effects.

Learning Points

- Job share processes have to be transparent and understood.
- Everyone must be aware of expectations from them in regards to quality of work life and consider the profile of working population in developing such arrangements.
- It is important to maintain good communication between job sharers' working groups and management so that any required changes can be implemented quickly.
- It can be useful to form a team to identify any issues with the new QWL initiatives.

Discussion Questions

1. How does Motorola's job sharing system fit with their business needs?
2. What particular needs do female employees face in QWL arrangements such as job sharing?
3. What are the advantages and disadvantages of job sharing to job sharers and their managers?
4. What factors come into play in introducing job sharing into other organizations?

CASE STUDY #3

Health Problems at IKEA

Background

IKEA is a Swedish home furnishing retailer that sells well-designed, functional furniture at low prices. It is a global business with over 150 stores in more than 20 countries around the world. IKEA's dream is "to create a better everyday life for the many people."

In IKEA's language, the dream's realization lies in the combination of the company's "business idea" and its "human resource idea", which is "to give down-to-earth, straightforward people the possibility to grow, both as individuals and in their professional roles, so that together we are strongly committed to creating a better everyday life for ourselves and our customers."

IKEA's Swedish heritage is important in the company, as demonstrated by its training for staff on Swedish culture. The Swedish national values of commitment to, and time with, family and community, combined with concern for a healthy environment, are strongly reflected in the company's organizational culture and management practices.

These values can be seen in its strategic approach that acknowledges quality of work life, to its recognition of the importance of coffee breaks in a pleasant environment for all staff for social interaction. The Quality of Work Life is expressed, for instance, in paid days off for all staff for first day of school leave, marriage leave and "moving house leave".

It is also expressed in the following areas of existing work life balance offerings, including flex time (variation in start and finish times), full-time and part-time work, special shift arrangements (early shifts only), non-standard work weeks (longer but fewer work days per week), emergency leave (for a domestic crisis like a flooding), public/community service leave (such as working on a public service board), leave for caring for dependents, parental leave, sick children leave, information about childcare, employee assistance programs, information and advice on the quality of work life and health promotion.[3]

The most recent initiative in IKEA's health promotion program is an upcoming Fit for Work week. IKEA will offer a range of fitness and occupational health activities during that week. The high rates of staff participation for previous Fit to Work weeks indicate that this program has been well-received by staff. Outcomes on an individual level,

The Quality of Work Life (QWL) programs help people balance work with other life factors. Employee feedback has shown that quality of work life arrangements have a positive effect on attendance and staff retention as it raises the profile of fitness and health and lets staff see that there is an investment in them.

Key performance indicators such a higher-than-industry average in employee retention, lower-than industry average in absence rates, and frequent employee referrals to new recruits strongly point to tangible benefits of quality of work life balance activities. In this way, IKEA is open to new ideas for QWL programs.

Way Forward

Development of quality work life initiatives is seen in positive terms with an open-minded attitude. The possibility of working from home within operational constraints is being considered. So, too, is initiating and funding social events for all staff and their families.

Learning Points

- Quality of work life is tied closely to organizational culture.
- QWL is not just about flexibility in work for life outside work, it also works the other way around—"by bringing aspects of wider life (health initiatives and socializing)—into work thereby making it fun" (HR motto of the company).
- The company ideology is the best way to engage more people in QWL programs is to let co-workers who have experienced it advocate it by word-of-mouth.

Discussion Questions

1. What aspects of world culture could be considered in the Quality of Work Life arrangements in IKEA stores?
2. What potential cultural work-life and life-work conflicts can you identify in IKEA's approach to the Quality of Work Life (QWL) initiatives in different countries?
3. Which of IKEA's quality of work life arrangements are innovative in Indian context?
4. What are the implications of operating these arrangements for managers and employees in Indian stores?

CASE STUDY #4

Work Life Quality at India Post

Background

For more than 150 years, the Department of Posts (DoP) has been the backbone of India's communication and has played a crucial role in the country's social economic development.

It touches the lives of Indian citizens in many ways: delivering mails, accepting deposits under Small Savings Schemes, providing life insurance cover under Postal Life Insurance (PLI) and Rural Postal Life Insurance (RPLI), providing retail services like bill collection, sale of forms etc.

It also acts as an agent for Government of India in discharging other services for citizens such as the Mahatma Gandhi National Rural Employment Guarantee Scheme (MGNREGS) wage disbursement and old age pension payments. With more than 1.55 lakh post offices, DoP has the most widely distributed postal network in the world.

India Post is a government operated postal system in India, which is under the jurisdiction of the Department of Post, Ministry of Communications of the Government of India. Generally called "the Post Office" in India, it began operations as Postal Service following Warren Hastings initiative under East India Company in 1766.

It was initially established under the name "Company Mail" and was later modified into a service under the Crown in 1854 by Lord Dalhousie Dalhousie introduced uniform postage rates (universal service) and helped to pass the India Post Office Act, 1854 which significantly improved upon the Post Office Act, 1837 that had introduced regular post offices in India. It created the position of Director General of Post for the country as a whole.

Governance System

For providing postal services, the entire country has been divided into 23 postal circles. Each circle is co-terminus with a state except for Gujarat Circle (which also administers the Union Territories of Daman & Diu and Dadra & Nagar Haveli), Kerala Circle (which includes the Union Territory of Lakshadweep), Maharashtra Circle (which has within its jurisdiction the State of Goa), North East Circle (which comprises six

North Eastern States of Arunachal Pradesh, Manipur, Meghalaya, Mizoram, Nagaland and Tripura), Punjab Circle (which has within its administrative jurisdiction the Union Territory of Chandigarh), Tamil Nadu Circle (which also administers the Union Territory of Puducherry) and West Bengal Circle (which also administers the state of Sikkim and the Union Territory of Andaman and Nicobar Islands).

Each of these Circles is headed by a Chief Postmaster General. Each Circle is further divided into regions comprising field units called Divisions (Postal/RMS Divisions). Each region is headed by a Postmaster General. Every circle and Region has other functional units like Circle Stamp Depots, Postal Stores Depots and Mail Motor Service etc. The divisions are further divided into sub-divisions.

Besides these 23 Circles, there is another Circle, called Base Circle, to cater to the postal communication needs of the Armed Forces. It is headed by an Additional Director General, Army Postal Service (APS) in the rank of a Major General.

The officer cadre of the Army Postal Service comprises officers on deputation from the Civil Posts. Seventy five percent of other ranks of the Army Postal Service are also drawn from the Department of Posts while the remaining personnel are recruited by the Army.

One of the highest post offices in the world is located at Hikkim, Himachal Pradesh, which is operated by the India Post at an altitude of 14,567 feet (4,440 metre).

Business Objectives

India Posts has bifurcated its objectives in two categories. They are:

1. Vision
    - A socially committed organization connecting individuals and businesses.
2. Goal
    - Post within easy reach of all.
    - To be a focal point for delivery of all social security schemes of the State.
    - To be a self-sustaining organization.
    - To increase financial inclusion of the unbanked population by at least 10 percent.

Outcomes

India Post provides last mile delivery to a number of important government schemes and related services. These programs directly impact the common citizen of the country. The administration of India Post is now successfully innovating and diversifying their products & services and further leveraging the trust of customers by entering into new areas such as telephony, financial services, etc.

Way Forward

To innovate training methodologies to bring about active participation knowledge acquisition in postal work with its extension to organising co-operative ventures of different kinds within the training campus. Active involvement in some major aspects of daily life would also provide an edge to learning in an office role with remote control coordination of training activities. This will add new dimensions to the overall work.[4]

Learning Points

- Modernizing postal network, post offices, mail offices and core operations.
- Developing initiatives for modernizing and expanding core businesses to meet customer expectations.
- Implementing job restructuring initiatives for judicious use of a skilled manpower.

Discussion Questions

1. How can India Post deal with congestion in office space, antiquanted and dysfunctional furniture, inadequate lighting etc?
2. What steps have been initiated to empower network for promoting rural development?
3. Can the India Post human resource be trained to effectively use computers and telecommunications?
4. How well is the India Post personnel reciprocating to QWL initiatives?

CASE STUDY #5

Job Rotation at Heavy Electrical Equipment Plant (HEEP)

Background

The Heavy Electrical Equipment Plant located at Haridwar in northern India is one of the major production units of Bharat Heavy Electricals Limited (BHEL). It is a large public sector unit employing nearly 10,000 employees with technical collaboration from a similar plant in Leningrad, Russia.

It is engaged in the design, engineering, manufacturing, construction, testing, commissioning and servicing of a wide range of products, systems and services for the core sectors of the economy such as power, transmission, industry, transportation etc.

HEEP has a huge network of infrastructure that allows it to execute more than 150 projects at sites across India and abroad. The company has the capability to address the growing demand for power generation equipment.

It has retained its market leadership position in power sector. An improved focus on project execution has enabled HEEP to enhance its stature in domestic and international markets. It has also been exporting its power and industry segment products and services for over 20 years.

The company's global references are spread across all six continents of the world. Its manufactured power plants are exported to nearly 21 countries including Malaysia, Oman, Iraq, UAE, Bhutan, Egypt and New Zealand. Their physical exports range from turnkey projects to after sales services.

Effective Management

By carefully analyzing feasibility, anticipating implementation issues, communicating with and ensuring the support of senior and line managers, and setting up realistic schedules for each position, the governing management has been able to derive value from a job rotation program.[5]

Its key features are:

1. Formulating clear policies regarding who will be eligible for the program, whether employees will be restricted to certain jobs or will be open to all job classifications.
2. Determining how the employees will be selected. Will the program be mandatory or will employees be allowed to 'opt-out'.
3. Involving employees and managers in planning specific job rotations so that there is a clear understanding of mutual expectations.
4. Have a clear understanding of exactly which skills will be enhanced by placing an employee into the job rotation process.
5. Using job rotation for employees in non-exempt jobs, as well as those in professional and managerial jobs.

Outcome

Leveraging HEEP's enviable strengths, glorious past and contribution towards nation building, the company has put together a series of initiatives focusing on sustaining growth and profit, asserting leadership in core business sectors, developing people, enhancing digital capabilities and building potentials in new and diversified businesses as well as technologies for sustained growth.

It is commonly believed that the organization's management is Responsive, Robust and Rising to the needs of customers, shareholders, employees and society.

Way Forward

Make strides to become an Indian multinational engineering enterprise providing total business solutions through quality products, systems and services in the field of energy, transportation, industry, infrastructure and other potential areas.

Learning Points

- The zeal to excel and zest for change.
- Strict coherence to commitments and ensuring speedy response.
- Fostering learning, creativity and team work.
- Respecting dignity and potential of individuals.

Continuing to develop associates is seen as central to sustaining the corporate culture and principles that foster quality of work life at WL Gore.

Discussion Questions

1. Were the employees free to rotate their jobs themselves along with adhering to internal norms to maintain discipline?
2. Was the supervisor released from routine supervisory role so that he could handle employee grievances?
3. Were the members of this experimental group invited to different seminars to share their experiences on job rotation?
4. What efforts have been made to redress certain doubts related to the QWL program?

CASE STUDY #6

Anti-Stress Pilot Program in the Workplace

Background

A Mental Health Trust employs some 846 people and provides mental health services to a large catchment area in Britain. The trust's data showed that stress-related illness was responsible for 25% of all absence. To address this issue, the trust implemented the Health Education Authority's anti-stress pilot program designed to reduce the anxiety and tension of employees within the organization.

The program was introduced at a time of major organizational change at the trust. As a result of it, absenteeism due to stress-related conditions was reduced. Moreover, a "general sense" of improved morale among the employees was noted.

Outcome

Predominantly, the employees expressed the following two responses in the listening group:

- The staff felt uninvolved in the planning and process of change, leading to a loss of control, of choice and ownership and a sense of devaluation and powerlessness.
- The staff did not know what was happening when it happened. Decisions could change from one week to the next.

Many were struggling to cope with changes in their work environment, such as service relocations and new methods of recording information.

Way Forward

1. Sickness absence in mental health.
2. Proportion of sickness absence due to stress.

Learning Points[6]

There were several take-away in the form of:

- Employees' comments after participation—Managers were generally more enthusiastic about the program than staff.

- Most participants in workshops or action groups felt they had benefited.
- Several described the program as "therapeutic" and constructive.
- Communications were better, more information was getting through, the lead up to the move was better.
- It felt as though there was more support and team effort. They felt that things are changing in my department and there is more on offer such as training and support. However, most do not know if it's the result of this intervention.
- A few identified other beneficial changes in attitudes or culture. Before the project it had not been possible to admit to certain feelings, such as being upset about the closure, but now it was.
- Some felt more confident that things could be influenced from the bottom up.

Discussion Questions

1. Can the formation of a Stress Management Group (SMG) manage the program? Elaborate on it.
2. Who all does a listening group comprise? And what is its modus operandi?
3. What is the purpose of organizing an organizational stress workshop?
4. Following the recommendations of action groups, how is an action plan formulated?

CASE STUDY #7

Improving India's Mental Healthcare

Background

COVID-19 has revealed the importance of having a robust and well-funded public healthcare system. Research suggests that the subsequent health crisis faced by India will likely be related to mental health—characterised by increased anxiety, depression, substance abuse and suicides. Hence, it has never been more necessary to integrate mental health into our understanding of public healthcare.

The Government of India attempted to do this through measures like the National Mental Health Policy in 2014 and the Mental Healthcare Act (MHCA) in 2017. Although these are significant steps in the right direction, the fundamental problem is with the execution of these policies.

In fact, most states do not even have state-level policies or action plans to ensure implementation. Kerala is one of the few states that has a mental health policy and is also ahead in terms of funding, awareness, adolescent care and the number of available professionals in most districts.

Therefore, it might be helpful for other states to understand the successes and limitations of the Kerala model—so that they can tailor their own state-specific systems.

The Right Approach

Kerala is pioneering mental health integration in schools. If mental illnesses in children are not accurately diagnosed and treated, there is an increase in the probability of health issues in adulthood. The state administered UNARV, a model for adolescent mental health in schools at a district level in 2007.

Students with behavioural and academic problems from class VIII to XII were counselled by their teachers, who were trained in adolescent developmental psychology and mental health disorders.

If their problems persisted, they were given cognitive behavioural therapy, problem solving skill therapy and anger management skills at a clinic. If there were family problems at home such as alcoholism or domestic violence, their parents were also given family therapy.[7]

This innovative program ensured that students who might have been suspended or dismissed from school were now treated for their issues.

Within this sample, 95 per cent of the students returned to school. This was done by integrating school teachers curtailing possible social stigma and developing a model that can be implemented in areas with resource constraints, by any district-level administration.

The state has many other mental health programs at the school-level such as 'Thalir', a scheme that focuses on eliminating similar psychological issues in all districts. Kerala also has one of the highest budgetary allocations for mental health—1.16% of its total health budget. Most other states do not even allocate separate funds for mental healthcare.

In fact, India as a country spends only approximately 0.05% of its total health budget (around Rs 345 crore) on mental health. To put this in perspective, a cautious estimate of the cost of executing the 2017 MHCA is around INR 94,073 crore.

Funding is one of the most significant hurdles when it comes to implementation. Further, a lack of investment is likely to cause a larger financial burden on the government—around 6.5 times more than actually implementing these policies would.

Additionally, Kerala is the only state that meets the requirement of at least one psychiatrist per lakh population and also has the greatest number of clinical psychologists (0.6 per lakh population).

In the 12 states that were surveyed in the 2019 National Mental Health Survey, the availability of psychiatrists per population of one lakh was found to be 0.05 in Madhya Pradesh. In an attempt to bridge this gap, the District Mental Health Program was created to ensure the availability of minimum mental healthcare by encouraging community participation and self-help.

Out of the total states, Kerala and Gujarat are the only states wherein several districts routinely conduct Information Education and Communication (IEC) campaigns to spread awareness on mental health issues. India's low mental health literacy, high levels of stigma and large treatment gaps illustrate the need for such efforts. Teetotaller

Outcome

A significant issue that even Kerala is facing is related to the lack of coordination between different sectors. There are several sections within the Ministry of Health and Family Welfare (MoHFW) as well as departments in other ministries that are involved in mental healthcare.

On both national and state level, these sectors do not function in a uniform nor coordinated manner. They all have varying sources of funding, nodal agency and staff patterns. They often do similar work, which drains resources without creating significant change.

Closely related to this is a lack of monitoring of the implementation of these policies in every state. There should be state-level advisory and monitoring committee to ensure transparency, accountability, and coordination with other department linkages.

Way Forward

Although Kerala does have a separate mental health budget, only 0.18% of the budget was utilized in 2019. A large portion of existing funds aren't fully utilized due to an absence of clarity and muddled responsibilities between the central and state governments in terms of activity designation, well-timed allocation and human resource constraints.

Kerala also has a significant treatment gap (around 84 percent) which is lower than most states but is still high. It also has an extremely high suicide rate—around 23.9 per 1 lakh population and high levels substance abuse disorders.

Learning Points

Although, Kerala is ahead of most Indian states in several avenues, there are significant ways in which:

- Its mental healthcare can also improve. This is likely because there is still a certain level of stigma regarding mental health interventions.
- The restructuring of mental health hospitals and an increased focus on easy access to this facility could help mitigate this.
- It is also necessary to look deeper into the principles that guide these policies, so that mental health is not just viewed as a health issue but as a social problem that requires collective engagement, community intervention, and a preventive focus.

Discussion Questions

1. What significant steps have been taken to evaluate specific mental health issues like suicide, substance abuse and other disorders prevalent in the state?

2. Can the stakeholders ensure that intervention strategies can be context-specific and more effective?
3. Is there a nation-wide necessity for state-specific policies and action plans?
4. Can an adequate and streamlined funding, robust mental health research, awareness building, mental health interventions in schools and strong monitoring mechanisms make up for holistic mental health program?

CASE STUDY #8

CDC's Workplace Health Program

Background

The Centers for Disease Control and Prevention (CDC), United States, has created a workplace health program to address the leading health-related cost drivers for employers (such as heart disease and stroke, obesity, diabetes). This program encompasses:

- Provides employers with tools and resources that build their skills to implement effective and sustainable workplace health strategies.
- Conducts research to identify and test promising strategies and interventions.
- Monitors and reports trends in employer programs, policies and practices to identify needs and gaps.
- Helps workplaces identify changes they can make to support employees who want to protect and maintain their health.

One hundred and forty six million Americans spend the majority of their waking hours at work each day. Many employers today are seeking ways to support employees who want to protect their health. Sixty percent of companies expect to increase their wellness offerings in 2021-2022.[8]

CDC focuses on small and mid-size employers who often lack internal capacity. Eighty nine percent of American employees work for smaller companies (with strength of 3 to 100 employees). Participating organizations reach adults that might not otherwise engage with the public health system.

Outcome

Through the Work@Health® employer training program, CDC has trained more than 300 employers and train-the-trainer participants from 42 American states, territories and the District of Columbia. Members of the CDC Workplace Health Research Network are conducting innovative research to advance their knowledge of effective health interventions that can be applied in worksites.

Way Forward

Over the last 18 months, the percentage of employees who participated in the National Healthy Worksite Program—who met CDC recommendations for physical activity—increased from 30% to 38%.

Besides, the percentage who consumed at least 5 daily servings of fruits and vegetable increased from 6% to 13% and the percentage who was current smokers decreased from 14% to 12%. Using the CDC Worksite Health Scorecard, over 1,200 worksites representing 40 states have assessed how proven health promotion strategies are used in their worksites.

Learning Points

- Training and Technical Assistance—Expand opportunities using the Work@Health® curricula, which is a science-based comprehensive approach to build effective and sustainable workplace-based health promotion, including a scalable and replicable Train-the-Trainer model.
- Data-Driven Decisions—Provide employers and states with data through the Workplace Health in America survey on current employer investments in workplace health programs including strengths, gaps and emerging trends.
- Provide Access to What Works—Launch a centralized information clearinghouse of effective, science-based tools and resources from a broad array of publically available information sources.
- Fill the Gaps—Expand opportunities to understand and improve employee health and develop best practices through research.

Discussion Questions

1. Can an effective workplace health program redress mental health issues?
2. What strategy should an organization apply to identify depression in the workplace?
3. How can one increase an employee's health knowledge and skills?
4. What can be done to reduce employees' on-the-job exposure to substances and hazards that cause diseases and injury?

CASE STUDY #9

Spiritual Intelligence and Work Satisfaction

Background

A majority of the developed world is in a post-materialistic period, in which not only people's basic needs but also their needs in the workplace are changing. Because jobs have largely transformed from routine to more creative positions in which the main components are abilities and competence of the human mind, higher-order needs have emerged.

To satisfy these needs, leadership must be based not on profits, but on values. Such a leader has not only a high-level of cognitive intelligence, but also a high degree of emotional and spiritual intelligence. Cognitive and emotional intelligence constructs are fairly well known. Meanwhile, the theory of spiritual intelligence is in the early stages of development.

Working without purpose and meaning leaves people unsatisfied and causes organizations to struggle to create an identity in the market and contribute to the communities they serve. Both leaders and employees are equally important group entities for a successful organization.

With a high-level of spiritual intelligence, we can use our spirituality to bring meaning, importance, and general enrichment to our lives. This helps us achieve personal integrity, determine the purpose of our lives, and stay on the right path. Because of spiritual intelligence, we are integrated—rationally, emotionally, and spiritually—creatures/individuals.[9]

Spiritually Intelligent

Leaders: The new paradigm of spiritual leadership focuses on vision, empowerment, risk, creativity, harmony, trust, honesty and compassion. The terms that accompany this new paradigm are spiritual leadership, moral conduct, authentic leadership and ethical conduct. Leaders who exhibit grace and values such as joy, beauty, optimism and confidence are more likely to inspire their employees.

Employees: Despite the fact that spiritually intelligent employees are of great value for organizations, work life balance experts stress that no universal prescription exists for how to seek and find spiritual intelligence. Each individual has to find it for himself/herself, and only he/she knows how to obtain it. Such challenges are much more present for employees during difficult times, when values are not the priority for their leaders and employees are seen only as tools for gaining profits.

Organization: The organizational environment in the 21st century is chaotic and requires rapid response from highly committed, productive, intrinsically motivated learning organizations. In order for organizations to meet the great challenges they face successfully, they have to make a radical shift and transformation to a new business model—a spirituality-based organization.

Outcome

As per a widespread survey conducted by the European Foundation for the Improvement of Living and Working Conditions in 2007, work satisfaction trends influence the functioning of labor market and labor productivity, work effort, work absenteeism and staff resignations.

Way Forward

Companies that engage not just the minds, but also the hearts and emotions of their employees will be more profitable. Therefore, an organization that earnestly treats its employees and leaders as part of its community and emotionally engages them in the organization's purposes, which makes all the difference in the world and will attract a higher level of leaders and employees' motivation and loyalty, ultimately leading to higher organizational performance.

Learning Points

- Leaders with a higher level of spiritual intelligence have a higher level of work satisfaction.
- Employees with a higher level of spiritual intelligence have a higher level of work satisfaction.
- An organization can be truly effective and successful only if it works towards satisfying a majority of individuals.

Discussion Questions

1. How to find an external power & vitality and give it meaning and significance for all external events?

2. Is the spiritual intelligence of leaders and employees positively correlated with their level of work satisfaction?
3. Can spiritual intelligence be considered a method for improving the well-being of management executives as well as organizational well-being?
4. Will it be okay to say that human resource managers should formulate strategies for developing and increasing employees' spiritual intelligence? Elaborate.

CASE STUDY #10

Spiritual Intelligence and Job Performance

Background

Employees today face tremendous stress at the workplace due to increased competitiveness, changing and evolving technologies and lack of work life balance. As a result, they feel hollow and dissatisfied at workplace resulting in negative impacts on their job performance.

Howard Gardner's theory of multiple intelligences[10] proposes that people are not born with all of the intelligence they will ever have. Robert Emmons draws on Gardner's definition of intelligence and proposed that spirituality cam be viewed as a form of intelligence because it predicts functioning & adaptation and offers capabilities that enable people to solve problems and attain goals.

Sometimes, spiritual intelligence is misunderstood as something related to religion while in reality it is not possible to be 'spiritual' without being religious. Spiritual teachers believe that spiritual intelligence can be applied to solve specific problems by tapping specific abilities such as using intuition or taking a holistic systems' perspective to solve problems more globally.

It also focuses on the fact that other than solving specific problems, spiritual intelligence can be applied in every moment of daily life to experience greater meaning and wellbeing by exercising its abilities such as mindfulness and presence of mind even in pain and suffering.

Outcome

People who regularly practice meditation have higher workplace spirituality scores than people who do not regularly practice meditation. A quasi-experimental study found that people practiced insight meditation.

Way Forward

An attempt has to be made to explore the relationship between various aspects of spiritual intelligence and job performance. The next step would be to train employees on spiritual intelligence to improve upon their job-related attitudes.

Learning Points

The effect of spiritual intelligence on job performance will result in:

- **Consciousness:** It is the development of refined awareness and self knowledge, featuring intuitive trans-rational knowing, mindfulness and spiritual practices.
- **Grace:** Living with alignment with the sacred, manifesting trust in and love for life that is based on gratitude, beauty and joy.
- **Meaning:** Experiencing significance in daily activities through a sense of purpose and a call for service, including in face of pain and suffering.
- **Transcendence:** Going beyond the separate egoist self into an inter-connected wholeness including a holistic system worldwide and nurturing human relationships through empathy, compassion, love, kindness and I-Thou orientation.
- **Truth:** Living in open acceptance, forgiveness, curiosity and love for all creations, including respect for the wisdom of multiple spiritual traditions.

Discussion Questions

1. How does a manager's spiritual intelligence affect employees' job performance?
2. What is the relationship between spiritual intelligence and job enrichment?
3. What impact does employee and organizational performance have when the workplace spirituality values framework is definable?
4. How does spirituality improve an educator's performance and institutional effectiveness?

CASE STUDY #11

Spiritual Intelligence at the Workplace

Background

Despite all our gains in technology, product innovation and world markets, most people are not thriving in the organizations they work for. They are neither fulfilled nor excited. If one walks into any organization, it is full of fear, anger, resistance to change, and employees who are there just for the pay-check.

The best employees are usually looking to go elsewhere, and the employees who are not so marketable are trying to stay under the radar and just hang on for dear life. They are not clear about where the organization is headed or what its highest priorities are. They are bogged down and distracted. Most of them do not feel they can change much.

In the late 1970s and throughout the 1990s, an expansion of management theories included focus not just on the workers as physical beings, or as emotional beings but also as thinking beings. Corona virus that hit the world in 2019 has given a fresh lease of life to spiritual intelligence at the workplace.

With recent research in quantum physics and holistic medicine, people are coming to accept that humans are also spiritual beings, that we are the sum of body, mind emotion and spirit. As crass as this may sound, spirituality is the new competitive edge.

Most organizations are physically efficient, and they attend to the emotional and social needs of employees to some degree. They have learned how to involve employees in decision making and to tap their intellectual abilities. But how many of them have learned to tap into the human spirit?

Organizations which have long been viewed as rational systems are considering making room for the spiritual dimension, which has less to do with rules & order and more with meaning, purpose and a sense of community.

Outcome

Mature leadership and high Spiritual Quotient (SQ)[11] is not about warm and fuzzy feelings. It is deep compassion manifesting in wise action. It is a profound personal integrity—an alignment with purpose and values.

The high SQ leader understands natural emergent processes at play and can work with them for the best outcomes, all while he/she stays focused on the big picture—remaining untriggered by old egoistic reactions.

Developing spiritual intelligence is a requirement if we want to access the highest stages of adult development and become truly mature leaders—leaders ready for the challenges we face. The world desperately needs a shift in consciousness in business, and every organization that takes steps in the direction of greater spirituality in the workplace is making a significant difference.

Way Forward

To find out the reasons and present compelling argument for why spirituality may be that ingredient—when consciously acknowledged and channeled into an organization's day to day operation—can institute hope and enhance the Spiritual Quotient (SQ) in the workplace.

Learning Points

- The downsizing, re-engineering and lay-offs of the past decade, which have turned the workplace into an environment where employees are demoralized.
- The workplace is increasingly seen as a primary source of community for many people because of the decline of neighbourhood chat groups, civic groups and extended families as principal places for feeling connected.
- The increased access to and enhanced curiosity about meditation have emphasized values such as group loyalty and finding one's spiritual centre in every activity.
- The fact that aging baby boomers are moving ever close to life's greatest uncertainty—death and thereby—are developing a growing interest in contemplating life's meaning.
- There is increasing pressure of global competition which has led organizational leaders to realize that employee creativity needs nurturing.

Discussion Questions

1. How does an organization continually adapt to its changing business environment?

2. What is the driving force that makes people creative and innovative in the workplace?
3. How can personal goals and objectives of people be brought in alignment with an organization's objectives and targets?
4. How to make employees more responsible and accountable for their work in proportion to their competencies?

Conclusion

The success of any organization is contingent on how it attracts, recruits, motivates and retains its workforce. The employees who were initially treated as laborers or commodity are now considered as free and empowered energy. In this contemporary scenario, managing these free and empowered energies by improving quality of work life (QWL) seems to be a new mantra on Indian corporate landscape. QWL is the favorableness or unfavorableness of a job environment. It is a multi-facet construct as it comprises of subjective and objective indicators. The subjective indicators of QWL include individual's level of satisfaction in context to mental and physical health, personality and job related attitudes etc. Objective indicators includes work load, compensation and benefits, career development to name a few.

Today's organization need to be more flexible and provide conducive environment to promote positive metal health of employees. However, the pressure of an increasingly demanding work culture is one of the biggest challenges to mental health at individual and organizational level. At individual level it causes anxiety, stress and various forms of disabilities while at the organizational level it leads to poor work habits, absenteeism, interpersonal conflict, low job satisfaction and performance. Various employee wellness programs (EAPs), counseling, supportive supervisors, review and evaluation of mental well-being etc. are various measures that are implemented to promote mental health and psychological well-being. These initiatives further strengthen the best practices recommendations and are helpful in building 'Spiritual Organizations'.

Organizations that foster spirituality are considered to be more visionary and employees in these organizations become more conscious of their higher selves and are aware of the purpose of their life. The spiritual workplace is characterized by shared power, higher tolerance for diversity, learning environment and need for self transcendence. Employees at different levels are respected, valued and reciprocal cooperation and understanding is nurtured.

Quality of work life and mental health thus can be referred as jewels for workplace spirituality. Whilst quality of life has been more widely studied, it remains relatively subjective in nature. Mental health on the other hand is a psychological construct and is influenced by various personality and situational constructs. It is the prime responsibility of leaders to make the workplace environment conducive to enhance organizational effectiveness. Leaders can organize various employee assistance programs, in service events, encourage tolerance and inclusivity, provide autonomy to do meaningful work that can enhance psychological well-being and spiritual awareness at individual and organizational level. Leaders play a crucial role in developing spiritual organizations and guiding employees to follow the principle of 'Nishkama Karma' and 'Sakam Karma' which are two aspects of 'Karma Yoga' for spiritual ideology.

I am hopeful that the people stories and case studies on quality of work life, mental health and workplace spirituality inspire readers to create a meaningful change in the world and connect them to higher divine. Once people begin to search for those who weave their work lives with spirituality in mutually enriching ways, they will go on to find many exemplars to add to the ones I have presented here. They will put to rest the myth that one cannot achieve excellence in work without forsaking the rest of one's life.

Bibliography

Unit I

1. https://www.economicsdiscussion.net/human-resource-management/quality-of-work-life/32426
2. Garg, C.P. *et al.* "Quality of work life an overview", *International journal of physical and social science*, 2012, Vol. 2, issue 3, pp. 231–242.
3. Staines, G. (1980). "Spillover versus Compensation: A Review of the Literature on the Relationship between Work and Nonwork." Human Relations 33:111–129.
4. Hersey, H. and Goldsmith, M. (1980). 'A situational approach to performance planning', *Training and Development Journal, Madison*, Vol. 34, No. 11, p. 38.
5. Lawler, E.E., III. (1982). "Strategies for Improving the Quality of Work Life." *American Psychologist* 37:486–493.
6. Rain, J.S., Lane, I.M. and Steiner, D.D. (1991). "A Current Look at the Job Satisfaction/Life Satisfaction Relationship: Review and Future Considerations." *Human Relations,* 44:287–307.
7. Harish, K.L. and Subashini, K. (2014). "Quality of work life in Indian industries—A case study", *International Journal of Innovative Research in Science, Engineering and Technology,* Vol. 3, Issue 10, pp. 16799–16804.
8. Balaji, R., Mariadhas, J. and Rajamani, K. (2019). Quality of Work Life (QWL) in IT Sector—Indian Scenario. https://www.semanticscholar.org/paper/Quality-of-Work-Life-(QWL)-in-it-Sector/9857d80919da55e2705f9397704e226c3d859626
9. https://www.sodexo.com/research-and-reports/responding-to-a-quantum-shift-in-work.html
10. https://www.indianresearchjournals.com

Unit II

1. https://ifioque.com/career-workshop/QWL
2. https://en.wikipedia.org/wiki/Sociotechnical_system
3. https://work.chron.com/job-restructuring-17903.html
4. https://www.verywellmind.com

5. https://greatergood.berkeley.edu/article/item/the_four_keys_to_happiness_at_work
6. https://www.gdrc.org/uem/qol-define.html
7. https://www.sciencedirect.com/science/article/pii/S1877042814011537

Unit III

1. https://www.semanticscholar.org/paper/A-Model-of-Quality-of-Work-Life
2. http://www.abepro.org.br/biblioteca/enegep2008_ti_st_072_509_12395.pdf
3. https://link.springer.com/article/10.1007/s11482-019-09730-3
4. https://www.slideshare.net/EshwariEshu2/measurement-of-qwl
5. https://depts.washington.edu/fammed/wpcontent/uploads/2019/09/SDT_needs_work.pdf

Unit IV

1. Introduction to Mental Health Issues in the EU. Helsinki, Finnish Ministry of Social Affairs and Health, 1999 (www.stakes.fi/mentalhealth).
2. Strategies, Employment, Mental Illness: Strategies to Secure and Maintain Employment for People with Long-term Mental Illness. United States National Institute on Disability and Rehabilitation Research (NIDRR), 1993, XV (10).
3. The Cost of Mental Health Problems: The Fundamental Fact. The Mental Health Foundation, UK, 2000 (www.mentalhealth.org.uk//ffcost.htm).
4. Conti, D.J., Burton, W.H. The Economic Impact of Depression in a Workplace. Journal of Occupational Medicine, 1994, 36:983–988.
5. Jenkins, R. Mental health at work—Why is it so under-researched? Occupational Medicine, 1993, 43:65–67.
6. US National Institute for Occupational Safety & Health (NIOSH). Stress at work. 1998.
7. Miller, D. Work problems caused by mental ill health and their management. In: Jenkins & Coney, Prevention of mental ill-health at work: a conference. 1992.
8. Lehtinen, V., Riikonen, E. and Lehtinen, E. Promotion of mental health on the European agenda. STAKES National Research & Development Centre for Welfare and Health, 1998.

9. Dooley, D. *et al.* Depression and unemployment: panel findings from the Epidemiologic Catchment Area Study. *Journal of Community Psychology,* 1994, 22(6):745–765.
10. Kalimo, R. Balanced mentally healthy working life. *Finnish Institute of Occupational Health,* 1999.
11. Burgess, A., Davidoff, I. and Goff, V. Investing in workplace productivity: Innovation in managing indirect mental health costs. Washington Business Group on Health, *National Institute of Mental Health, National Worksite Program,* 1999.
12. Stein, L.I., Test, M.A. and Marx, A.J. Alternative to the hospital: A controlled study. *American Journal of Psychiatry,* 1975, 132:517–522.
13. Allness, D. and Knoedler, W.H. The PACT Model. Arlington, VA, NAMI Anti-Stigma Foundation, 1998.
14. Goldfinger, C. The Future of Work. UNESCO Courier, December 1998.
15. Vardhan, M., Facts about Mental Illness, December 2000.
16. Sullivan, A. *et al.* Choose/Get/Keep: A Psychiatric Rehabilitation Approach to Supported Education. *Psychosocial Rehabilitation Journal,* 1993, 17(1).
17. Employing and Accommodating Workers with Psychiatric Disabilities. Cornell University, School of Industrial & Labour Relations, January 1994.
18. United Nations. The Standard Rules on the Equalization of Opportunities for Persons with Disabilities. Adopted at the 48th Session, 20 December, 1993 (Resolution 48/96).
19. World Development Report. Investigating Health (Executive Summary). Washington, DC, World Bank, 1993.
20. Andrew, G., Sanderson, K. and Beard, J. Burden of Disease. *British Journal of Psychiatry,* 1008, 173:123–131.
21. WHO. Basic Documents, 8th Edition. Geneva, 1990:1.
22. WHO. Alma Alta 1978. "Health for All" series No. 1. Geneva, 1978.
23. ILO. A summary review of the replies to the ILO General Survey on Convention 159 and Recommendation 168. Geneva, 1997.
24. Harnois, G.P. Mission Report to WHO Regional Office for South-East Asia. October 1999.
25. Mancuso, L.L. Reasonable Accommodation for Workers with Psychiatric Disabilities. *Psychosocial Rehabilitation Journal,* 1990, 14(2), 3–19. https://doi.org/10.1037/h0099449

26. Managing for Mental Health—The Mind Employers Resource Pack. Guide No. 2. Mind Publications, 2000.
27. Janardhan, V., Mental Health at Work. 1993:65–67.
28. Grove, B *et al.* The Social Firm Handbook. South Hampton, Ashford Press, p. 11.
29. Chafkin, R. Supported Employment. InfoLines, 2000, 11(2).
30. Palmer-Erbs, V., Donegan, K. Promoting the Importance of Work for Persons with Psychiatric Disabilities—The Role of the Psychiatric Nurse. *Journal of Psychosocial Nursing and Mental Health Services,* April 1998: 13–25.

Unit V

1. Danah, Zohar and Dr Ian, Marshall (1999: p. 25–45), Bloomsbury, USA.
2. Skelley, M.F. (1996). Creating a spirituality of work for organizational change New Theology Review, 9(2), 59–74.
3. Ver Beck, K. (2000) Spirituality a development taboo, Development in Practice, Vol. 10, No. I, February, Oxford.
4. Feldman, Robert (1987). Understanding Psychology, McGraw Hill.
5. Public Management Reform: A Comparative Analysis—New Public Management, Governance, and the Neo-Weberian State (2000: P 352). Oxford University Press.
6. Mitroff, I. and Denton E.A. (1999). A study of spirituality in the workplace Sloan Management Review, 40(4), 83–92.
7. Dhiman, S. (2000). Course syllabus: Spirituality in the workplace. Woodbury University (Online). Available www.spintatwork.com/knowledgecenter/university/syllabı/Dhiman
8. Skelley, M.F. (1996). Creating a spirituality of work for organizational change New Theology Review, 9(2), 75–80, Biberman, J.A. and Whitty, M. (1999). Twenty-first century spiritual paradigms-possibilities for organizational transformation. *Journal of Organizational Change Management*, 12 (3), 170–174.
9. Mitroff, I.I. and Denton, E.A. (1999). A study of spirituality in the workplace. *MIT Sloan Management Review,* 40(4), 83.
10. Reed, J. (1996: P 28–37). *Journal of Managerial Psychology.*
11. Karakas, F. (2010: P 29–34). Journal of the British Educational Management and Administration Society.
12. Fenwick, T. and Lange, E. (1998). Spirituality in the workplace. The new frontier of HRD. *The Canadian Journal for the study of adult education*, 12(1), 63–87.

13. Biberman, J.A. and Whitty, M. (1997). A postmodern spiritual future for work. *Journal of Organizational Change Management,* 10 (2), 130–138.
14. Ashmos, D.P. and Duchon, D. (2000). Spirituality at work: A conceptualization and measure. *Journal of management inquiry,* 9 (2), 134.
15. Swami, Vivekananda (1900). World Parliament of Religions, Chicago.
16. Swami, Vivekananda (1900). World Parliament of Religions, Chicago.
17. Delbecq, A.L. (2010). *Journal of Management, Spirituality and Religion,* Vol. 7, No. 1, pp. 51–71. Neal, JA (1997) https://doi.org/10.1177/105256299702100111.
18. Craigie, F.C. (1999). The spirit and work Observations about spirituality and organizational life. *Journal of Psychology and Christianity,* Number 18, pp. 43–53.
19. Biberman, J.A. and Whitty, M. (1997). A post-modern spiritual future for work. *Journal of Organizational Change Management,* No. 10(2), pp. 140–145.
20. Giacalone, R.A. and Jurkiewicz, C.L. (2003). Right from wrong: The influence of spirituality on perceptions of unethical business activities. *Journal of Business Ethics,* Number 46 (1), pp. 85–97.
21. Westgate, C.E. (1996). Spiritual Wellness and Depression. *Journal of Counseling & Development,* Number 75, pp. 26–35. https://doi.org/10.1002/j.1556–6676.1996.tb02311.
22. Kolodinsky, R. *et al.* (2008). Workplace Values and Outcomes: Exploring Personal, Organizational, and Interactive Workplace Spirituality. *Journal of Business Ethics,* 81(2), pp. 465–480.
23. Saks, A.M (2011). Workplace Spirituality and Employee Engagement. *Spirituality and Religion,* Vol. 8, pp. 317–340.
24. Lee, C. and Zemke, R. (1993). The search for spirit in the workplace Training Magazine, pp. 21–28.
25. Bhindi, N. and Duignan, P. (1997). Leadership for a new century Authenticity intentionality. Spirituality, and sensibility. Educational Management and Administration: *Journal of the British Educational Management and Administration Society,* 25(2), p. 117.
26. Boozer, R.W. and Maddox, E.N. (1992). An exercise for exploring organizational spirituality: The case of teaching transformation. *Journal of Management Education,* 16 (4) 503–510.

27. Garcia-Zamor, J. C. (2003). Workplace spirituality and organizational performance. *Public Administration Review,* 63 (3), pp. 355–363.
28. Krishnakumar, S. and Neck, C.P. (2002). The "what", "why" and "how" of spirituality in the workplace. *Journal of managerial psychology,* 17 (3), pp. 153–164.
29. Mohamed, A., Wisnieski, J., Askar, M. and Syed, I. (2004). Towards a theory of spirituality in the workplace. *Competitiveness Review: An International Business Journal,* 14 (1/2), pp. 102–107.
30. Bhunia, A. and Das, A. (2012). Workplace Spirituality and Job Satisfaction, pp. 82–109.
31. Harrington, W., Preziosi, R. and Gooden, D. (2004). Worldview resiliency of business degree graduate students—An examination of spiritual experiences and psychological attitudes. *Association of Employment Practices and Principals,* p. 119.
32. Feldman, M.S. and Rafaeli, A. (2002). Organizational Routines as Sources of Connections and Understandings. *Journal of Management Studies,* 39 (3), pp. 309–331.
33. Van den Brande, C. *et al.* (2016). Workplace spirituality and organizational commitment: An integrative model. *Journal of Management, Spirituality & Religion,* 8(3), pp. 211–232.
34. Hoobler, J.M. *et al.* (2010). Bossess' Perceptions of Family-Work Conflict and Women's Promotability: Glass Ceiling Effects. *The Academy of Management Journal,* 52 (5), pp. 939–957.
35. Wheatley, M. (1996). A Simpler Way, Berrett-Koehler Publishers, pp. 91–100.
36. Karman, R. and Hormann, J. (1990), Creating value for customers, Designing and implementing a total corporate strategy, Harmony Books.
37. Robbins, L. (ed.) (2003) Management and Spiritual Energy, Report on the Hope of the Managers, Academy of Management.
38. Wagner-Marsh. E. and Conley, J. (1999), The fourth wave: the spiritually based firm, Journal of Organizational Change Management, MCB University Press, Volume 12, Number 4, pp. 292–301.
39. Biberman, J. and Whitty, M. (1997). A post-modem spiritual future for work, Journal of Organizational Change Management, MCB University Press, Volume 10, Number 2, pp. 130–138.

40. Wong, P. (2003). Spirituality and Meaning at Work. Available http://www.meaning.ca/articles/presidents_column (10:10:03).
41. Rogers, H. (1995). Bringing Life to Organisational Change, Barkana Institute.
42. Vaill, P. (1998). Spirited Leading and Learning. Process Wisdom for a New Age, San Francisco, Jossey-Bass.
43. Kulesa, P. (2003). Keeping the Good Apples, Security Management, 47 (8), p. 32.
44. Dr Lyons, Lawrence (2001). Henley Management College in his article 'HR Specialists Will Lead'.
45. Mitroff, I. and Denton, E. (1999). A Study of Spirituality in the Workplace, San Fransico Jossey-Bass, pp. 55–64.
46. Swami, Jitatmananda (1995). is a monk of the Ramakrishna order who is an exponent of Neo-Hinduism lecturing at international platforms including the United Nations and UNESCO.
47. Miller, C. (2007). The Paradox of Stretch Goals: Organizations in Pursuit of the Seemingly Impossible, Academy of Management.
48. Chawla, V. and Guda, S. (2013). Workplace Spirituality as a Precursor to Relationship-Oriented Selling Characteristics, *Journal of Business Ethics,* 115(1).
49. Escrivá, J. (1968). A Catholic Spirituality for Business, Catholic University Press of America. https://doi.org/10.2307/j.ctvh9w0p7.
50. Rosner, B. (2001). Is there a room for the soul at work? Workforce, 80(2), 82–83.

Unit VI

1. http://aims.fao.org/information-and-communication-technologies-ict
2. Venkata Ratnam, C.S. (2001). Globalisation and Labour Management Relations, p. 303, Response Books.
3. Adapted from www.work.htm
4. https://www.mercer.com/our-thinking/career/covid-19-global-survey-coronavirus-impact-to-global-market.html)
5. Venkata Ratnam, C.S. (2001). Globalisation and Labour Management Relations, p. 303, Response Books.
6. http://www.indiancommunities.org/2020/03/13/theory-of-trade-unionism
7. https://www.wbdg.org/resources/changing-nature-organizations-work-and-workplace

8. Casner-Lotto, J. and Barrington, L. (2006). Are they really ready to work? United States: The Conference Board, Corporate Voices for Working Families, Partnership for 21st Century Skills and Society for Human Resource Management.
9. https://www.ustravel.org/research/state-american-vacation-2018
10. Success Stories Archive, https://www.global-integration.com/success-stories
11. https://nextbillion.net/social-protection-digital-innovative-whatsapp-paraguay
12. https://nextbillion.net/india-covid19-workplace-wellness-revolution
13. https://www.gartner.com/smarterwithgartner/9-future-of-work-trends-post-covid-19

Unit VII

1. https://www.shrm.org/resourcesandtools/tools-and-samples/toolkits/understandinganddevelopingorganizationalculture.aspx
2. https://www.betterlyf.com/corporate-wellness
3. https://www.sciencedirect.com/science/article/pii/S0277953620308121
4. https://www.jstor.org/stable/4375055
5. Connor, R.J. (2016). Excellent Job Design: A Handbook for Recruiting Managers and HR Professionals, p. 73–109.
6. https://hbr.org/2019/11/making-work-less-stressful-and-more-engaging-for-your-employees
7. https://www.kingsfund.org.uk/publications/quality-improvement-mental-health
8. https://www.betterup.com/solutions/betterup-care
9. https://ideas.repec.org/a/vrs/ngooec/v62y2016i2p51-60n6.html
10. https://www.verywellmind.com/gardners-theory-of-multiple-intelligences-2795161
11. http://integralleadershipreview.com/5502-feature-article-why-spiritual-intelligence-is-essential-to-mature-leadership